INTERNATIONALISATION STRATEGIES

From the same publishers

INTERNATIONAL BUSINESS AND EUROPE IN TRANSITION
Edited by Fred Burton, Mo Yamin and Stephen Young

Internationalisation Strategies

Edited by George Chryssochoidis, Carla Millar and Jeremy Clegg

St. Martin's Press
New York

INTERNATIONALISATION SRATEGIES

For information, address:

St. Martin's Press, Scholarly and Reference Division,
175 Fifth Avenue, New York, N.Y. 10010

First published in the United States of America in 1997

This book is printed on paper suitable for recycling and made from fully managed and sustained forest sources.

Printed in Great Britain

ISBN 0–312–16407–6

Library of Congress Cataloging-in-Publication Data
Internationalisation strategies / edited by George Chryssochoidis, Carla Miller, and Jeremy Clegg,
p. cm.
Includes bibliographical references and index.
ISBN 0–312–16407–6 (cloth)
1. International economic integration. 2. International business enterprises—Management. 3. Investments, Foreign. 4. Strategic alliances (Business) I. Chryssochoidis, George. II. Millar, Carla. III. Clegg, Jeremy, 1955–
HF1418.5.I587 1996
338.8'8—dc20 96–26116
CIP

Contents

List of Figures vii

List of Tables viii

Preface xi

List of Contributors xii

Acknowledgements xiv

PART ONE ENVIRONMENTAL INFLUENCES

1 **Introduction**
George Chryssochoidis, Carla Millar and Jeremy Clegg 3

2 **Trading Blocs, Trade Liberalisation and Foreign Direct Investment**
Roger Strange 19

3 **Global Integration: Changing Bilateral Trade and Investment Relations between Canada and the UK**
Peter J. Buckley, Christopher L. Pass and Kate Prescott 43

4 **Internationalisation of Service Firms: Strategic Considerations**
Niklas Arvidsson 71

5 **Industrial Restructuring and the Control of 'Concentrations' in the European Market**
Eleanor J. Morgan 91

6 **National Culture, Corporate Culture and Economic Performance: An Interdisciplinary Synthesis and Implications for Internationalisation Strategy**
Christos Nicolaidis and Carla Millar 113

PART TWO INTERNATIONALISATION METHODS

7 **International Franchising: Market versus Hierarchy** 135
Fred Burton and Adam R. Cross

8 **A Study of EC Firms' Choice of Entry Mode into the Chinese Market: Licensing or Joint Ventures?** 153
Wei-Ping Wu

9 **International Joint Ventures in China from a Managerial Perspective: A Comparison between Different Sources of Investment**
Haochun Dong, Peter J. Buckley and Hafiz Mirza 171

10 **The Impact of Strategic Choice on the Internationalisation of the Firm**
Timothy Clark and Geoff Mallory 193

11 **Global Procurement: A Strategy For Improving International Business Competitiveness**
Shan Rajagopal and Kenneth N. Bernard 207

Bibliography 227

Index 247

List of Figures

4.1	The relation between customisation, physical goods, services and interaction between seller and buyer during the production process	77
4.2	The internationalisation of a firm in relation to the internationalisation of its business environment	80
6.1	Schein's framework of organisational culture	123
6.2	Corporate culture: a synthetic view	126
7.1	Various structures of international franchise entries	140
7.2	Continuum of resource commitment to the local market	141
10.1	*Between* and *within* mode foreign market servicing shifts	198
11.1	A model of incremental internationalisation in the purchasing process	211
11.2	A matrix of generic choices for global procurement strategies	212
11.3	A typology of global sourcing strategies	213
11.4	A framework for developing a global sourcing strategy	215
11.5	Modes of international sourcing entry strategies	216
11.6	Profiling globalisation of procurement process by country of domicile	223

List of Tables

1.1 Foreign direct investment stock, percentage distribution for the leading regions of the world, 1980–1990 11
2.1 A typology of the entrepreneurial motivations for foreign direct investment 22
2.2 The effects of liberalisation measures on flows of foreign direct investment into a trading bloc/common market 25
3.1 The sample of firms: firm codes 45
3.2 Summary of foreign market servicing strategies and effects of regionalisation 48
5.1 National, community and international majority acquisitions (including mergers), number and increases in annual activity 92
5.2 Decisions after full proceedings (to 1 March 1993) 99
7.1 Characteristics of international franchising cited in the literature 139
7.2 Principal differences between the licensing and franchising entry modes 143
7.3 Some recommended terminology for international franchising 144
8.1 Summary of hypotheses: joint ventures versus licensing 159
8.2 Results of logistic regressions for the choice between licensing and joint ventures 163
9.1 Sample pattern summary 177
9.2 Comparison of foreign partners' motivations (Mann–Whitney test) 178
9.3 Comparison of local partners' motivations (Mann–Whitney test) 179
9.4 Comparison of differences in selecting local partner (Mann–Whitney test) 180
9.5 Comparison of differences in selecting foreign partner (Mann–Whitney test) 181
9.6 Foreign partners' rates of control: comparison of the differences (Mann–Whitney test) 183
9.7 Comparison of local and foreign partners' rates of control in Group 2 (N=77) (Wilcoxon matched-pairs signed-ranks test) 183
9.8 Comparison of local and foreign partners' rates of control in Group 1 (N=37) (Wilcoxon matched-pairs signed-ranks test) 184

9.9 Comparison of foreign partners' rates of conflict (Mann–Whitney test) 186
9.10 Comparison of local and foreign partners' rates of conflict (N=114) (Wilcoxon matched-pairs signed-ranks test) 187
9.11 Comparison of partners' perceptions of JV performance (Mann–Whitney test) 188
9.12 Comparison of local and foreign partners' perceptions of JV performance (Wilcoxon matched-pairs signed-ranks test) 188
10.1 Foreign market servicing options 201
10.2 Types of foreign direct investment shifts 203
10.3 Types of mixed marketing approaches and their frequency 204
11.1 Principal expectations regarding motivations for internationalisation by country of domicile 222

Preface

The 20th Annual Conference of the UK Region of the Academy of International Business (AIB) took internationalisation strategies as its theme. A total of 38 articles were presented at the Conference. All papers were subjected to a blind refereeing process, in which each was reviewed by three members of the Editorial Board. In addition to the editors, the Board included:

Professor Stephen Young, University of Strathclyde and Chairman of the UK AIB
Professor Peter J. Buckley, University of Bradford
Fred Burton, UMIST
Professor Hafiz Mirza, University of Bradford

The papers which were later selected to form this volume were subjected to a further review by the Editorial Board, assisted by external reviewers. We would like to place on record our thanks for the invaluable efforts of the following in helping to ensure the high quality of the final selection of papers:

Professor Mark Casson, University of Reading
Professor Rob Goffee, London Business School
Professor Ben Kadia, Memphis State University
Professor Andrew Pettigrew, University of Warwick
Professor Peter Turnbull, UMIST
Dr Michael McDermott, University of Strathclyde

We should also like to extend our thanks to the participants at the Conference, particularly those who chaired sessions and those who acted as discussants.

Our gratitude also goes to the University of Glamorgan for its support, and to Mr Pascal Grippai for his assistance in the organisation of the event.

Cardiff, London and Leeds

GEORGE CHRYSSOCHOIDIS
CARLA MILLAR
JEREMY CLEGG

List of Contributors

Niklas Arvidsson Research Associate, Institute of International Business, Stockholm School of Economics, Sweden

Kenneth N. Bernard Lecturer in Marketing, Department of Marketing, University of Strathclyde, UK

Peter J. Buckley Professor of International Business and Director, Centre for International Business, School of Business and Economic Studies, University of Leeds, UK, and Visiting Professor of Economics at the University of Reading, UK, and at La Sorbonne, Paris, France

Fred Burton Senior Lecturer in Economics, School of Management, UMIST, UK

George Chryssochoidis Lecturer in Marketing, Cardiff Business School, University of Wales, UK

Timothy Clark Research Fellow in International Management, Open University Business School, The Open University, Milton Keynes, UK

Jeremy Clegg Senior Lecturer in International Business, Centre for International Business, University of Leeds, UK

Adam R. Cross Lecturer in International Business, Centre for International Business, School of Economic and Business Studies, University of Leeds, UK

Haochun Dong Visiting Fellow in International Business, University of Bradford Management Centre; and Manager (Business Development China), Holset Engineering Co. Ltd, UK

Geoff Mallory Lecturer in Strategic Management, Open University Business School, The Open University, Milton Keynes, UK

Carla Millar Director, Management Development Centre, City University Business School, London, UK

Hafiz Mirza Professor of International Business, University of Bradford Management Centre, UK

Eleanor J. Morgan Senior Lecturer in Business Economics, Centre for International Business Research, School of Management, University of Bath, UK

Christos Nicolaidis Director of MAK Agricultural Machinery Manufacturing and Management Consultancy; and Visiting Lecturer in Strategic Management and Organisational Behaviour, Department of Economics, Aristotle University of Thessaloniki, Greece

Christopher L. Pass Reader in Comparative Industrial Economics, University of Bradford Management Centre, UK

Kate Prescott Lecturer in International Business, University of Bradford Management Centre, UK

Shan Rajagopal Academic Director, Singapore Institute of Purchasing and Supply, and formerly Lecturer in Marketing, Department of Marketing, University of Strathclyde, UK

Roger Strange Senior Lecturer in Economics, The Management Centre, King's College London, UK

Wei-Ping Wu Lecturer in Asian Business and Management, and Director, Institute of Pacific Asia Studies, University of Hull, UK

Acknowledgements

The editors and publishers are grateful to the following for permission to reproduce copyright material: United Nations Conference on Trade and Development for table 2 of the Annex of the *World Investment Report 1993*; Routledge for tabular material from R. Strange (1993) *Japanese Manufacturing Investment in Europe: Its Impact on the UK Economy*; Croom Helm for a figure from J. Johanson and L.-G. Mattsson (1986) 'International Marketing and Internationalisation Processes – A Network Approach' in S. Paliwoda and P.W. Turnbull (eds) *Research in International Marketing*, and a table from P.W. Turnbull and J.-P. Valla (1986) *Strategies for International Industrial Marketing*; McGraw-Hill for a table from A.M. Rugman *et al.* (1988) *International Business: Firm and Environment*, 3rd edn. Every effort has been made to contact all the copyright-holders but if any have been inadvertently omitted the publishers will be pleased to make the necessary arrangements at the earliest opportunity.

Part One

Environmental Influences

1 Introduction

George Chryssochoidis, Carla Millar and Jeremy Clegg

Internationalisation strategies concern the internationalisation of the firm in order to service international markets and to enhance or maintain competitiveness, including competitiveness in the home market. An internationalisation strategy involves the adoption of at least one of the modes of international business, although having such a strategy does not necessarily imply that the firm should aim ultimately to become a foreign direct investor (that is, a multinational enterprise), although many firms will indeed attain this state.

For some time it has been suggested that internationalisation should be restricted to the question of 'How to enter and develop international markets' (Young, Hamill Wheeler and Davies, 1989, p. 2). In a similar way, Buckley, Pass and Prescott (1990) use the term 'foreign market servicing strategies' in the context of internationalisation. However, the complexity of international business forces most of the boundaries of current definitions to remain controversial. For instance, would backward international vertical integration be excluded as a form of internationalisation? If so, then the internationalisation of the procurement process would not be reckoned as an internationalisation strategy. Broadening the definition of internationalisation is the simplest answer. A definition that includes any growth that extends the horizons of the firm internationally encompasses all the possibilities.

Providing an accurate measurement of the extent of internationalisation is less tractable. It is important to acknowledge the distinction between 'internationalisation' and 'international operations'. Thus, internationalisation may be said to be concerned with entering and initially developing operations in another country. The conceptualisation of passing from one phase to the other, however, is misleading. Companies do not go through stages, but through states. The initial Johanson and Vahlne (1977) model discussed state aspects, selecting market commitment and knowledge as representative features. The term 'state' was employed to describe the degree of involvement in international operations rather than to denote 'condition' or 'situation' of development. Market commitments and knowledge are only two elements in complex company behaviour concerned with the internationalisation of operations. A fuller explanation of the shortcomings of the 'stages' approach can be found in Clark and Mallory's contribution later in this book.

The crossing of national boundaries in the process of a firm's growth may be argued to be a meaningless threshold (Buckley, 1990). However, development through internationalisation is significantly different compared with development in the narrower domestic environment (Buckley and Ghauri, 1993) and merits individual attention. Naturally, an internationalisation strategy may involve a sequence of international business modes. Research in this area has customarily trodden the path of identifying what firms actually do (description and analysis), rather than of prescribing what firms should do. This reflects the considerable problems of generalising from limited samples, and raises the obstacle of a highly variable body of research, from which it is arduous to distil. It is possible to construct typologies of determinants of internationalisation – promoting and constraining factors. However, the forms of international business continually evolve, and no typology can hope to be prescient enough to remain valid.

The greatest bestowal of the academic literature has been to set out logically the alternatives available to firms, and to give indications as to the circumstances in which certain strategies are worthy of especial consideration. Firms face great uncertainty and information costs, and there is always the risk that they might choose a less effective form of international business as a result, with a consequential loss of competitiveness. While firms generate their own knowledge on internationalisation strategies, the scope for learning from novel sources is widening all the time.

At the same time, new challenges to existing ways of thinking about internationalisation are continually posed by empirical reality. For instance, the emergence of sectors that are new to full-bodied international business, such as telecommunications and a number of other services. One does not have to look far to detect fundamental shifts in environmental factors bearing on internationalisation. There have been innovations in and by the institutions that govern large portions of world trade and investment: the new rules of the General Agreement on Tariffs and Trade (GATT) and the World Trade Organisation (WTO), European Union market integration and the North American Free Trade Agreement (NAFTA), and the general wave of liberalisation and deregulation in previously embargoed industries, as well as instances of the less welcome new protectionism.

The consequences of the Uruguay Round of GATT negotiations are of worldwide significance. The achievements with respect to intellectual property rights and counterfeiting will have impacts on firms' internationalisation strategies. The more secure is a firm's technology in a foreign market, the more willing it will be to engage in non-affiliate licensing; that is, the dissemination of technology will be encouraged. The ratio of foreign direct investment (FDI) to non-affiliate licensing is typically higher in less-developed host countries (LDCs) than in developed hosts, precisely because of the risks of technological dissipation via licensing in the LDCs. Strengthened protection of technology will encourage licensing, wherever this is the lowest-cost method of servicing a host market.

The service sector has historically not been subject to GATT rules until the Uruguay Round. Because many services are non-tradable, freedom to compete in foreign markets requires the right of establishment. The fact that services are now covered for the first time will raise the internationalisation prospects of service industries. While market opening moves are yet to be settled in financial and telecommunications services, the importance of the service sector in international business is in general below its potential level. Services account for around 20 per cent of world trade, over 45 per cent of world FDI, and about 60 per cent of global production. It follows that internationalisation strategies involving trade and foreign investment in services are bound to gain importance.

Protection and liberalisation both have impacts on internationalisation strategy. While tariff and trade barrier-jumping are well documented, it is also the case that firms internationalise in order to learn from newly deregulated markets, in order to improve their competitiveness and to heighten their readiness for deregulation at home and in third markets. This puts an extra twist into the incrementalistic model of internationalisation, founded on progressive market entry and commitment. It is internationalisation strategy, rather than myopic gradualism, that has become the underlying concept. Equally, the impression given by mainstream theory that firms adjust their international business profile slavishly in response to their stock of intangible assets is clearly an over-simplification.

It can be argued persuasively that time horizons in internationalisation strategy have become extended, and that firms' behaviour has become more cognitive. As the world is seen as becoming inexorably more 'borderless', it behoves firms to anticipate developments in the international environment earlier rather than later. Apart from environmental initiatives, technical and technological forces are also at work, influencing internationalisation strategies. It is widely observed that product life cycles have become progressively shorter, meaning that firms have a shorter time over which to recoup their research and development costs. This fact tends to favour the marketing of new products worldwide, without the lag identified in the original product cycle model (Vernon, 1966).

ASPECTS OF INTERNATIONALISATION STRATEGIES

The tendency is to over-simplify when analysing international strategies. The limitation of existing reductionist frameworks of internationalisation is that they overlook the fact that firms make simultaneous use of various internationalisation modes, not only in different markets, but also within the same markets. Greater complexity tends to arise with the maturing of a firm's international activities. Nevertheless, it is generally recognised that the rise of international business is linked to foreign market size and growth, and therefore to the business cycle.

There are two leading impacts of the size and growth of foreign markets on internationalisation. Firstly, as the size of national markets has grown, it has become economic to differentiate products and services to a higher degree. This is a pressure in favour of local production, as differentiation and customisation generally require greater proximity to the market. Therefore, internationalisation modes will tend to evolve into local forms, although local production may not represent the full range of stages in the production process, nor be constituted as the traditional majority-owned affiliate.

Secondly, as the standard economics-based sequential internationalisation model suggests, there is a tendency for the replacement of lower-commitment market servicing modes by higher-commitment modes as foreign markets grow (Buckley and Casson, 1981). The modes chosen reflect comparative advantage and the barriers to international business at the industry, country and firm-specific levels, and the costs of overcoming these in terms of spatial and transaction costs (Buckley and Casson, 1976). The conventional textbook account emphasises the efficiency motives for internationalisation. This is to be read as efficiency from the viewpoint of the firm. In the case of imperfections in intermediate markets, the transaction costs incurred are seen as the costs of doing business. When imperfections are in final markets, the market power motive for internationalisation is in clear evidence; that is, the motive identified in the earlier literature of Hymer (1960), Kindleberger, (1969) and Knickerbocker (1973). Disentangling these fine theoretical distinctions in empirical research is problematic, and not very fruitful.

An important development in internationalisation strategy theory relates to business networks. This body of research analyses how companies in international markets establish, develop and maintain lasting relationships with other business actors (Hakansson, 1982; Turnbull and Valla, 1986). Every firm is engaged in business relationships with customers, customer's customers, competitors, suppliers, supplementary suppliers, distributors and agents as well as regulatory agencies (Johanson and Vahlne, 1990) forming a network of relationships (Johanson and Mattsson, 1986). In these networks, operating companies occupy a clearly defined position (Johanson and Mattson, 1986; 1988), which governs the relationship of each firm with every other firm. According to this view, internationalisation means joining networks that are active across national boundaries.

Industry-related Factors and Internationalisation

At an aggregate level, the growth of internationalisation via exporting is constrained by trade elasticities. Trade elasticities (the responsiveness of trade to economic growth) are determined by industry-specific factors such as tradability and protection against imports. Elasticities are greatest in manufactures, lower in the less-tradable services, and traditionally lowest in protected industries such as agriculture. That is to say that elasticities are greatest in the liberalised sectors. However, this is not a one-way causality, because underlying elasticities are greatest in these sectors; this has predisposed the developed countries to make the largest reciprocal tariff reductions under the GATT in these products, as they offer the greatest scope for export growth.

Liberalisation in trade has promoted simultaneous exporting and multinational production strategies by firms, as witnessed by the growth of international intra-firm trade. International intra-firm trade arises when exports flow between firms within the same multinational group. For developed-country multinationals operating in the developed world, intra-firm exports from the parent to affiliates (or between affiliates) typically consist of finished or nearly-finished products, or of intermediate goods produced under conditions of scale economies. Exports from an affiliate in a less-developed country to the (developed country) parent are usually intermediate products closer to the raw material stage, or products with value added by low-wage labour. A number of studies have suggested that intra-firm trade is considerable. Certainly, within the world's largest firms the proportion of intra-firm trade in visibles is substantial: an average of 50 per cent for those in high research intensity industries, 37 per cent in medium research intensity industries and 6 per cent in the least research intensive industries (Dunning and Pearce, 1981). Because assessments of the extent of intra-firm trade are restricted to visibles, the importance of integrated exporting and foreign production strategies will be even more compelling when services are included.

The most rapid growth of intra-firm trade dates from the introduction of value-added tariffs by the US in the 1960s. The influence of import tariffs on final goods is to cause the bulk of production to locate in the market country. However, value-added tariffs can have a more subtle effect, causing a stage of production to move to a foreign location where a specific factor of production is available. This is best exemplified by the provisions adopted first by the United States in 1966, under tariff schedules 806.30 and 807.00, which taxed only the foreign value-added component of United States imports. This initiative is accepted to have provided an impetus to United States firms, including many multinationals, to export intermediate or semi-finished products to low-labour-cost countries (especially in South-East Asia) for processing, assembly and subsequent re-import to the United States. This pattern of offshore production then became commonplace for multinationals from other developed countries.

In an international context, a distinctive feature of intra-firm trade is the scope which exists for the firm to set prices which may not align with those which would exist between independent importers and exporters. While this may not be a leading strategic motive for internationalisation, it certainly may be a benefit to multinationals which have extensive intra-firm trade coupled with marked preferences for recording profits in particular countries; for example, those with strong currencies or low corporate tax rates.

As intra-firm trade has grown, so has intra-industry trade and intra-industry foreign direct investment; that is, trade and investment classified to the same industry and flowing both ways between partner countries. Intra-industry foreign direct investment is a symptom of an increasing tendency in internationalisation strategies. While it is partly a statistical artefact created by the breadth of industrial classifications, it does reflect the fact that, increasingly, firms from developed countries feel it imperative to mutually penetrate each other's markets in order to remain competitive.

One reason for this interpenetration is the importance of market proximity for the competitiveness of firms. The need to acquire knowledge directly about markets, coupled with barriers facing non-local producers, militates in favour of local presence. The intention to create a Single European Market constitutes a movement towards liberalisation and deregulation which heightens the importance of local market presence. It therefore is a strong stimulant to the operations of non-European Union firms in the European Union (EU) market.

Furthermore, firms will always attempt to re-establish the security they felt prior to liberalisation through novel means, such as alliances and political lobbying. Firms established within the EU will have an incentive to raise barriers against firms on the outside. The most visible manifestation of this to date has been in the form of anti-dumping actions by the EU. This is clearly trade bloc-based protectionism against *de novo* entrants and other more competitive outside producers. Such behaviour also constitutes an incentive to firms that wish to sell in the major markets to also produce within them.

Trade Policy and Internationalisation

There is the view that in the postwar period the power of sovereign territorial states over political and economic affairs has been gradually eroded and replaced by international structures created by firms. The control of multinationals over trade, in particular over intra-firm trade, has already been noted. It can therefore be said that, to some extent, the role of managing the world economy has moved away from the virtually exclusive control of nation states and their creations, such as the GATT.

The shift from old-style protection via tariff barriers to the new protectionism, based on non-tariff barriers and abuses of GATT provisions, is normally explained as a response to changing comparative advantage that generates painful adjustment costs in (mainly Western) domestic markets. The great progress in tariff barrier reduction in successive GATT rounds has disabled the tariff as a regular method of protection. However, trade frictions still induce protectionist responses in the form of non-tariff barriers or anti-dumping actions. One possible outcome might be an international alliance between producers, or an alliance might occur to pre-empt foreseeable frictions. The experience of manufacturing industries such as automobiles and semiconductors conform with this account (Cowhey and Aronson, 1993).

International corporate alliances are structures that have become increasingly popular since the 1980s, and to some extent are mechanisms via which firms are able to circumvent imperfections in international markets. Rather than lobby governments for domestic protection as a lever to gain foreign market access, firms that have international horizons are best advised to pursue their own solutions. In effect, to disengage themselves from the bargaining problems of nation states. This desire is most pronounced when firms operate in industries where high technology and learning opportunities are present, and particularly in service industries where foreign production is more important than trade. In contrast with firms, states are more concerned with favouring domestic production and national champions, and prefer measures that predominantly bolster domestic economic performance.

The implications for internationalisation have been visible in the new forms of international business chosen by firms. The shift from wholly or majority-owned multinational production as the traditional solution to foreign market access difficulties, in favour of alliances, is a reflection of the market barriers that face firms, and particularly those in industries new to international business. International alliances swiftly enable foreign firms to wear the mantle of a domestic producer, often through involvement in some form of joint venture to exploit local procurement bias or to gain local knowledge.

Telecommunications is an industry which is now characterised by international alliances. In this case, the recent changes in firms' strategy is the direct outcome of national liberalisation programmes, where trade was formerly severely limited by national monopolies. Alliances have emerged as information and market-knowledge sharing arrangements, and as a means of securing strategic positions. Firms internationalise into liberalising markets based both on strength (experience of operating in liberalised markets) and on the strategic need to gain experience of a competitive environment, where a firm's home market may not yet have liberalised. While alliances, in their various forms, produce a flush of competition, firms that have been national monopolists naturally might aim to return to some degree of market stability. Indeed, alliances can be viewed as an attempt to make a partial return to the *status quo ante*, as they may bolster barriers to entry to future potential entrants in the longer term.

Firms seeking to export to certain less-developed countries face further types of obstacle, such as requirements for them to participate in countertrade. Countertrade can be defined as a contractual arrangement under which the export of a good is linked to the import of other goods. Countertrade is often not the first choice of Western firms wishing to export, but some have become proficient in arranging countertrade contracts. In the circumstances where a partner-country firm, typically in a less-developed country, lacks the necessary marketing expertise (or cannot acquire it), a firm with the expertise (or access to it) may be an attractive countertrade partner. The underlying problems of countries that have a high incidence of countertrade tend to relate to foreign exchange difficulties, a reliance on a narrow range of exports (often of low quality), country indebtedness, a low indigenous technological capacity, and a concomitant disposition to restrict foreign ownership (Casson and Chukujama, 1991).

REGIONAL PATTERNS OF MULTINATIONALISATION

The internationalisation process for many leading firms results in the globalisation of their business. Globalisation means that investment becomes mobile between countries, but on a global scale. The creation and extension of regional trading blocs has important implications for the strategies of firms. In essence, the more regionalised trade becomes, the more introspective (within each bloc) investment is likely to be. Trade arrangements that foster trade blocs are pursued in the full knowledge that market size and market growth attract investment. To this extent, a degree of trade-bloc rivalry over investment is inherent in regional integration. Above this, certain regional trading arrangements may actually be protectionist, in effect even if not in intent.

The regional trends in multinational activity encapsulate some of these key issues in international business. Table 1.1 shows that the collective grasp on world inward foreign direct investment (FDI) by the three major trade blocs, Western Europe, North America, and Asia Pacific, amounted to 84 per cent in 1980 and 1985, rising to 92 per cent in 1990. This is actually a greater grasp on inward investment than the developed countries of the world taken as a whole. Looking at the detail, it would appear that the hold of Western Europe on inward FDI, predominantly that of the EU(12), slipped in the early 1980s, to recover by 1990. This recovery may have owed something to the announcement of the programme to integrate the European Market. To this extent, the evidence is consistent with firms' foreign investment market servicing strategies having been stimulated by the planned integration of the EU market.

The period of the data presented in Table 1.1 precedes the North American movement towards free trade. Indeed, the North American share of inward FDI fell slightly in the late 1980s. Historically, it can be seen that Canada has been losing its share of inward FDI, while the United States' share has consolidated and that of Mexico has held up. It is to be expected that NAFTA will act as a fillip to foreign investment into North America. The Asia Pacific region accounted for a rising share of world inward FDI throughout the 1980s. Although the share of Japan in world inward FDI is considerably below what might be expected for a country of its market size, its share has clearly been increasing. Internationalisation into the Japanese market has undoubtedly been fraught with difficulties for foreign investors.

The outward investment figures have to be interpreted particularly cautiously, because they are unable to say anything about the split between

Table 1.1 Foreign direct investment stock, percentage distribution for the leading regions of the world, 1980–1990

Regions	*Inward stock*			*Outward stock*		
	1980	*1985*	*1990*	*1980*	*1985*	*1990*
Western Europe	*40.72*	*31.80*	*40.77*	*43.81*	*43.10*	*46.88*
EU(12)	37.39	28.83	37.65	37.73	36.85	41.32
Other Western Europe	3.33	2.97	3.12	6.08	6.25	5.57
North America	*31.94*	*38.18*	*36.23*	*47.09*	*41.98*	*30.87*
Canada	11.52	9.11	7.22	4.38	5.61	4.63
United States	18.53	26.94	26.99	42.71	36.37	26.24
Mexico	1.89	2.13	2.03	0.00	0.00	0.00
*Asia Pacific**	*11.72*	*14.43*	*14.51*	*7.75*	*13.50*	*21.49*
Japan	0.66	0.93	1.23	7.08	12.12	19.27
Western Asia	*0.77*	*4.01*	*1.90*	*0.00*	*0.16*	*0.07*
Latin America and the Caribbean	*6.92*	*6.65*	*4.47*	*0.16*	*0.27*	*0.19*
Africa	*5.20*	*3.28*	*1.30*	*0.08*	*0.06*	*0.03*
Other developed countries	*3.71*	*1.65*	*0.83*	*1.11*	*0.94*	*0.47*
Developed countries	78.61	74.38	82.23	99.58	99.22	99.33
Less developed and Industrialising countries	22.36	25.62	17.77	0.42	0.78	0.67
Total	100.00	100.00	100.00	100.00	100.00	100.00
Value US$M (current prices)	448 248	685 293	1 496 114	515 537	690 227	1 612 980

Notes: Figures may not sum precisely to 100 due to rounding
*Asia Pacific includes Australia and New Zealand

Source: Adapted from United Nations Conference on Trade and Development, World Investment Report (1993), Annex Table 2

intra-bloc and extra-bloc outward investment. A complete set of individual target country data would be needed to establish this distinction. The clearest fact to emerge is that outward investment from the countries of Asia Pacific has grown fastest, driven by the rapid multinationalisation of Japanese firms investing mainly in Western markets. The rapid internationalisation via FDI by Japanese firms has been a response to both market size and growth, but also to trade barriers. However, a word of caution is necessary, as Japanese multinational activity abroad is customarily measured using the cumulation of Ministry of Finance balance of payments flow data. This means that the FDI stock estimate can diverge significantly from the true figure. Historically this has tended to be an underestimate, but as profits are reinvested abroad and investments mature the position becomes more uncertain. This may alter the figures, but there is no argument over the direction of the Japanese trajectory.

The statistics agree with the contention that FDI is a strategy that is heavily oriented towards the developed markets, and towards the regional blocs. In contrast, less-developed host regions, notably Africa (which excludes South Africa for statistical purposes), have consistently lost share on account of the relative lack of attractiveness, in terms of size, growth and risk, of the African market. The reasons why regional blocs elicit such an impact on inward FDI have been put above. There had been created a total of 85 regional trading arrangements by autumn 1993, with as many as 28 being new additions since 1992 (Evans and Walsh, 1994). It is not the place here to speculate over the protective effects of these measures, but firms' perceptions will undoubtedly have shaped their internationalisation strategies.

ENVIRONMENTAL INFLUENCES

The book is divided into two parts. In Part One, Chapters 2 to 6 concern environmental influences on internationalisation strategies; and in Part Two, Chapters 7 to 11 focus on aspects of internationalisation modes. The general theme of the contributions runs counter to the textbook presentation of research on internationalisation: that the influences on and behaviour of firms is reducible to a fairly limited number of determinants, and that firms process through a predictable number of phases of internationalisation. Rather, the contributions suggest, certain firms, and certain industries, may find particular forms of international business to be most appropriate to their needs. The standard factors at the levels of the industry, country and firm have a role, but the specialisation of firms within industries and within stages are also of paramount importance.

Internationalisation strategies can be linked to the desire not only to sell abroad and to produce abroad, but also to buy abroad and to influence government decision-making abroad, as well as to a host of other considerations. Following a brief overview of some of the issues, this introduction will then turn to the contributions themselves and to how they advance our understanding of internationalisation strategies.

Chapters 2 and 3 treat the effects of trade blocs: the first, by Roger Strange, provides an historical account of the creation and development of trade blocs as well as a discussion on the link between regional developments and foreign direct investment. It is argued that the Single European Market, the European Economic Area and NAFTA all move significantly beyond trade integration and include important provisions to promote intra-bloc flows of factors of production. Consequently, these developments are expected to greatly influence intra and extra-bloc internationalisation strategies.

A finer resolution on the impact of the integration of the European Union and the creation of NAFTA is furnished in the subsequent chapter by Peter Buckley, Chris Pass and Kate Prescott. Based upon their own empirical research, this contribution studies the actual bilateral internationalisation strategies adopted by UK and Canadian firms. The early signs are that regional concerns have dominated perceptions, such that both governmental and corporate decision-making have raised the spectre of inwardness. This implies protectionism and the potential sidelining of GATT, with the re-emergence of bilateral bargaining between trading groups.

However, it has become apparent that the threat of 'Fortress Europe' was overstated, and little evidence emerges of renewed European protection, either tariff or non-tariff. Where barriers are alluded to, the focus is mainly on remaining barriers between the EU markets as opposed to trade barriers with non-members. This challenges the proposition that regionalisation inevitably results in free trade internally and protectionism externally. Nevertheless, the potential threat of renewed protectionism is sufficient to fuel the belief that it is necessary to establish within the European Union in order to take full advantage of the freedoms being offered by the Single Market. The authors also find that strategies of internationalisation differ between industries, depending on whether industries are global in nature or more regional (or national) in character. The nature of industries in this respect has been greatly influenced by technological aspects. Clear evidence is offered that technological developments are taking place outside economic unions, which are then exploited on a global scale.

In Chapter 4, Niklas Arvidsson extends the argument that arose in the previous chapter: that there are substantial differences in the choice of internationalisation strategies arising from the nature of the industry, and the nature of products (for example, services versus goods). Arvidsson focuses on services and explores how the distinctive characteristics of services impact upon internationalisation. It transpires that the critical strategic choices that have to be made by service companies contrast strongly with those of manufacturing companies. Three main categories of abilities appear to influence the success of strategic choices for internationalising service firms. Firstly, the ability to build relationship-driven product offerings to the customers. Secondly, the ability to select effectively from the numerous investment alternatives. Thirdly, the ability to develop network contacts. However, the importance of these three capacities varies as internationalisation progresses.

The initiation of internationalisation in services is highly influenced by network contacts and the firm's abilities or desires to become international. Further expansion is more influenced by knowledge previously gained, and the need to maintain standards of quality. International competition in services tends to require production within foreign markets earlier than in manufactured products, and this paper provides substantiation of this.

Eleanor Morgan bases her chapter (Chapter 5) on evidence from the common competition rules of the European Union. This chapter demonstrates how the regulatory environment evolves, and how it can constrain investment strategies. The rules have dual objectives, between which there is a degree of tension. On the one hand, they are designed to remove obstacles to the Europeanisation of firms' activities by ensuring that anti-competitive behaviour does not keep the internal market divided. On the other, they are intended to ensure that consumers enjoy the potential efficiency benefits from market integration.

The progressive removal of barriers to trade as part of the single-market programme encouraged corporate reorganisation through mergers and merger-like arrangements, which threw the inadequacies of EU controls into sharp relief, increasing the pressure for new merger regulation at the Union level. The introduction of EU merger regulation in 1990 represented an important development in European competition policy. It was intended both to facilitate mergers by reducing transaction costs, and to give the Commission specific power to control those which appeared anti-competitive.

Closing Part One, Chapter 6, by Christos Nicolaidis and Carla Millar, lays the foundations for an explanation of how both national and corporate cultural elements influence decision-making in internationalisation strategies. Entrepreneurs in different nations are influenced in their decision-making, throughout the internationalisation process, by general national and corporate cultural values. This, in turn, implies that a nation's culture may be integral to the process of creating and developing a firm's distinct competitive advantage. It follows that internationalising companies will tend to reproduce significant features of their national cultures in their structure and functioning in cross-border activities.

INTERNATIONALISATION METHODS

The contributions in Part Two show how the individual modes adopted (for example, international franchising, licensing or joint ventures) or the nature of the function (for example, purchasing, production or marketing) are shaped internationally. It transpires clearly that the choice of mode in internationalisation is a dynamic and continuously evolving phenomenon.

Fred Burton and Adam Cross provide a fresh approach to international franchising in Chapter 7. They offer and develop new ideas on the factors affecting the choice between the various different types of international franchising. Firms employing franchising contracts in their internationalisation process can, and frequently do, invest significant amounts of equity in host-country franchise sub-systems. These equity investments challenge many of the simplistic assumptions traditionally held by scholars of foreign market entry. Agency theory issues, and transactional and internalisation aspects are each involved in the choice of the precise type of low or high-equity international franchise entry method.

Entry modes in the Chinese market are the focus of both Chapters 8 and 9. Wei-Ping Wu examines some of the variables which differentiate firms that opt for the use of licensing from those whose preference is for joint ventures. The joint venture is a higher resource commitment entry mode than licensing. Amongst other things, at the firm level, his findings suggest that licensing is preferred by smaller firms that perceive the potential risks of the Chinese market to be higher, and by firms that have a commitment to servicing world markets via exports. At the industry level, the degree of standardisation of the product favours licensing. At the country level, the author's measure of cultural distance shows no effect; however, firms that perceived a greater political and economic distance between China and their home EU country were found to be reluctant to commit higher levels of resources. For the host country, the finding that equity-based transfers convey more know-how, including tacit know-how, than licensing, is a vindication of the policy stance in favour of the joint-venture mode of foreign involvement.

Haochun Dong, Peter Buckley and Hafiz Mirza focus on the motivations for joint-venture formation, and the factors involved in partner selection, control and conflict of joint-venture partners in key decision areas. Their findings strongly indicate the importance of national characteristics (country-specific factors) in determining differences in performance between joint ventures, according to the country of origin of the foreign partner. Generally, investments from North American and European companies are larger and are of a longer duration, and are more market-orientated when compared with overseas Chinese investments, which are more profit oriented. North American and European investments are technologically more advanced and are likely to be in technology-intensive industries, such as electronics, pharmaceuticals and motor industries, in contrast with investments from overseas Chinese.

The authors of Chapter 9 also report that local partners in joint ventures with Western multinational corporations (MNCs) were relatively more satisfied with their joint venture's performance than those in joint ventures with overseas Chinese, and the Western partners' level of satisfaction is much lower than their local counterparts. The longer-term outlook suggests that Western and Japanese joint ventures are conducive to a higher level of performance satisfaction than the profit-orientated outlook of overseas Chinese partners. At the firm level, a clear locational strategy emerges. Companies with a high inclination to export tend to choose a location in coastal areas, and particularly in special economic zones where fiscal incentives for offshore production are most favourable. Firms with a long-term commitment to targeting the domestic market are more likely to select a fairly central location, such as Beijing, Tianjin or Shanghai.

In Chapter 10, Timothy Clark and Geoff Mallory give an account of the shifts between and within market servicing modes, as well as shifts between forward and reverse modes. Their results demonstrate that whilst firms may expand on a country-by-country basis, they do not apply the same foreign market servicing strategy in each market. New forms of foreign market servicing are pursued, according to interdependencies with existing foreign operations. Firms continually monitor their overseas operations, both as separate entities but also in terms of their interrelationships. The sequential approach suggested by the stages theory of internationalisation is appropriate for some firms in some markets, but the firm may use its accumulated experience from operating internationally, or that of the group of which it is a part, to jump intermediate steps and adopt a direct route to FDI.

Recognition of the importance of international sourcing decisions is highlighted in Chapter 11, by Shan Rajagopal and Kenneth Bernard, in their analysis of the internationalisation of the procurement process. They argue that global procurement is increasingly important in the competitive strategies of firms, regardless of whether the final output of these firms is itself for world markets or for domestic markets. In other words, firms may become internationally oriented or multinational simply on account of the imperative to source internationally. This is not an unfamiliar proposition in the case of natural resource-oriented foreign direct investment nor, for example, in the case of foreign affiliates based on manufacturing stages that are intensive in low-wage labour. However, the generalisation of the phenomenon does imply the restructuring of the internal relationship between the supply side and the marketing functions in an ever larger number of firms.

PRELUDE TO THIS COLLECTION

This introduction has sought to draw attention to a few of the developments in research, and in the international economy, that bear upon internationalisation strategies. The detailed treatments of the subject material are the domain of the individual papers. Each of the chapters has something distinctive to contribute to the discussion. The editors have encouraged this diversity. In presenting the contributions, we have not sought to impose a uniformity of approach or standard usage of terms, either for geographical areas or in respect of more idiosyncratic concepts. As is common in international business research, authors use alternative terms. A good example of this is the variety in terminology to denote the multinational enterprise (MNE), most notably TNC (transnational corporation, the United Nation's preferred usage) and MNC (multinational corporation). The renaming of institutions, in particular the European Community (EC) as the European Union (EU) has inevitably meant that both are referred to within this volume, either for reasons of historical accuracy, or quite simply because of the aesthetic desirability of consistency within chapters.

It is clear that the subject of internationalisation strategies is accessible from a variety of discipline standpoints and topic areas. This is exactly as it should be. The broadening out of international business research is synonymous with its deepening, and is essential to the maturing of the subject. Internationalisation strategies cannot be approached from a single point. To this extent it is evident that the wider the forum, then the better it is for research. This is very much the view of the Academy of International Business and of its UK regional branch, which is responsible for the annual conferences held in the United Kingdom.

The topics included in this collection are in no way exhaustive of the possible contributions to the subject of internationalisation strategies. However, the general themes of internationalisation in the face of regionalisation and regulation, coupled with the special issues raised by internationally-oriented services, and by cultural factors, are representative of the range that international business research must comprehend.

Research must also have something to say about how firms actually compete in international markets, in particular about internationalisation methods. The study of international business must contribute to an understanding of the choices that confront firms. These are many, not least because of the great variety of internal and external factors bearing on firms. As is represented in this volume, a blend of theory, empirical work and the study of policy is essential to meet the challenges of as dynamic an area as international business research.

2 Trading Blocs, Trade Liberalisation and Foreign Direct Investment

Roger Strange

INTRODUCTION

Two of the most interesting phenomena in the contemporary world economy are the explosive growth of foreign direct investment (FDI) and the emergence of new and/or the extension of existing regional trading blocs. In the 1950s and 1960s, a first phase of regional integration saw the formation of the European Economic Community (EEC) and the European Free Trade Area (EFTA), together with a number of other short-lived trading blocs in Latin America, the Caribbean and Africa. A second phase in the late 1980s and early 1990s has brought initiatives not only in Europe and Latin America, but also in North America, Australasia and South-East Asia. Furthermore, this new phase of 'regionalism' has generated considerable concern about whether the relatively open, multilateral world trading system will be superseded by a small number of large, relatively closed regional blocs.[1]

The effects of most (if not all) of these preferential trading arrangements on trade have been analysed extensively, both at the theoretical and the empirical level.[2] In contrast, the effects of such arrangements on FDI have received far less attention despite its increasing importance. The main purpose of this chapter is to attempt a partial remedy for this neglect, and to explore the relationship between regional integration and FDI in the context of the world trading system in the mid-1990s.

The chapter is organised as follows. The next section examines the theoretical link between regional integration and FDI, and it is argued that the relationship depends upon the underlying entrepreneurial motivation for the investment, and upon the liberalisation provisions of the integration. The role of the General Agreement on Tariffs and Trade (GATT) in promoting multilateral trade liberalisation and in implementing rules governing the application of trade-related investment measures (TRIMs) is then considered. The following section traces the historical development of the major trading blocs in the world, and discusses how their creation and/or extension are interrelated and linked to the GATT process. The penultimate section highlights important trends in the growth of FDI during the 1980s and early 1990s. Attention is drawn not only to the effects of regional integration, but also to the liberalisation of the regulatory framework for FDI in many host countries, recent substantial inflows of direct investment in service industries, and the rise of FDI from Japan. In the final section, three interrelated issues are considered. First, do any parallels exist between the first phase of regional integration in the 1950s/1960s and the second phase in the 1980s/1990s? Second, has the process of regional integration helped or hindered the GATT process? Third, what effects will the second phase of regional integration have upon FDI through the 1990s?

REGIONAL INTEGRATION AND FOREIGN DIRECT INVESTMENT

Regional integration which involves arrangements for preferential trade may take a number of forms. The term *trading bloc* is usually reserved by economic theorists[3] for arrangements which take the form either of a free trade area or of a customs union. A *free trade area* involves the elimination of tariffs on trade between the member states, but each member maintains its own national policy towards trade with third countries. Customs inspectors monitor trade at the frontiers between the member states in order to tax trade that might otherwise circumvent high tariff barriers by entering the area through the member state with the lowest external tariff. In contrast, member states of a *customs union* adopt a common external tariff. Commodities thus flow freely between member states, and there is no need for customs inspection at national borders.

Trading blocs involve the removal of trade barriers, but stop short of further economic integration. A *common market* allows not only for the free movement of commodities, but also for the free movement of factors of production. Finally, *economic union* is used to describe the situation where member states not only participate in a common market, but also promote a high degree of integration in their fiscal, monetary, commercial and welfare policies.

Compared to the ideal of free world trade, any preferential trading arrangement which discriminates against third countries typically leads to an inefficient pattern of production.[4] In reality, however, the world is already characterised by widespread barriers to trade, and thus the pattern of production is already inefficient. Regional integration typically leads to reductions in tariffs and other barriers to trade between the member states, and this liberalisation has a number of effects on both trade and FDI. First, there are the static effects of trade creation and trade diversion.[5] Then there is the dynamic effect on trade through the creation of a large unrestricted domestic market which allows efficient domestic manufacturers to take advantage of economies of scale, with a resultant fall in average costs of production.

The trade liberalising aspects of regional integration also have repercussions for FDI. To the extent that firms (either domestic or foreign) increase their investment in response to a larger market, or rationalise their production to lower-cost locations within the bloc, then there will be benefits in terms of efficiency and welfare. On the other hand, if trade diversion provides the catalyst for FDI, there will be a loss of economic efficiency and welfare. Other provisions of deeper regional integration will also have an effect on FDI. The removal of restrictions on the movement of factors of production (especially the movement of capital) should facilitate both intra-bloc FDI, and FDI from third countries. And FDI should also be stimulated by the relaxation of ownership and entry requirements, and other liberalising measures to open markets to greater competition.

The liberalisation measures associated with regional integration will, however, typically impact in different ways upon intra-bloc FDI and upon FDI from third countries, and will also have differential effects according to the underlying entrepreneurial motivation of the investing firm. Firms are motivated to invest overseas for a variety of reasons, and six stylised 'types' of FDI may be identified[6] – see Table 2.1.

- The first type of FDI is that undertaken to gain access to specific factors of production (for example, resources, technical knowledge, managerial know-how, patents or brand names) owned by a firm, or firms, in the host country. If such factors of production are not available in the home economy of the foreign firm, and are not transferable at arm's length, then the foreign firm must invest locally in order to secure access. This will typically involve an equity stake in an appropriate host-country firm (if the factor is firm-specific), although the factor in question may take the form of a public good available to all firms in the industry. An example of the latter would be an industry consortium to pool research and development (R&D) resources, and whose results were only available to members.
- The second type of FDI is that identified by Raymond Vernon in his celebrated product cycle hypothesis (Vernon, 1966), and considers investment to gain access to cheaper factors of production (for example, low-cost labour). This type of FDI may be encouraged by the government of the host country if it is pursuing an export-oriented development strategy, in which case it may well provide some form of investment incentive (subsidies, grants, tax concessions and so forth) to the foreign firm. If the government is following an import-substitution policy, on the other hand, foreign firms may only be allowed to participate in the host economy to the extent that they possess technical or managerial know-how that is not available to domestic industry. Such know-how may be transferable on an arm's length basis, in which case the foreign involvement may take the form of a licensing arrangement or other form of contractual resource transfer. Or, if the know-how is not transferable in this way, then a foreign minority stake may be encouraged in a joint venture with a local partner.

Table 2.1 A typology of the entrepreneurial motivations for foreign direct investment

Motivation for FDI	*Competitive environment*	*Policy response of host country government*	*Likely characteristics of FDI*
Access to factors of production	Host country firm(s) have access to certain factors of production (materials, technology etc.) not available/transferable to foreign firms	Passive (unless deemed against national interest) as host country firms are assumed to hold competitive advantage	Acquisition of host country firms
Access to cheaper factors of production (Product cycle hypothesis)	Shift of comparative advantage from emergence of cheaper factor costs in host country	Conditional upon development strategy and requirements to promote technology transfer. Protection of domestic industry by import quotas/tariffs and controls on foreign equity participation	Contractual resource transfers and joint ventures with minority equity participation by foreign firms
Access to products (MPI scenario)	International competition among similar products. Technical change leaves firms in different countries with competitive advantages in different sub-products	Passive, as mutual benefits perceived for foreign and host country firms	Mutual equity participation
Access to customers	International trade and competition are limited because of punitive transport costs, or because customers require local production/service	Passive, as foreign firms will be operating in the host country on the same basis as domestic firms	Full manufacturing/service operations, together with local design facilities
Access to markets (Tariff-jumping FDI)	International competition among similar products. Technical change shifts comparative advantage in favour of foreign firms. Import penetration in host country increases	Protection of domestic industry through import quotas/tariffs etc.	Assembly operations. Continued parts/components from abroad. Investment-shunting. Subsidiaries are wholly-owned or involve majority equity participation by foreign firms
Access to future markets (*Quid pro quo* FDI)	As above	Threat of protection for domestic industry	Full manufacturing operations, together with local sourcing of parts/components and local R&D facilities. Joint ventures/technical agreements with host country firms

Source: Strange (1993) pp. 40–1

- The third type of FDI involves international competitors undertaking mutual investment in one another (either through cross-shareholdings, or through the establishment of joint ventures), in order to gain access to each other's product ranges. The background to this type of FDI is increased competition among similar products as a result of R&D-induced specialisation. Both firms find it difficult to compete in each others' home markets, or in third-country markets for each other's products. If neither product (and hence neither firm) gains the dominant advantage, then the two firms may well invest in each other's area of expertise, and thus promote sub-product specialisation in production.
- The fourth type of FDI relates to that undertaken by firms in order to secure access to customers in the host-country market. No underlying shift in comparative advantage either to or from the host country is observed, but exporting from the firm's home base may be impossible (for example, certain services), punitively expensive because of transport costs (for example, bricks), or unfeasible because customers insist on short supply lines (for example, components) or the capability to request immediate design modifications and/or amendments. In particular, the limited tradability of many services (for example, banking, other financial services or retail and wholesale distribution) has been an important factor promoting the growth of FDI in these sectors.
- The fifth type of FDI relates to the trade diversionary aspect of regional integration. This is commonly known as 'tariff-jumping' FDI and occurs when there are locational advantages for foreign firms in their home country, but the firms are prevented from exporting to the host economy by the existence of tariffs or other barriers to trade. The foreign firms therefore jump the barriers by establishing a local presence within the host economy in order to gain access to the local market. The local manufacturing presence need only be sufficient to circumvent the trade barriers,[7] as the foreign firm will want to maintain as much of the value-added in its home economy, hence simple assembly operations will be the norm.
- The final type of FDI is that undertaken by foreign firms not with the intention of jumping protective barriers, but with a view to defusing the threat of protection itself. As with tariff-jumping FDI, this follows a systemic shift in comparative advantage in favour of the foreign producers as a result of R&D-induced changes in know-how. The defusion may be achieved either by enhancing directly the benefits (on employment and so on) that FDI confers on the host economy, or by co-opting local firms in joint ventures and thus allocating them a share of the potential benefits. Such *quid pro quo* FDI is thus likely to take the form either of full manufacturing operations together with local sourcing of parts and components, or of strategic alliances with selected competitors in the host economy.

How then are these six types of FDI affected by the various measures which may accompany regional integration? Table 2.2 provides a summary of the expected effects of the main provisions, upon both intra-bloc FDI and FDI from third countries.

Clearly the relaxation of ownership and entry requirements to restricted industries will stimulate both intra-bloc FDI and FDI from third countries. This will be the case whether the motivation is to gain access to factors of production, products or markets, or whether liberalisation permits foreign firms access to new customers. The liberalisation of intra-bloc labour movement will have little effect on any type of FDI flow, except for intra-bloc FDI which is undertaken to gain access to customers and where the investing firm's competitive advantage lies in the expertise of its workforce. Various service industries (for example, finance, insurance or consulting) would fit this pattern. The liberalisation of intra-bloc capital movements should have little effect upon FDI from third countries, except perhaps through easing the formation of joint ventures with local partners. But freer capital movement will aid all types of intra-bloc investment for obvious reasons.

Of most interest, however, are the differential effects on FDI of the reductions in intra-bloc barriers to trade that accompany regional integration. The reduction of such barriers should have little effect on FDI undertaken to gain access to specific factors of production, as the acquisition of know-how, expertise and so on was the primary motivation, not trade. Intra-bloc FDI to gain access to cheaper factors of production will increase as firms within the bloc rationalise their production activities. FDI from third countries may also increase as cheaper locations entice some foreign firms to pursue production within the bloc for export to the higher-cost markets. FDI to gain access to products will also be promoted by reduced barriers to trade as the potential market for the joint venture will be enlarged. In contrast, FDI to gain access to customers should not be significantly affected as, by definition, international trade is either impractical or unfeasible.[8]

The final two types of FDI are both related to the discriminatory aspect of regional integration. Any reduction in intra-bloc barriers to trade will increase the competitive disadvantage (within the bloc) suffered by firms from third countries in relation to firms from within the bloc, and will lead to trade diversion. FDI by the firms from the third countries is therefore a possibility, as they attempt to secure access to the protected market. On the other hand, intra-bloc trade will be stimulated by the reduction in the barriers, and any intra-bloc FDI previously undertaken to secure access to the markets of partner countries may well be reduced.

The various provisions of regional integration agreements thus have quite different effects upon FDI from within the bloc, and from third countries outside the bloc. Furthermore, these effects differ according to the underlying entrepreneurial motivation of the direct investment. Second-round effects may also be identified. For example, much investment in services is linked to investment and/or trade in manufacturing.

Table 2.2 The effects of liberalisation measures on flows of foreign direct investment into a trading bloc/common marke

Motivation for FDI	*Source of FDI*	*Relaxation in ownership and entry requirements*	*Liberalisation of intra-bloc labour movements*	*Liberalisation of intra-bloc capital movements*	*Reduction of intra-bloc barriers to trade*
Access to factors of production	Within bloc	++	0	+	0
	Outside bloc	++	0	0	0
Access to cheaper factors of production	Within bloc	++	0	+	+
	Outside bloc	++	0	0	+
Access to products (MPI scenario)	Within bloc	++	0	+	+
	Outside bloc	++	0	+	+
Access to customers	Within bloc	++	++	+	0
	Outside bloc	++	0	0	0
Access to markets (Tariff-jumping FDI)	Within bloc	++	0	+	–
	Outside bloc	++	0	0	++
Access to future markets (Quid pro quo FDI)	Within bloc	++	0	+	–
	Outside bloc	++	0	0	++

Notes:
++ indicates a strong positive effect of the liberalisation measure on foreign direct investment
\+ indicates a weaker positive effect of the liberalisation measure on foreign direct investment
0 indicates little or no significant effect of the liberalisation measure on foreign direct investment
– indicates a negative effect of the liberalisation measure on foreign direct investment

Finally, it is important to note that regional integration may play a role in promoting international policy convergence towards FDI.[9] This may occur if integration results in the convergence of the regulatory regimes of the member states, or if pressure may be exerted on non-member countries to bring their policies into line with those adopted by member states,[10] or if the activities of international firms exert pressures to harmonise policies at the global level. Such policy convergence can only serve to promote further foreign direct investment.

THE GENERAL AGREEMENT ON TARIFFS AND TRADE

The General Agreement on Tariffs and Trade (GATT) was established in 1947,[11] and has become the main forum for the promotion of orderly world trade relations. Three basic principles underscore the various Articles of the Agreement, viz.: non-discrimination, reciprocity and transparency. The principle of non-discrimination – or the Most Favoured Nation (MFN) rule, as it is also known – requires that all countries should treat all other signatories in the same way with regard to trade concessions and/or barriers. In theory, it thus prohibits any form of preferential trading arrangement, though in practice the situation is rather more permissive. The principle of reciprocity requires a country benefiting from a tariff reduction to make a corresponding concession. The MFN rule then leads to such concessions being enjoyed by all the GATT signatories. Finally, the principle of transparency requires that countries replace quotas and similar quantitative restrictions with more visible tariffs.

Various exceptions to the principles are allowed within GATT in certain circumstances. Non-tariff measures may be extended on a temporary basis in times of balance-of-payments difficulties, or to protect agricultural industry. Discrimination is permitted against imports dumped by specified countries, through the use of anti-dumping and/or countervailing duties. And Article XXIV provides for the establishment of free trade areas and customs unions, under which member states may exercise discriminatory treatment in favour of each other, and for preferential trade between a country and its colonies or dominions.

The first seven rounds of GATT negotiations (Geneva, 1947; Annecy, 1949; Torquay, 1950–51; Geneva, 1955; Dillon, 1959–62; Kennedy, 1964–67; and Tokyo, 1973–79) all essentially concentrated on the reduction of tariff barriers to trade.[12] Furthermore, the tariff reductions were largely confined to trade in manufactured goods, while certain 'sensitive' sectors (for example, textiles, agriculture and services) were exempted.

The eighth and most recent round of GATT negotiations began at Punta del Este in Uruguay in September 1986, and was originally scheduled for completion in 1990. The agenda was far more ambitious than those of previous rounds, and the potential difficulties were reinforced by the large number of participants (with different and often conflicting objectives) and the complex and interlinked set of issues. These included not only tariff and non-tariff barriers to trade in industrial products, but also trade in services, agriculture and textiles, as well as various features of the GATT system, and other issues such as the protection of intellectual property rights, and trade-related investment measures (TRIMs).

The original deadline was comprehensively missed amidst much acrimony, but agreement by the 117 participants was finally reached on 15 December 1993.[13] Twenty-eight accords were covered, and were to be implemented from January 1995. Tariffs on industrial goods were cut by an average of 40 per cent worldwide. Subsidies and barriers[14] to trade in agricultural produce were reduced over a period of six years, thus bringing trade in the sector under multilateral rules for the first time. Textiles and clothing too were brought under GATT rules, with the quotas under the Multi-Fibre Arrangement (MFA) to be gradually eliminated after 1995 and finally abolished after ten years. New and/or revised rules were laid down *inter alia* on rules of origin, anti-dumping, subsidies and countervailing measures, and safeguards. And a World Trade Organisation was established from July 1995, encompassing GATT and sister bodies on services and intellectual property, which would have substantial powers to resolve disputes between members. Estimates vary as to the scale of the effects on the world economy, but it is likely that they will be in the region of 1 per cent of gross global income by the year 2002.

With regard to services, the Uruguay Round established a comprehensive framework of multilateral rules to govern trade in services, and various national commitments to a continuing process of liberalisation. Individual countries promised market-opening measures in a range of industries including tourism, construction, consultancy and professional services. But general agreement was not forthcoming in a number of important industries. Air transport was not included in the negotiations from the outset. Further talks were planned during 1994–95 on liberalisation in the telecommunication, financial services, audio-visual services, and maritime transport industries.

The accord on the protection of intellectual property rights encompassed agreement on the protection of patents, copyright, trademarks, industrial designs, semiconductor layout designs and trade secrets as well as rules on geographical indications. Industrial countries were given one year, and most developing countries were given five years, to implement the accord in their national legislation. Additional time was allowed for the least developed countries.

TRIMs are imposed by some host country governments on foreign investors, often in conjunction with some form of investment incentive and/or trade protection. They may be input-based (for example, local content requirements) or output-based (for example, export performance requirements), and may either restrict or augment trade.[15] It is these trade-distorting aspects that underpinned US insistence that TRIMs be included on the agenda for the Uruguay Round, but there was a broad spectrum of opinion on the appropriate treatment by GATT in the various submissions that were made. The thrust of the submissions from developed countries was that TRIMs had trade-distorting effects, and should in some way be controlled by GATT. In contrast, the submissions from developing countries typically stressed that TRIMs were primarily investment measures and thus beyond the GATT mandate.

The final accord prohibits the use of TRIMs which are inconsistent with either Article III (national treatment) or Article XI (prohibition of quantitative restrictions) of the GATT. Local content requirements and trade balancing requirements are included in the list of TRIMs which are deemed to be so inconsistent. All non-conforming TRIMs are subject to mandatory notification and elimination within two years in the case of developed countries (five years for developing countries, and seven years for the least-developed countries), and the implementation of these commitments is to be monitored by a newly-established Committee on TRIMs.

THE HISTORICAL DEVELOPMENT OF THE MAJOR TRADING BLOCS

The late 1950s and early 1960s witnessed the creation of various trading blocs and other preferential trading arrangements in the world economy. The most notable of these were the European Economic Community, the European Free Trade Area, the Latin American Free Trade Area, and the Canada–US Autopact; but there were numerous other examples in Africa, Latin America and the Caribbean.[16] The late 1980s and early 1990s have seen the extension of existing blocs and/or creation of new blocs in a second phase of regional integration. Here, one may draw attention to the moves towards the Single European Market and the European Union, the European Economic Area, the North American Free Trade Area, the ASEAN Free Trade Area, the Australia–New Zealand Closer Economic Relations Trade Agreement and various groupings in Latin America. This section outlines the historical development of these major trading blocs, and discusses how their creation and/or extension are related.

The European Union

The European Economic Community (EEC) was established by the 1957 Treaty of Rome, and the original signatories were Belgium, France, the Federal Republic of Germany, Italy, Luxembourg and the Netherlands.[17] Its formation was due in part to the slow progress on trade liberalisation in the early GATT Rounds. The 1947 Geneva Round of GATT negotiations had brought agreement to make tariff concessions on items covering about one-half of world trade at the time. Negotiations in this and the subsequent five rounds were all conducted on an item-by-item basis, and thus, as Williamson and Milner note:

> The pace of trade liberalisation associated with early rounds could not be maintained. This was due in part to the cumbersome nature of item-by-item bargaining on a multilateral basis. More important, however, was the fact that the process encountered political resistance. In the early rounds, item-by-item bargaining proved acceptable because it allowed negotiators to select items for concessions where tariff redundancy allowed 'liberalisation' with limited need for adjustment, but eventually countries with low tariffs were concerned that a continuation of the item-by-item process would eventually leave them in an exposed position relative to countries with high tariffs.
>
> As a response to dissatisfaction with item-by-item negotiation it was suggested as early as 1951 that tariffs be lowered on an across-the-board basis, and that the reductions should be planned and staged. This proposal was not endorsed by the United States or Britain, and the continental European nations channelled their energies into economic integration instead. The outcome was the creation of the EEC in 1956 and the European Free Trade Area (EFTA) in 1959 [*sic*]. This preoccupation with regional liberalisation undoubtedly undermined interest in multilateral liberalisation via GATT in the 1950s.[18]

A timetable was specified in the Treaty of Rome for the abolition of customs duties on intra-EEC trade, and for the establishment of a common external tariff for imports from third countries.[19] The harmonisation of external tariffs was subsequently speeded up and the customs union was realised eighteen months ahead of schedule in 1968.

Notwithstanding the early achievement of customs union and the subsequent enlargement of the Community,[20] concern had been growing about the less than impressive economic performance of the Community through the 1970s and early 1980s. Attention was subsequently focused on the plethora of non-tariff barriers which nullified many of the potential benefits of the 'Common Market', as the European Community was mistakenly known. The conclusion was that border controls and customs red-tape, divergent standards and technical regulations, conflicting business laws and protectionist procurement practice all contrived to maintain 12 distinct national markets.

The issue of non-tariff barriers had been addressed in both the Kennedy and Tokyo Rounds of GATT negotiations, but little agreement had been reached. As in the 1950s, the European countries instead pursued their own unilateral initiative. In 1985, the European Commission published a White Paper on *Completing the Internal Market*[21] which set out a detailed legislative programme for creating a real common market in Europe by the end of 1992. The White Paper foresaw the removal of non-tariff barriers in Europe catalysing a supply-side shock to the Community economy. Costs would be reduced, and prices would then fall under the pressure of competition. Lower prices would in turn stimulate demand and give companies the opportunity to increase output, to exploit resources more efficiently, and to take advantages of scale economies in European competition. Financial markets (banking, insurance and securities) would be liberalised, which would enable the wider availability of credit and better allocation of financial resources across the Community. Macroeconomic benefits were also predicted. Public deficits would be eased under the dual impact of open public procurement and the regeneration of the Community economy. Any tendency to inflation would be offset by the drop in prices provoked by open markets. The improvement in competitiveness would mean that economic growth would not damage the external trade position of the Community. And, last but not least, substantial job creation was envisaged.[22] The Single European Act was agreed in December 1985, and the Single European Market (SEM) came into being on 1 January 1993. Thereafter, the Community became (at least in theory) a true common market.

Meanwhile, further initiatives were underway both to widen and to deepen the Community. The treaty establishing the European Economic Area with the seven EFTA nations – see below – was signed in October 1991. Hungary, Poland and Czechoslovakia all concluded agreements on association with the Community in December 1991.[23] These agreements took effect on 1 March 1992, and were aimed at promoting the free flow of goods within ten years. All three Eastern European countries are likely to press for full EU membership in the future. And, in December 1991, the Maastricht Treaty signalled significant moves to progress towards greater economic, monetary and political union. The Treaty contained new agreements on consumer protection, health, education and trans-European networks in telecommunications, transport and energy projects, and set a date (1999) for European Monetary Union. The Treaty came into effect on 1 November 1993, and thereafter the correct title for the Community became the European Union.

The European Free Trade Area

The United Kingdom had declined to be one of the original members of the EEC, largely because of her ties with the Commonwealth and hence her traditional access to cheap food supplies. As a reaction to the formation of the EEC, she had instead established (with Austria, Denmark, Norway, Portugal, Sweden and Switzerland) the European Free Trade Area (EFTA) through the 1960 Stockholm Convention. The aims of EFTA were rather more modest than those of the EEC. Tariffs on intra-EFTA trade in manufactured goods were to be removed in stages, but a common external tariff was not adopted, neither was a common agricultural policy envisaged. The United Kingdom could thus continue to accord preferential treatment to goods, especially agricultural produce, originating in the Commonwealth. Finland and Iceland joined EFTA as associate members in 1961 and 1970 respectively, and Liechtenstein some time later. After the withdrawal of Denmark and the United Kingdom to join the European Community, the remaining EFTA members negotiated the phased removal of tariffs on trade in manufactured goods between them and the EEC from 1972.[24]

The passing of the Single European Act forced a reassessment of the role of EFTA, and of its relationship with the larger Community. A series of negotiations led, in October 1991, to an agreement to create a European Economic Area (EEA) with effect from January 1993. Subsequent legal problems meant that the EEA did not come into force until 1 January 1994, and that only five of the EFTA countries (Austria, Finland, Norway, Sweden and Iceland) were signatories.[25] The main features of the EEA accord[26] are unrestricted trade in goods and most services (including banks and financial services), and the creation of a single labour market. Labour and capital will be able to circulate freely within the EEA, except for some restrictions on direct investment in areas such as fisheries and property in the EFTA countries.[27]

The EEA is thus not a customs union with a common external tariff, and frontier controls will still remain between the EFTA states and the European Union. Yet, the EEA accord also contains a number of provisions that promote the movement of factors of production, and the EEA is thus more than a simple trading bloc. In addition to the free movement of capital, EEA companies will be permitted to establish affiliates in all other EEA countries, either through acquisition or new investment, and will be granted national treatment therein.

The North American Free Trade Agreement

The passing of the Single European Act in 1985 provoked Canada and the United States to conclude a Free Trade Agreement (FTA)[28] on 4 October 1987. Charles notes that:

> The US Congress . . . was becoming more and more protectionist . . . Canada was also aware that 1992 in Europe may create a major trading bloc with protectionist walls about it. It feared US and Japanese retaliation. This would mean Canada, as the smallest of the Group of Seven developed economies, would be on its own against the major trading blocs. For both economic and geographic reasons, the United States was the natural trading partner with which to establish a free trade agreement.[29]

The agreement became effective on 1 January 1989, and provided for the phased elimination (over a maximum period of ten years) of all bilateral tariffs on manufactured goods, the reduction of many non-tariff barriers to trade in goods and services, and the liberalisation of direct investment flows. The two countries agreed to provide national – that is, equivalent – treatment to investors from the other. Restrictions on the establishment of new firms were eliminated. Canadian screening of indirect acquisitions by US investors was to be phased out. The FTA did not, however, establish a common external policy, nor did it allow unrestricted labour mobility.

Soon afterwards, Mexico approached the United States to negotiate a bilateral free trade pact to run alongside the Canada–US FTA. Canada was eventually drawn into the negotiations, and the result was the North American Free Trade Agreement (NAFTA) signed in August 1993. NAFTA came into effect on 1 January 1994. Its main provisions[30] include the elimination of tariffs and other trade barriers between the three countries over a period of 15 years (depending upon the industrial sector), and the removal of investment restrictions in most sectors. Labour mobility was excluded, though some movement of white-collar workers was eased.[31]

The NAFTA represents both a deepening and a widening of the Canada–US FTA, and is noteworthy in that it involves countries with significant differences in wage levels and living standards. Such differences explain the NAFTA restrictions on full labour mobility, and the fact that each country has been allowed various temporary reservations with regard to investment and services.

Preferential Trading among Developing Countries

The establishment of free trading areas, customs unions and/or common markets has a long, but not particularly distinguished, history among many developing countries.[32] An early example was the Latin American Free Trade Area (Mexico and all the South American republics), which was created in 1960 but which had effectively split into smaller groups by 1969. Various initiatives in Africa and the Caribbean have also proved to be short-lived.

The appeal of such preferential trading arrangements to developing countries is that they potentially create markets large enough to support the economies of scale needed for 'home' producers to compete effectively with the more advanced countries. The main problem is the unequal distribution of benefits from the new import-competing industries, with the gains inevitably concentrated in one, or a few, locations. Together with a lack of effective mechanisms for sharing these benefits through some form of income distribution, the resultant political tensions have all too often destroyed the union.

Nevertheless, some preferential trading arrangements have persisted and there are signs of renewed interest in regional integration in a number of areas of the world. In Latin America, for example, a number of trading blocs currently exist:[33] the Central American Common Market (Guatemala, El Salvador, Honduras, Nicaragua, Costa Rica and Panama); the Caribbean

Community (Antigua and Barbuda, Barbados, Belize, Dominica, Grenada, Guyana, Jamaica, Montserrat, St Kitts and Nevis (including Anguilla), St Lucia, St Vincent and the Grenadines, Trinidad and Tobago); the Andean Pact (Venezuela, Colombia, Ecuador, Peru and Bolivia); and the Southern Cone Common Market (Mercosur), whose members are Brazil, Paraguay, Argentina and Uruguay. Mexico is already a member of NAFTA, and Chile has started negotiations on accession. Many of the above countries have recently cut tariffs unilaterally to the outside world, with a resultant surge in regional trade. Further integration is also likely as a result of the NAFTA agreement, as the Latin American countries seek to maximise their bargaining power.

Other examples include the Association of South-East Asian Nations (ASEAN), whose members are Brunei Darussalam, Indonesia, Malaysia, the Philippines, Singapore and Thailand. Established in 1967 largely in response to an external security threat,[34] a preferential tariff arrangement was implemented in 1977 but this

> fell into disrepute when it became clear that most of the items on the list were put there because they were so little traded. Indonesia generously offered a 10 per cent cut in tariffs for snowploughs; Malaysia granted preferential tariffs on a list of rubber products of which it is the only large ASEAN producer.[35]

As Kirkpatrick notes,[36] the pattern of East Asian trade and investment expansion through the 1970s and 1980s occurred independently of any significant institutional integration agreement within the region, and was based on progressive, unilateral, non-discriminatory liberalisation of trade and capital movements.[37] The rapid growth in the region was based largely on exports to Europe and North America, and trade expansion in East Asia thus began as a process of worldwide integration. Given these outward-oriented development strategies and the countries' heavy involvement in world markets, the ASEAN nations were concerned about developments in Europe and North America in the early 1990s.[38] Notwithstanding the protestations of the participants, both the SEM and the NAFTA were seen as (potentially) protectionist, and these worries were reinforced by the uncertain outlook for the Uruguay Round of GATT negotiations. The ASEAN nations were particularly concerned that the preferential access to the EU market granted to selected Eastern European countries, and Mexico's membership of NAFTA, would both result in significant trade and investment diversion away from the East Asian region.

The countries in the region thus began to look at options for greater regional cooperation and integration, and one tangible result was the agreement in October 1992 between the ASEAN countries to establish an ASEAN Free Trade Area (AFTA).[39] The agreement brought together 320 million consumers in one of the world's fastest growing areas, and envisaged the reduction of tariffs to a maximum of 5 per cent over a 15 year period from January 1993. An initial list of 15 products, including cement, rubber, wooden furniture and textiles, was slated for attention in the first seven years while more sensitive items (for example, cars and components) were deferred for later action.

GLOBAL TRENDS IN FOREIGN DIRECT INVESTMENT

Foreign direct investment (FDI) emerged as a major phenomenon in the world economy in the 1960s:

> Prior to that decade, most multinational enterprises (MNEs) had the bulk of their foreign investment in the developing countries, and the dominant organisational pattern was for each affiliate to be as self-contained as possible – small clones, scattered around the world, of the mother company. Developments in transport and communications technology permitted the emergence in the 1960s of a more centralised organisational structure, where production and financing decisions were taken at headquarters and allocated across subsidiaries.[40]

FDI through the 1960s grew at twice the rate of GNP in the OECD countries, with US companies accounting for a substantial proportion of the cross-border investment. In particular, there was a surge of FDI from the United States in the newly-formed European Economic Community.[41] The growth of FDI worldwide was checked by the oil and other commodity price shocks of the early 1970s, and it was not until the mid-1980s that the strong upward trend was resumed. Between 1983 and 1990, FDI outflows rose at an average annual rate of 27 per cent – about four times faster than the growth of world output and three times faster than the growth of exports – to $234 billion in 1990.[42] In 1991, the outflow fell to $180 billion, and preliminary estimates for 1992 show a further fall to $150 billion.[43] The developed countries accounted for about 97–98 per cent of total worldwide outflows of FDI through the 1980s and early 1990s, with the five G-5 countries (that is, the United States, the United Kingdom, Japan, Germany and France) accounting for two-thirds of the total.

As regards FDI inflows, the G-5 countries accounted for about 56 per cent of the total over the period 1980–1990.[44] The share taken by all the developed countries rose from 74 per cent over the period 1981–1985, to 83 per cent over the period 1986–1990. This increasing trend seems to have been reversed in the early 1990s, with the developing countries receiving 25 per cent of all FDI inflows in 1991 and almost one-third ($40 billion) in 1992.

The major stimuli to the surge in FDI during the 1980s are perhaps fourfold.

First, there was a phenomenal explosion of FDI from Japan, reflecting the growing internationalisation of the Japanese economy.[45] FDI from Japan doubled between 1975–1977 and 1981–1983, and then increased eight-fold between 1981–1983 and 1987–1990. Second, many developing countries showed more interest in FDI as a source of capital, technological know-how and managerial skills. This gave rise to greater liberalisation of trade and of the regulatory framework for FDI, particularly in Latin America and South-East Asia.[46] The liberalisation process accelerated during the late 1980s, and occurred largely independently of moves towards regional integration in these areas.

Third, the rapid growth of FDI was marked by significant changes in its sectoral composition. In the 1950s, much of FDI was concentrated in resource-based activities. In the 1960s – as noted above – developments in transport and communications technology enabled more FDI in manufacturing. In the 1980s, services and technology-intensive manufacturing accounted for the largest proportion of new FDI. In particular, the increased role for services FDI came about because of the increased demand for services as a result of higher real income per capita in many countries. It has been facilitated, moreover, by major changes in information technology which have not only made existing markets more accessible, but have also created markets for new services. Many services are non-tradable, and thus FDI is the only way to participate in foreign markets. But FDI has been widely prohibited in many service industries, in both developed and developing countries, for a variety of reasons. The rise of FDI in services was thus held back until the liberalisation of these industries had caught up with the domestic process of structural change. In many developed countries – beginning with the United States and spreading to the G-5 countries and elsewhere – the process of deregulation gathered momentum through the 1980s, and FDI rose concomitantly. In the European Community, for example,

> obstacles to foreign direct investment and trade in services remained untouched until the late 1980s when the 1992 project began. The mere announcement of the Single Market and the process to remove these obstacles has led to a massive reorganisation of service industries in the Community and has created a substantial interest on the part of transnational service corporations from all major home countries which rapidly started positioning themselves in the large and dynamic Community market. As a result, the share of services in total foreign direct investment in the European Community by both third-country and Community transnational corporations rarely fell below 60 per cent in each of the years during the 1984–1988 period.[47]

Fourth, and of most importance in the context of this chapter, there have been the moves towards regional integration, notably in Europe and North America. Empirically, the SEM programme has been contemporaneous with an increase in intra-EC FDI and an increase in FDI from third countries, particularly Japan. As argued above, however, this increased FDI arises for a variety of entrepreneurial motivations and in response to a variety of measures, some associated with the process of regional integration and some not. Unfortunately, it is not possible to discern from data on FDI flows whether the FDI is of the product life cycle type, whether it is of the 'tariff-jumping' type, and so on. Neither is it possible to discern whether it has been stimulated by reductions in barriers to trade, by the liberalisation of certain industries, or by the liberalisation of movement of factors of production. All play a part, and the effects – some positive, some negative – are confused. Japanese direct investment in the European Community, for example, has been motivated by different reasons in different industries[48], and is certainly not all of the tariff-jumping variety. Much of the intra-EC FDI in the late 1980s was stimulated by the liberalisation in service markets, though some was motivated by firms' desire to rationalise their operations on a Community-wide scale.[49] Finally, it is important to draw attention to the Latin America/East Asian experience where unilateral, non-discriminatory liberalisation, rather than regional integration, has provided the stimulus to substantial inflows of FDI.

CONCLUDING REMARKS

Three issues are considered in this section. The first issue relates to whether any parallels exist between the first phase of regional integration in the late 1950s/1960s and the second phase in the late 1980s/1990s. The answer is yes, but with certain reservations. Both phases of regional integration have been catalysed by periods of slow progress in multilateral trade liberalisation. In the 1950s, it was dissatisfaction with the item-by-item negotiations of the early GATT rounds that encouraged the continental European countries to create the European Economic Community. And the creation of the EEC stimulated the creation of the European Free Trade Area. In the 1980s, it was partly dissatisfaction with the slow progress of the Tokyo and Uruguay Rounds on items such as trade in services, dumping and non-tariff barriers to trade that prompted the Single European Market initiative.[50] And this initiative led to the creation of the European Economic Area, and to the Canada–US Free Trade Area and subsequently to the North American Free Trade Area. NAFTA is expected to promote further integration in Latin America, and the formation of the ASEAN Free Trade Area is a response to both NAFTA and the EEA.

On the other hand, there are important differences in the scope of the agreements in the two phases. First, both the EEC and EFTA accords were concerned with the liberalisation of trade flows. In contrast, the Single European Market, the European Economic Area, and NAFTA all move significantly beyond trade integration and include important provisions to promote intra-bloc flows of factors of production and the liberalisation of services. These differences are mirrored in the agendas of the various GATT rounds. Second, the Latin American, African and Caribbean agreements of the 1960s were motivated primarily by national import-substitution policies, and thus actively promoted trade diversion. In contrast, the regional agreements of the 1990s have accompanied and promoted trade liberalisation, and may well prove more successful as a result.

The second issue relates to whether the process of regional integration has been compatible with multilateral trade liberalisation. Again the answer is a qualified yes. It is evident that many of the major agreements have pre-empted multilateral measures introduced through the GATT negotiations, and it has been argued, for example, that the creation of the EEC stimulated the Dillon and Kennedy Rounds of GATT negotiations. It is also generally accepted that the formation of the EEC, in particular, brought substantial trade creation.[51] Furthermore, it is arguable that the existence of powerful trading blocs has forced concessions from other participants, and has thus aided the process of multilateral trade liberalisation.[52] On the negative side, there is testimony that European attention to the creation of the EEC undermined interest in the GATT process in the 1950s, and it is likely that similar US, Canadian and European preoccupations delayed the conclusion of the Uruguay Round. Furthermore, the growing profusion of managed trade deals and other bilateral arrangements which distort free trade have probably been facilitated by the existence of ever more powerful trading blocs.

The third issue concerns the prospects for FDI through the 1990s. One indisputable fact is that FDI is already a major phenomenon in the world economy.

As the UN Conference on Trade and Development reports, there were 170 000 foreign affiliates of some 37 000 parent companies in 1990. Worldwide sales of these affiliates was approximately $5.5 trillion, compared to world exports of goods and non-factor services of $4 trillion. Furthermore, the figure of 37 000 covers only those firms that have equity stakes of more than 10 per cent in foreign affiliates. It does not include

> firms that control assets abroad through various non-equity ties (for example, management contracts, transfer-of-technology contracts, subcontracting agreements, franchising) and that are linked with other firms through strategic alliances. No data are available on those, but estimates are that strategic alliances number in the thousands and subcontracting agreements alone in the hundreds of thousands.[53]

As the authors of the report argue, these activities promote significant integration between countries even in the absence of trading blocs.

In the future, it is likely that the pattern of FDI will continue to be dominated by the factors identified in the previous section, but with the additional influence of greater multilateral regulation of FDI provided by the World Trade Organisation.

The process of regional integration will be furthered in Europe (with the accession of the EFTA countries, and perhaps the Eastern European countries, to the European Union), in America (with the accession of Chile, and perhaps other Latin American countries, to NAFTA), and in East Asia (with the possible establishment of an Apec Free Trade Area). Although it has been argued that the link between regional integration and foreign direct investment is by no means a simple causal relationship, these initiatives are likely to promote further FDI in the aggregate. In the European Union, FDI will be stimulated by the removal of barriers to trade, the greater freedom of movement for factors of production, and the liberalisation of ownership and entry requirements in service industries. FDI between the EU and EFTA will be furthered in the short term by the provisions of the EEA agreement with regard to the free movement of capital, the granting of national treatment, and the liberalisation of labour movement. In the longer term, it seems inevitable that the EFTA countries will seek, and obtain, full EU membership, and this should stimulate further investment flows. In North America, the NAFTA will also promote intra-bloc FDI, though it may be some time before the full effects are felt due to the lengthy phasing-out period of many trade barriers and the remaining restriction on labour mobility and investment. Considerable FDI from third countries in low-cost Mexico for export to both the United States and Canada is also likely.

In East Asia, as noted above, regional integration has played less of a role in promoting FDI. Much of the recent economic success of the region has been fuelled by inward investment, and the ASEAN governments are keen to prolong the inward flows of foreign capital. The success of their liberalisation policies is likely to promote yet more liberalisation in the region, and also to set a trend for other developing countries to follow. The emergence of China (and India) as major investment locations will certainly add to the inward flows of foreign investment in the region.

The deregulation of service industries worldwide should also progress in the 1990s. The process will be furthered within the European Union and North America by the measures introduced as part of the SEM and NAFTA programmes respectively. FDI in service industries worldwide should also increase as the Uruguay Round accords give the process additional multilateral momentum.

FDI from Japan and other East Asian countries may be expected to increase substantially through the 1990s. Japanese FDI fell back in 1991, largely in response to the domestic slowdown and the worldwide recession. There are clear signs, however, that Japanese firms, having invested substantially in North America and Europe through the 1970s and 1980s, are now turning their attention once again to East Asia, and particularly China. Furthermore, outward investment from South Korea, Taiwan, Singapore and so on is also likely to rise dramatically as a consequence of their development success. The share of total worldwide inflows of FDI to developing countries should therefore rise, as too should the share of worldwide outflows from the developing countries.

Finally, the increasing importance of FDI flows worldwide has raised a whole range of issues related to the international regulation and promotion of direct investment. Balasubramanyam and Greenaway (1993) note that as,

> borders shift back with increasing openness, and the role of conventional trade instruments (most notably tariffs) declines, issues that were formerly regarded as non-border measures – investment policies, regulation of services, protection of intellectual property, competition policy – are increasingly becoming the subject of trade friction within and between regions.[54]

The accords concluded in the Uruguay Round on the protection of intellectual property, TRIMs, the provision of investment incentives and the liberalisation of services are particularly relevant here. For example, the accord on intellectual property rights should provide a stimulus to FDI and technology transfer, particularly to developing countries. With regard to TRIMs, if they are binding they act as a disincentive to FDI in that they require the foreign investor to do something that it would not otherwise have done. The prohibition of certain TRIMs should therefore promote FDI in the affected industries, though it might also reduce FDI in intermediate goods industries.[55] These and related issues are certain to appear high on the agenda of the newly-established World Trade Organisation.

Notes

1. United Nations Department of Economic and Social Development (1992), p. 44.
2. Srinivasan *et al.* (1993) review various empirical studies on the impacts of regional agreements.
3. In this chapter, the term will be used as a shorthand to cover any form of preferential trading arrangement.
4. Although individual countries may be better off in a tariff-ridden world.
5. Trade creation occurs when a country starts to import a commodity from a fellow member state that it had previously produced domestically, and this serves to increase welfare and efficiency within the bloc to the extent that expensive (domestic) supplies have been replaced by cheaper imports from the partner. On the other hand, the formation of the bloc may encourage member states to expand trade with each other to the exclusion of non-member countries. Trade diversion occurs when a country starts to import a commodity from a fellow member state that it had previously imported from the outside world, and this serves to reduce welfare and efficiency within the bloc to the extent that cheap imports from outside the bloc have been replaced by more expensive imports from fellow member states. The net welfare effect depends upon whether the

gains from trade creation outweigh the losses from trade diversion, or vice versa. The relative size of these effects depends upon a number of factors notably the price elasticity of import demand, and any cost differentials between the home country, its fellow member states, and suppliers from the outside world. The most favourable conditions for welfare-improvement are typically found for trade in manufactured goods among industrialised countries; the least favourable conditions for trade in agricultural goods among developing countries.

6. See Strange (1993), pp. 33–42, for further discussion of this classification.
7. The local operations may, however, be circumscribed by local content requirements, and other trade-related investment measures. See Greenaway (1990) for a discussion of the economic effects of various TRIMs.
8. Indeed, it is unlikely that industries which fall in this category will be heavily protected by tariffs and so forth, as such protection would be superfluous.
9. See United Nations Department of Economic and Social Development (1992), p. 45.
10. This may be the case when countries wish to join the trading bloc (for example, EFTA and the European Union, Latin American countries and NAFTA).
11. The Charter contained 38 Articles, and there were 23 signatories.
12. The Kennedy and Tokyo Rounds did see *inter alia* attempts to control the growth of non-tariff barriers (quotas, voluntary export restraints and so on) to trade, and the introduction of codes on anti-dumping, subsidies, and technical barriers to trade.
13. The Final Agreement was signed in Marrakesh in April 1994.
14. All quantitative restrictions were converted to tariffs in line with the GATT principle of transparency.
15. See Greenaway (1990) for further discussion.
16. The Council for Mutual Economic Assistance (CMEA or COMECON) is not included in this discussion as it was not a trading bloc in the accepted sense of the term, but more of an agreement on the division of labour among the participant countries. CMEA was formed in January 1949, and the six original members were Bulgaria, Czechoslovakia, Hungary, Poland, Romania and the Soviet Union. Albania and the German Democratic Republic signed up later in the year (Albania left in 1962). Mongolia (1962), Cuba (1972) and Vietnam (1978) subsequently joined, and several other countries had observer status. One commentator suggested it might be called a 'trade-destroying customs union'. See Holzman (1985).
17. The same six countries were also founder members of the European Coal and Steel Community (ECSC) established by the Treaty of Paris in 1951, and the European Atomic Energy Community (Euratom) set up by a second Treaty of Rome in 1957. In 1965, a single Council and a single Commission were established to replace institutions pertaining to the individual communities, and the whole was thereafter referred to as the European Community (EC).
18. Williamson and Milner (1991), p. 332.
19. The common external tariff was set equal to the arithmetical average of the import duties of the six Member States, and was thus GATT-consistent.
20. The United Kingdom, together with Denmark and the Irish Republic, joined the European Community in 1973. Greece became a member in 1980, and Spain and Portugal increased the membership to 12 in 1986. The Federal Republic of Germany merged with the German Democratic Republic to form a united Germany in October 1990.
21. Commission of the European Communities (1985) *Completing the Internal Market.*
22. Cecchini (1988) p. xix.
23. The European Community has for many years had association agreements with

a large number of countries, which provide for preferential access for specified goods to the EC market. The Lomé Convention has since the 1960s allowed access to specified quantities of certain goods from a number of African, Caribbean and Pacific countries – largely countries with ex-colonial links. Twelve Mediterranean countries also have concessionary access. See Winters (1993), pp. 117–19. The agreements under the Lomé Convention led to trade diversion away from competitive producers in Latin America and other areas not eligible for associate status. This prompted UNCTAD, after much negotiation, to introduce the Generalised Scheme of Preferences (GSP) in 1971. See Williamson and Milner (1991) p. 349. Wolf (1993) reports that, in 1991, EFTA accounted for 22.4 per cent, the Mediterranean countries for 7.1 per cent, the Lomé countries for 3.9 per cent, and other developing countries under GSP for 6.2 per cent of EC external imports, and that the agreements with the eastern European countries must be added to the list. He concludes that the 'EC sits at the centre of a spider's web of discrimination, discriminating itself and a source of discrimination in others'.

24. Each EFTA country had a separate but similar agreement with the European Community. 'The EFTA agreements arose from the need to reduce market losses in industrial goods when the UK acceded in 1973. The UK had industrial free trade with these countries by virtue of its membership of EFTA, and provided a major market for their exports; the sudden application of the common external tariff would have damaged EFTA economically and the EC politically.' See Winters (1993), p. 118.
25. Switzerland rejected the EEA accord in a referendum in December 1992. As a result, Liechtenstein could not join the EEA until it had changed its customs union with Switzerland.
26. *Financial Times* (1 January 1994), pp. 1 and 22.
27. Furthermore, the two blocs will maintain separate agricultural regimes, and there will be some special provision on fisheries, energy and transport.
28. A forerunner of the FTA was the 1965 US–Canada agreement (Autopact) on automobile manufacture and trade. It is also interesting to note that Canada and the United States were both members of a free trade area as long ago as 1854, but the agreement was abrogated in 1866 as a response to British interference in the US Civil War. Thereafter, protectionist instincts in one or both countries forestalled any new agreement until 1987. See Charles (1989), pp. 18–20.
29. Charles (1989), p. 20.
30. See United Nations Conference on Trade and Development (1993), pp. 51–2.
31. In addition, two side accords were concluded which provide for fines and/or sanctions if a panel finds repeated non-enforcement of environmental laws, and for penalties for non-enforcement of child, minimum wage, and health and safety laws. Agreement was also reached to negotiate an anti-dumping and subsidy code by 31 December 1995.
32. See Greenaway and Milner (1990) for further details.
33. *Financial Times* (19 November 1993), p. 25.
34. Kirkpatrick (1994), p. 197.
35. 'Fortress Asia?' *The Economist* (24 October 1992), pp. 79–80.
36. Kirkpatrick (1994), pp. 195–7.
37. As such, it is very different from the pattern in Europe and North America.
38. Anderson and Blackhurst (1993), p. 3.
39. The six members of ASEAN, together with Australia, Canada, Japan, South Korea, New Zealand and the United States, were the original members of the Asia Pacific Economic Co-operation (Apec) group which was founded in 1989 at the suggestion of Australia. China, Hong Kong and Taiwan joined the group

in 1991. The group is a forum for discussion of economic issues though the United States, in particular, has indicated an interest in expanding Apec's role and creating new formal structures in which to discuss trade liberalisation. A suggestion that the group should agree to set a timetable for the achievement of an Apec Free Trade Area was not met with enthusiasm at the 1993 meeting in Seattle, though the idea will probably reappear in the future. See the *Financial Times* (16 November 1993, p. 8 and 18 November 1993, p. 4).

40. Julius (1990), p. 4.
41. Balasubramanyam and Greenaway (1993), p. 147.
42. United Nations Department of Economic and Social Development (1993), p. 1.
43. United Nations Conference on Trade and Development (1993), p. 16.
44. United Nations Department of Economic and Social Development (1993), p. 17.
45. See Strange (1993), pp. 64–71 for further discussion.
46. United Nations Centre on Transnational Corporations (1992), pp. 1–15.
47. United Nations Centre on Transnational Corporations (1991), p. 20.
48. See Strange (1993), pp. 357–73.
49. It is doubtful, however, if such rationalisation was the main stimulus to intra-EC FDI as some authors have suggested. For example, see United Nations Department of Economic and Social Development (1993), p. 31.
50. The frustration with multilateral negotiations is also evident in the growth in the numbers of managed trade agreements (particularly between the United States, the European Community and Japan) in sensitive sectors such as automobiles, textiles, semiconductors and steel. The agreements typically take the form of either voluntary export restraints or voluntary import expansions, and fall outside GATT rules because they are 'voluntary'.
51. The trade creation effects of EFTA were more limited. It is obviously too early to assess *ex post* the effects of the SEM, EEA and NAFTA initiatives, though the various *ex ante* studies suggest substantial net benefits for the participants.
52. Certainly the objective of increased economic clout has been in the minds of many who champion the formation of trading blocs. See the comments above with regard to the Latin American accords.
53. United Nations Conference on Trade and Development (1993), p. 19.
54. Balasubramanyam and Greenaway (1993), p. 163.
55. For example, Japanese investment in the UK automobile component industry was prompted by the local content requirements imposed on the UK factories of Nissan, Honda and Toyota.

3 Global Integration: Changing Bilateral Trade and Investment Relations between Canada and the UK[1]

Peter J. Buckley, Christopher L. Pass and Kate Prescott

INTRODUCTION

Over the last couple of decades, dramatic changes have been witnessed in the international business environment. Internationalisation of business has continued apace, driven partly by stagnant domestic markets and partly by the need to expand abroad to spread risks and compete on a par with leading multinational players. As a result, the international business arena is no longer dominated by large multinationals emanating from the world's leading developed markets; the newly industrialising countries (NICs) have spawned a number of global players, and small firms have begun to take on a more significant role in international business activity. Typically nationally constrained industries, those comprising 'the service sector' in particular, have as a result of liberalisation and deregulation opened up to international competition, further fuelling changes in international competitive activity, and adding to competitive intensity.

Internationalisation has also acted as a spur to technology development, promoting innovation, dramatically reducing technology life-cycles and creating a sophisticated and demanding global customer base concerned with issues of quality and service. Research and development has consequently moved up the business agenda at a firm-specific level, and leading nations have been forced to reassess their competitiveness in terms of the commodity composition (technological sophistication) of their trade (and investment).

In the light of such changes and increased competitive pressure, the process of regionalisation is almost inevitable. Opening up markets and removing barriers which result in business inefficiency on a regional basis is an important way of promoting the competitiveness of firms within the region, better preparing them for competing successfully on a global scale. The Single European Market Act (1986) was designed to combat the problems which had typically been associated with the fragmented nature of Europe, consisting of a number of relatively small, highly distinctive national markets, wherein the need for market-by-market adaptation militated against firms' drive for efficiency. Its creation resulted in the largest consumer market in the world (365 million people) posing a threat to the USA and Japan, which had for some time exploited the advantages of their large domestic markets. In response to this threat, the Americans signed the North American Free Trade Agreement (1989) with Canada – with Mexico soon to be included in the union.

The impact of such regionalisation on the world economy has yet to be felt. The early signs, however, show that the dominance of regional concerns means that issues in both governmental and corporate decision-making have raised the spectre of 'inwardness', protectionism and the potential sidelining of GATT with the re-emergence of bilateral bargaining between trading groups. In essence, liberalisation within the regions – but barriers and protectionism between them.

This chapter seeks to explore the impact of regionalisation on the bilateral strategies of UK and Canadian firms, with the intention of discovering whether the Single European Market Act (SEM) and North American Free Trade Agreement (NAFTA) have facilitated or frustrated firms' developments within each others' trading region. The UK and Canada provide a very interesting case. Once linked by their Commonwealth affinity they now find themselves members of two distinct world trading blocs. As a result, the future of cross-Atlantic flows between the two nations (at least in their current guise) may be called into question.

However, as regionalisation is but one dynamic in the strategic decision-making process – firm-specific, industry-specific and country-specific factors, along with changes in the global environment discussed above, all acting as critical dependent variables – it is important to hold constant as many factors as possible so that a true assessment of the impact of NAFTA and the SEM can be made. The chapter therefore focuses on certain key propositions associated with regionalisation, drawn from a wide bank of literature on the subject. The nature of the interviews conducted, comprising open-ended, exploratory questions, means a full exploration of motivations and attitudes is possible.

THE SAMPLE OF FIRMS

Twenty-five interviews were conducted with ten Canadian and 15 UK firms between January and July 1992, almost exclusively with executive-level managers. The sample traverses a wide cross-section of industry and commerce, with sectors being chosen to reflect key industries in each country's economy: those in which one country is clearly dominant (pharmaceuticals

Table 3.1 The sample of firms: firm codes

Industries covered	*Firm codes* *UK*	*Canada*
Pharmaceuticals	1.1	
	1.2	
Wood, paper and pulp		2.1
Food and drink	3.1	3.4
	3.2	3.5
	3.3	
Transport equipment, systems and services	4.1	4.3
	4.2	
Financial services	5.1	5.4
	5.2	5.5
	5.3	5.6
Communications	6.1	6.2
		6.3
		6.4
General industrial equipment & systems	7.1	
	7.2	
Power supply & equipment	8.1	
	8.2	

for the UK and wood, paper and pulp for Canada); those demonstrating strong and growing bilateral flows (general industrial equipment, transportation equipment and services and food and drink); industries growing rapidly in the world economy (communications and financial services); and a number of sectors where major acquisitions have taken place in recent years (telecommunications systems and power).

Table 3.1 summarises and classifies the firms interviewed and industries covered. Firms have been allocated code numbers in order to preserve anonymity. What the table does not show, however, is the varying size and international experience of the firms in the sample. In terms of size (and associated resources available for international expansion), firms range from those with foreign turnovers of less than £50 million (with trade dominating their international activities) to multinational enterprises with a large number of foreign investments and turnover in excess of £200 million. Relating to experience, there are firms in the sample which are in the throes of internationalising for the first time and those which have, over many decades, built up significant trade and investment activities.

Consequently, the sample reflects both the essence of bilateral trade and investment between the two countries, as well as the changes taking place in the global environment alluded to earlier.

KEY PROPOSITIONS

A number of key propositions relating to the effects of regionalisation will be discussed in the light of attitudes towards regionalisation, and bilateral strategies employed by the firms in the sample. The propositions are drawn from the general literature on the impact of regionalisation on both member and non member countries.

Trade Creation and Trade Diversion

The concept of regionalisation contains an element of discrimination against non-member countries (El-Agraa, 1988) which means it involves a certain paradox – free trade on the inside, protectionism on the outside. This leads to two important economic effects – trade creation, increased trade and efficiency within the trading bloc, and trade diversion, wherein trade creation is at the expense of trade with non-member countries.

From a bilateral trade point of view, to test out these propositions it is necessary to explore the incidence of renewed trade restrictions from both a tariff and non-tariff perspective as well as the impetus for tariff/non-tariff barrier induced FDI.

Free Trade and Competition

Once operating inside a trading bloc, foreign firms are subject to the same competitive conditions as indigenous firms – the potential to operate freely across national borders and the increased competitive pressures engendered by free competition and improved efficiency. This gives rise to two further propositions: firstly, firms will utilise their established base within the Canadian or UK markets to exploit the wider opportunities offered by the opening up of markets (or will rationalise production into a single centre to promote efficiency); and second, intensified competitive activity will enforce a reassessment of strategy as a means of consolidating competitiveness. With non-member firms having to also combat the challenges of 'foreignness' within the trading bloc, there are grounds to suggest they are operating at a strategic disadvantage *vis-à-vis* domestic competitors, necessitating their developing strategies which permit full exploitation of compensating advantages.

Technological Advance

The 'virtuous circle' of economic benefits associated with regionalisation assumes that initial cost-cutting programmes, prompted by competitive pressure and the need to lower prices (facilitated by economies of scale) – static efficiency gains – will give way to differentiation-based competition which demands innovation and new product development as firms attempt to gain competitive advantages in the longer term – dynamic efficiency gains – (Cecchini, 1988). The development of new technologies, or access to technological advances, will therefore take on greater significance within the new economic groups. Therefore, it is necessary to explore firms' strategies from the point of view of enhancing technology.

Within the European Community, technological development is being promoted through a number of government funded research initiatives, many of which are expressly targeted at joint-development projects between firms based in different EU Member States. The aim is to facilitate the transfer of new technologies across the Member States to promote EU-wide competitiveness rather than monopoly power of individual players. With reciprocal programmes across the North American bloc, the impact of regionalisation on technological advance may potentially be to induce parallel technological developments between the EU and NAFTA, resulting in technological divergence, making it more difficult for intra-bloc trade.

THE EFFECTS OF REGIONALISATION

Table 3.2 summarises the main activities of the firms in the sample, their foreign market servicing strategies and the likely impact of regionalisation. The information provided forms the basis of the following discussion of the key propositions and, while it is impossible to assess each circumstance in any depth, the experiences of the sample of firms provides a bank of information from which common examples can be drawn.

Trade Creation and Trade Diversion – Attitudes to European Protectionism

The genesis of the Single European Market raised international political concerns over the establishment of 'Fortress Europe', and renewed protectionism against non-member countries. Some 'rumblings' of this nature were apparent among Canadian firms, principally in relation to non-tariff protectionism.

Canadian firms, like their US counterparts, have been frustrated by lack of access to the documentation of the new European standards setting committees – CEN (The European Committee for Standardisation) and CENELEC (The Committee for Electrotechnical Standardisation). In the communications sector, Company 6.4 (the aerospace manufacturer) referred to this as 'gamesmanship' – frustrating but fair, and over-stated as a source of competitive disadvantage given the propensity of technology-based firms to locate activities within the EU.

Similarly, Company 6.2 (the telecommunications equipment manufacturer) suggested lack of access to the new standards for Canadian firms was not the key issue – rather the fact that Alcatel and Siemens, the two leading

Table 3.2 Summary of foreign market servicing strategies and effects of regionalisation

Firm code/Business activity	*Current foreign market servicing strategy in Canada/UK*	*Likely impact of NAFTA/SEM*
1.1 Pharmaceuticals (UK) Ethical pharmaceuticals for clinical treatments	• Established Canadian sales office in 1950 • Acquisition of Canadian producer (1958) giving a 'secondary' manufacturing facility • Established US sales office in 1950 • Co-marketing agreement with Swiss company (1963) to sell key new drug in USA • Established major greenfield manufacturing/sales/R&D operation in USA in 1964	• Product line rationalisation involving greater intra-plant specialisation and cross exporting to enhance both 'presence' advantages (e.g. local product customisation) and plant operating economies
1.2 Pharmaceuticals (UK) Speciality ethical pharmaceuticals & over-the-counter branded products	• Began exporting to Canada in 1989 using local distributor (one product only)	• Initial signs have been promising & company looking at the possibility of selling more products through the distributorship. Also looking to expand into the USA (prompted by NAFTA) and are looking for new US distributors
2.1 Wood, paper & pulp (Canada) Forest and related products, building materials, communication papers, pulp, paperboard and packaging	• Established UK sales subsidiary (1967) (timber, wood, pulp) • Acquisition of UK manufacturer of wood products (1989) • Strategic alliance established in the Netherlands and being sought in Germany (sourced by exports from Canada)	• Further joint ventures being sought in mainland Europe. Deeper FDI involvement being sought to overcome the EU's 'protectionist stance' as well as increased investments by the Nordic timber producers
3.1 Food and drink (UK) Fresh meat (bacon & poultry) eggs and milling	• Acquisition of a major Canadian flour miller and food products company (1987) • Acquisition of Canada's largest food processing company (1990) • Joint venture company formed with US flour milling group (1992) • A number of subsidiaries in the USA, [illegible]	• NAFTA raising the company's interest in the USA where alliances with major US producers would help the company make a bigger impact with major US food store groups. NAFTA is expected to create new opportunities for selling the company's products on a pan-American scale

3.2 Food and drink (UK) Premium teas	• Exports to Canada through long-established distributorship • Initially exported to USA through regional distributors • The company was acquired in 1984 by a UK food company who then sold it to another UK food company in 1989. This latter company has a sales/marketing subsidiary in the USA which now handles the company's products in the USA	• NAFTA has led to a review of the company's overall North American operation and it is possible that the that the US sales subsidiary will take over responsibility for handling the company's brands in Canada
3.3 Food and drink (UK) Soft drinks	• Initially, exported small volumes to Canada via a distributorship established in 1985 (the distributor approached the company) • Currently some of the company's products are produced locally under licensing agreements which were organised by the distributor which continues to handle sales & marketing • No USA business due to the overriding dominance of the leading brands (Pepsi and Coca-Cola)	• Canada and the USA are viewed as very separate markets, USA being non-penetrable due to indigenous firm dominance (although the firm has been approached regarding the possibility of establishing a joint venture). While Canada is similarly dominated by US firms the large ex-patriate market offers scope for small scale activities
3.4 Food and drink (Canada) Beer	• Licensing deals were established in the UK with several local brewers to gain access to the 'tied' public house chains for 'standard' draught lager brand. Yeast ingredient exported from Canada • Wider distribution of 'premium' packaged brand through licensees/public houses • Strategic alliance/joint venture with local UK retailing group to build-up public house chain • Acquisition of two Italian brewers in Italy and other Continental acquisitions being reviewed	• Further European investments being sought to deepen the firm's involvement in the EU. Wide diversity of demand conditions requires acquisitions of, or strategic alliances with, local brewers with strong established brands. The company's own brands may be slotted into local product portfolios as appropriate

(*continued on p. 50*)

Table 3.2 *continued*

3.5 Food and drink (Canada) Frozen foods including: french fries, pizzas, vegetables, meats & burgers, fruit juice, cakes and desserts, prepared meals	• Established UK manufacturing subsidiary (1968) • Established and acquired manufacturing plants in Holland, Belgium, Spain and France and sales/marketing subsidiaries in a large number of EU markets • Cross-border exporting arising out of the need to maximise EU efficiencies through product specialisation and expand local portfolios	• Will establish/acquire businesses to increase market penetration • Growing possibility to maximise the advantages of a pan-European (global) brand
4.1 Transport equipment, systems services (UK) Hydraulic tipping hoists & cylinder skip loaders	• Originally exported to Canada via a distributorship established in the early 1960s • In 1983 a dispute between the company and its distributor led to the termination of the agreement and the withdrawal of the company's products from the Canadian market. (The distributor then set up a manufacturing facility producing '4.1 style products'.) • The company subsequently attempted to re-enter the Canadian market with a new distributor although this also ended in dispute • A US distributorship was established in the 1970s. In 1980 the company acquired its distributor, with the view that a company-owned network would provide a more dedicated basis for expansion • In 1984 the US operation was closed as part of a cost-cutting measure (the company having been seriously effected by the recession in the early 1980s) • The company's products are now handled by an independent distributor in the USA	• NAFTA is seen as offering opportunities for expansion. A dedicated sales/marketing subsidiary covering North America would be 'preferred', but as the company's financial situation is in poor shape, the possibility is ruled out at present

4.2 Transport equipment, systems & services (UK) Automotive components	• Established sales/distribution subsidiaries in Canada and the USA in 1948 to supply the 'aftermarket' in car parts (i.e. replacement equipment). Exports sourced from the UK • In 1959 the company established a greenfield plant in the USA to obtain 'original equipment' business. The company currently has six manufacturing plants in the USA • The Canadian market is now mainly serviced from the US plants	• The 1965 'Autopact' between Canada and the USA partially liberalised trade in cars and car parts leading to a substantial increase in cross-frontier trade • NAFTA further liberalised this sector and extends the new freedoms to Mexico. A substantial amount of car investment has been undertaken in Mexico. The company is well placed in this respect, having established a 'source' company in Mexico which services components from the US plants and the company's joint venture in Brazil • There remain some concerns that, despite NAFTA, the sensitivity of the car industry may lead to trade disputes between the leading North American markets
4.3 Transport equipment, systems & services (Canada) Water transport of dry bulk	• Established UK sales office (1986) to facilitate greater EU involvement	• Possible the company will establish offices in main European ports. The Single Market will benefit transportation companies in general although the company is concerned that the EU might impose a 'flag preference' system giving EU-owned vessels priority over foreign fleets
5.1 Financial services (UK) Insurance company division focusing on life assurance investment trusts	• Only recent involvement in N. American insurance market (described as market exploration). UK-based personnel are sent out to Canada and the USA to establish client contacts	• May establish a N. American sales/marketing office in the USA. Operationally, the Canadian and USA markets are, however, currently seen as separate given current legislative differences
5.2 Financial services (UK) One of the UK's top	• Acquired a Canadian bank in the 1950s • In the 1970s the company changed direction	• The company hopes that NAFTA will induce greater harmonisation in North American

(*continued on p. 52*)

Table 3.2 *continued*

four clearing banks focusing on service banking (corporate banking) in N. America	and focused the business on servicing the needs of major Canadian corporate clients • In 1989 the company closed 2 of its four Canadian offices as part of the company's efforts to consolidate their North American business, although a subsidiary in Canada remains essential due to continued legislative differences • The company established US corporate banking operations in the 1950s based in New York	banking legislation such that the Canadian offices can be managed from their New York office
5.3 Financial services (UK) Investment management services	• Currently operate an 'export type' operation in Canada and the USA. UK based personnel are sent out to the market to establish client contacts. Some business also picked up through local agents	• It is hoped that greater harmonisation of Canadian and US investment management rules and regulations will provide opportunities for a more integrated approach to North American operations There is some possibility of their establishing a sales operation in the USA in this respect
5.4 Financial services (Canada) General and life insurance	• Long established UK sales subsidiary (1893) which runs an extensive network of branch offices • Also established sales office in the Republic of Ireland but no other European business involvement	• The company has adopted a 'wait and see' posture for the present, unlike many UK insurers which have entered into strategic alliances with other European insurers and broad-based financial service groups. However, they see the single banking licence as offering potential for expanding across Europe under UK rules (with which they are completely familiar)
5.5 Financial services (Canada) Specialised treasury division of one of Canada's leading banks dealing in off-balance	• Long-established treasury office in the UK (1870) • Also acquired UK broking business to give the company European legal status –	• May establish offices in other EU financial centres (e.g. Paris, Brussels) if treasury business moves away from London. As with company 5.4 this company has adopted

sheet items such as foreign exchange, money market receipts and off-balance sheet trading	important in obtaining freedom of access under the 2nd Banking Directive. However, as yet, the company has no business outside of the UK – mainly because London remains the leading financial centre in Europe	a 'wait and see' stance. The issue of 'reciprocity' is being looked at by the EU and NAFTA authorities which may, ultimately, prove damaging to the company's EU-wide business prospects
5.6 Financial services (Canada) Professional re-insurance services	• Established UK sales subsidiary (1987) • Established sales branch office in Brussels (1989) to develop European business contacts and 'monitor' new legislation	• No immediate plans to set up further local offices, mostly due to the dominance of London as the main EU centre for re-insurance
6.1 Communications (UK) Provider of telecommunications systems and services	• Acquired 51% stake in Canadian telecommunication equipment manufacturer (1986). This has since been sold as the company has dedicated its focus on the provision of value-added telecommunication services • Various acquisitions in the USA from 1986 onwards taking the company into voice messaging, cellular and data communication services • Canada now serviced as part of a broader based pan-American operation centred in the USA	• The company's North American strategy is to provide telecom services to local and international companies. Deregulation of the telecoms market and NAFTA will help the company's position insofar as greater integration of client companies' North American activities will favour companies which are able to provide cross-border and global telecom services
6.2 Communications (Canada) Telecommunications equipment including: telecom switching and transmission equipment and fibre optic cables	• Established UK sales subsidiary (1978) sourcing products from overseas plants • Established various manufacturing operations in England, Wales and Northern Ireland (1980s) • Acquisition of major UK-based equipment manufacturer (1991) with European plants and sales networks • Strategic alliances established in Germany (1991), Poland (1992), Spain (1992) and France (1992) to provide further expansion	• Further strategic alliances are being sought to widen and deepen access to 'big ticket' procurement contracts. Some concern regarding moves to harmonise technical standards and local 'fiefdoms' in perpetuating procurement bias

(*continued on p. 54*)

Table 3.2 *continued*

	into Europe and potential for technological collaboration	
6.3 Communications (Canada) Mainframe computers and communications systems	• Established UK sales office (1970) sourcing computers and peripherals from US-based parent and Canadian subsidiary. • Established greenfield manufacturing plant in the Republic of Ireland (1988) as an export 'platform' into the UK and mainland Europe • Exports to mainland Europe via distributors, sourcing from overseas and the Republic of Ireland – supported by a distribution centre in Amsterdam	• Local content issues are very much to the fore as the company's Irish plant sources some components from its overseas plants (particularly Japan). The company is currently negotiating with the European Commission to clarify local content status, the likelihood being that more items will need to be sourced locally to qualify as 'authentic' European products and thus avoiding import restrictions
6.4 Communications (Canada) Aerospace including: space robotics, space stations, satellites and land and space communications	• Exports of 'know how' and space satellite equipment through UK and European strategic alliances (co-production and installation consortia) • Acquired US company (1989) producing related products, which brought with it a UK manufacturing subsidiary. This subsidiary is used to co-ordinate the company's participation in European alliances	• Continuance of the strategic alliance format inevitable in the future – although this is more to do with the nature of the business rather than integration. The company also expressed concern regarding technical standards and reciprocity.
7.1 General industrial equipment (UK) Fluid power components and systems	• Established a greenfield operation in Canada in 1975 • It has since consolidated its position through acquisition including a US-based subsidiary in 1987 and a further Canadian subsidiary in 1988 • The company has an extensive network of sales offices and a number of assembly plants in Canada and the US which produce customised fluid process systems for clients	• NAFTA is not expected to change things much. Sales offices provide a key customer linkage and the company is already well-represented across North America where 'on the ground' representation is crucial. In theory, assembly operations are more 'footloose' and thus there is some possibility for production rationalisation (although local sales/service centres will be retained)

7.2 General industrial equipment (UK) Precision measuring equipment	• Products exported to Canada are handled by a distributor. The Canadian distributorship was established in 1978 • The company appointed a US distributor in 1968. A second distributor was appointed in 1991 after the original distributor got into financial difficulties	• The NAFTA is expected to increase competitive pressures and break down regional 'spheres of influence' giving the company's products access to, and a profile in, areas where it has hitherto been under-represented. Longer term, sales offices may be established.
8.1 Power supply and equipment (UK) Producer and distributor of natural gas	• Acquired a 51% stake in a Canadian exploration and production company in 1988 • Acquired an 85% stake in Canada's largest gas distribution company in 1990 • This latter acquisition was divested in 1993 as the company decided to focus on higher value-added business on a global scale • In keeping with this latter move, the company has also acquired a number of oil and gas exploration concerns in the USA and entered into joint ventures with US companies	• Tight regulatory control of public utilities in Canada, and little evidence that NAFTA was offering a solution to such controls resulted in the company selling its distribution interests in Canada
8.2 Power supply and equipment (UK) Electric and electronic power systems, particularly gas turbines	• The company is a joint-venture concern between a UK and French company set up in 1989 to create a stronger international power systems business • Both parent companies operated sales offices in Canada prior to the formation of the joint venture and these were consolidated into a sales/marketing subsidiary • The company has a subsidiary in the USA which is mainly concerned with obtaining sales, although it undertakes a limited amount of production	• NAFTA has led the company to consider establishing a major manufacturing presence in North America (most probably in the USA). At the present time, however, the company has a highly successful technical collaboration agreement with the leading US power supplier. This may well inhibit further encroachment on the US market which would be seen as an aggressive attack on its partner's traditional business territory

European players in their sector, are attempting to put in place an interpretation of the laws which excludes North American standards. However, they hope that the committees will rule that the long-term effects of such a move would prove damaging to European firms, as it would mean their losing access to American technology which can provide an important source of information for new developments.

This exposes a key consideration in respect of the tendency for regionalisation to promote external protectionism. While the underlying ethos of regionalisation accepts that intensified competition within the union promotes efficiency and technological development, restriction of foreign competition and thus exposure to the most efficient and technologically advanced products in the world market place has the potential to douse the impetus for developing globally competitive products and services (Welford and Prescott, 1996).

Company 6.2 has also, for many years, been frustrated by access to public procurement contracts. Such problems characterised the company's efforts to penetrate the UK market in the early 1980s as the state-owned monopoly – British Telecom – continued to award the lion's share of its business to a locally-based equipment manufacturer. Real encroachment on the market was only achieved early in the 1990s when Company 6.2 gained full control of the equipment supplier, a move which was clearly induced by non-tariff procurement bias protectionism. While, in theory at least, this EU based operation is now in a position to exploit the opportunities offered by the liberalisation of public procurement within the EU (which dictates that governments must offer contracts for tender on an EU-wide basis and award contracts based on cost), there remain concerns that national preference will prevail. These concerns are shared by European firms – and are not restricted to foreign players (Buckley, Pass and Prescott, 1992).

The scope for governments to justify local preference on grounds other than cost (for example, quality, technological compatibility, or service and delivery) is immense, and continued technological divergence and decentralisation of government purchasing are frustrating the achievement of free market principles in government procurement on an EU-wide scale. As a consequence, procurement bias continues to serve as an inducement for both inter and intra-EU foreign direct investment (FDI). Company 6.2 is therefore committed to extending and consolidating production in a number of EU Member States. This decision has also been taken as a result of concerns over re-exporting and local content rules – concerns which are shared by Company 6.3 (the computer mainframe supplier).

Company 6.3 established a manufacturing facility in Ireland in 1988 as a result of the threat of greater protectionism and the need to facilitate access to public procurement. The success of the venture has, however, been hampered by a number of 'networking' problems arising from local content issues. Local content rules have been introduced across a wide number of industries in the EU to ensure that foreign manufacturers add-value locally.

There was a tendency in the early 1980s, by Japanese firms in particular, to circumvent trade restrictions by establishing 'screwdriver plants'. These plants, under the guise of local manufacturing centres, imported components and semi-processed product parts from domestic manufacturing plants, simply assembling them in the target market. Thus, they arguably served as 'windows' for cheaper imports, semi-processed components being subject to lower tariffs. By stipulating that a certain proportion of the final product is produced within the EU, firms were forced to source supplies from local manufacturers – thus adding value within the EU Member States (although there was a tendency for this to induce inward FDI by component manufacturers). Company 6.3 (a US–Japanese joint venture)[2], which sources many of its components exclusively from Japan in order to keep costs down, now faces problems relating to the 'authenticity' of its goods produced in Ireland which are subsequently not tradable across the EU without impediment. The company is currently negotiating with the EU authorities to clarify local content status.

The only mention of tariffs and quotas came from the Canadian wood, paper and pulp manufacturer (Company 2.1) which has, throughout its history in Europe, been troubled by tariffs, price controls and quotas. The acquisition of a Scottish-based manufacturer in 1989 enabled the company to by-pass some of these protectionist measures as well as assisting with dealings with 'officialdom' in negotiating standards and product specifications. The pursuit of greenfield manufacturing opportunities and joint ventures in other Member States is seen as allowing further by-passing of trade restrictions. It is also hoped that the harmonisation of product standards and liberalisation of public procurement will provide further scope for increased market penetration. While not specifically alluding to tariff protection, the attitude of Company 3.2 (the Canadian beer manufacturer) encapsulates the general attitude of many of the Canadian managers interviewed:

> Problems with GATT and the polarisation of economies into major trading blocs is raising barriers to business between the leading world markets such that a direct investment presence in key consuming markets is necessary to achieve profitable growth.

For Canadian financial service firms, many of which remain frustrated by differences in legislative environments between Canada and the US which severely curtail pan-American development, the new legislation in Europe which includes mutual recognition (automatic acceptance of services licensed in one Member State by the other 14 countries), home country control (domestic regulations extending to activities in other EU markets) and a single banking licence (permitting firms registered in one state to offer goods across the Member States of Europe) is greatly welcomed.

Companies 5.6 (the re-insurance firm), 5.4 (the insurance firm) and 5.5

(the treasury division of a leading Canadian bank) all alluded to the new 'openness' in Europe and the comprehensive scope of legislative change – although there remain some concerns in connection with reciprocity agreements as a result of an earlier test-case involving European firms in the USA wherein the EU authorities demanded that the new freedoms afforded to American companies in Europe should be replicated for European firms in America. The Americans rejected the proposition on the grounds that this would effectively mean European firms having a greater advantage over American indigenous financial institutions constrained in terms of inter-state financial provision. A compromise was reached, the Commission diluting their demand for 'reciprocal access' to one of 'national treatment that gives effective access', a stance which is now being taken in GATT negotiations on trade in services (Colchester and Buchan, 1990). Although the Canadian government is introducing new freedoms into the financial service industry, there remain fears that their actions do not go far enough, raising the possibility of an EU backlash.

From a European perspective, therefore, there is little evidence of greatly intensified protectionism in the wake of the Single European Market Act, casting some doubt over the reality of 'Fortress Europe'. What is evident, however, is that the potential threat of renewed protectionism has resulted in pre-emptive actions by many firms keen to ensure they are not exposed to the effects of protectionism were they to be used aggressively by the EU authorities – 'perceived threat'-induced FDI and business consolidation. However, it would be over-simplistic to assume that this serves as the only motivation for Canadian FDI. As will be discussed later, there are a number of competitive pressures making the establishment of a local presence increasingly attractive. Some evidence of discrimination against non-member countries did emerge in relation to technological standards and local content rules, although other barriers relate as much to intra-EU trade as inter-EU activity.

TRADE CREATION AND TRADE DIVERSION – ATTITUDES TO CANADIAN PROTECTIONISM

There was some underlying evidence of UK firms being frustrated by Canada's lack of openness – potentially an outcome of the country's efforts to improve its position in finished manufactures as opposed to commodities, in a number of key growth sectors. In the pharmaceutical industry, for example, the Canadian authorities' position on patent protection has caused problems for UK firms attempting to penetrate the market. Company 1.1 (the UK ethical pharmaceutical manufacturer) referred to the 'lax' policy on patents, designed to promote the indigenous generics market, and the consequent frustrations for ethical pharmaceutical producers for whom patent protection is an important means of securing profits for investment in new R&D initiatives. Whereas patent protection in Europe is 20 years and the USA 15 years, the effective patent life (the life of the product in the market place prior to patent expiry and the take-up of the product by generics producers) is approximately half this, following protracted testing and licensing procedures.

In 1987, Ottowa bowed to pressure from the multinationals and extended pharmaceutical patent protection from seven to ten years, although this still only constitutes five years in the market place. This was only granted in return for 'promises of sizeable investment in Canada', to which Company 1.1 has complied by raising its R&D spending in Canada. Unlike in Europe, where issues of this kind are being tackled at a supra-national level, no such common competition policy framework exists within NAFTA, meaning problems of this kind are likely to continue for the foreseeable future.

In the food industry, Company 3.1's (the major UK food group) development in Canada has been hampered by the local competition authorities. Following two major acquisitions of Canadian milling companies, and the subsequent merger of the two firms, the company agreed a joint venture with Canada's third largest milling group as a means of both companies competing more effectively against the big US millers. The authorities vetoed the deal because the combined group would have a dominant position in the Canadian market:

> A somewhat myopic view given the pro-competitive impetus of the NAFTA.
> (Manager of the leading UK foodgroup)

This raises an important issue in relation to national competition policy: the concerns of national authorities typically reflect the scope of activities within the nation state which rather ignores the impact of global competition and the opening up of markets. In the Single European Market, new competition directives cover such activities and are more concerned with EU-wide effects rather than individual Member State concerns (although mergers between firms with combined worldwide turnover of less than ECU 5 billion, and EU wide sales of ECU 250 million remain the concern of national authorities). Lack of an all-embracing policy within the NAFTA agreement means that wider concerns of competition within the union are not currently on the agenda. Divergence in competition rules between Canada and the USA was also highlighted by Company 4.2 (the UK vehicle components suppliers), such differences having the potential to cause trade frictions despite unification.

In the financial service sector, there have until recently been strict levels on the amount of investment funds which can be invested internationally, severely restricting opportunities for foreign firms. Recently, the level has been raised from 5–10 per cent, and there is hope that it will be raised further to 25 per cent. The UK insurer (Company 5.1) and the investment trust company (Company 5.3) welcome this new openness although there is still thought to be scope for greater liberalisation. The remaining UK financial service firm (Company 5.2) highlighted the problems of pan-American service provision as a result of continued differences in legislation between the two countries. It is hoped that NAFTA will spur on the eradication of such barriers although, currently, there is little evident activity in this respect.

Comparing these experiences with those of Canadian firms operating in the UK, it is clear that while EU competition policy has established common principles across Europe, no such framework is evident within NAFTA. Indeed, many Canadian firms expressed the belief that the SEM is more comprehensive than the NAFTA agreement, common rules facilitating strategic planning as regulations are more transparent. With less pervasive competition rules the threat of renewed protectionism on a trading bloc basis is not apparent, and while there are examples of firms replacing exports with local Canadian subsidiaries (be they sales and marketing or production) the motivation for such strategic shifts relates more to changes in competitive conditions rather than trade-barrier induced FDI.

FREE MARKETS AND COMPETITION – THE EUROPEAN UNION

There was some evidence, among the sample of Canadian firms, of the UK (or in one case Ireland) being used as a 'gateway' to Europe – a stepping stone into the wider European market. The wood, paper and pulp manufacturer (Company 2.1), the producer of mainframe computers (Company 6.3), the aerospace manufacturer (Company 6.4), the Canadian re-insurance firms (Company 5.6), the insurance group (Company 5.4), the division of the Canadian bank (Company 5.5) and the Canadian shipping company (Company 4.3) all commented on the possibilities for greater European expansion from the establishment of facilities in the UK. At face value, this appears to suggest their expanding activities through intra-European trade from their UK manufacturing base – although further analysis demonstrates this is not the case.

For most firms seeing the UK as a 'gateway' to Europe, further EU encroachment will necessitate the development of additional business facilities in the other Member States of Europe. Two main reasons support the motivation for such Europe-wide strategic development: cultural differences between the markets in Europe which act against the development of a common approach to markets; and the growing competitive pressures in many of the EU Member States which reinforce the need for 'local presence'.

On the first point, the issue of public procurement access, discussed earlier, dictates that the mainframe computer manufacturer (Company 6.3) maintains a network of sales and marketing subsidiaries in the Member States of Europe, and the telecommunications equipment producer (Company 6.2) retains its manufacturing facilities in a number of EU countries. In this latter case, the monopolistic character of EU markets (described as 'local fiefdoms') which remain despite privatisation and deregulation, further reinforces the importance of strategic development on a market-by-market basis. Similarly, the financial service sector is characterised by cultural diversity across Europe. Thus, while new legislation affords firms the potential to operate across borders, the need for a local presence makes such freedoms difficult to realise. For Company 5.6 (the re-insurance firm), with their customers being other insurance companies many of which are used to dealing with UK firms (due to the overriding dominance of Lloyds in the re-insurance market), the UK location affords a strong base from which to service the European market, although the company has established an office in Brussels to further penetrate the market and monitor changes in legislation.

For the remaining two firms it is rather the freedom to establish subsidiaries in other Member States, and the fact that these subsidiaries will be controlled on the basis of UK rules, which is proving attractive. For the insurance firm (Company 5.4), the highly dispersed customer base, and poor past performance with market-based intermediaries, means that expansion will inevitably take some form of FDI which supports the development of locally based sales forces. Conversely, for the treasury division of the Canadian bank (Company 5.5), foreign facilities are established to support financial investments in leading world financial centres rather than sales to customers, which means EU expansion will only follow with the rise in global importance of financial centres outside of London.

Similarly, in the beer industry, cultural differences between markets dictate the development of strategies on an individual market basis. This is nowhere more apparent than in the UK, where the 'tied-house' character of beer retailing raises the importance of distribution access which has led to Company 3.2 establishing a joint venture with a local pub retailing group, through which it may exploit the sale of its products produced through locally established licences with major producers. Conversely in Italy, where the retailing arm of the business is of less critical importance, the company has opted for takeovers of indigenous brewers.

Relating to the second issue, growing competitive pressures are raising the stakes of competition in many industry sectors. For example, in the wood, paper and pulp industry, the freedom of access to the EU for Nordic countries permitted by the development of the European Economic Area (and reinforced more recently through their impending access to the EU of Finland, Austria and Norway), and their propensity to consolidate their EU business dealings, particularly through vertical acquisition, has put pressure on Company 2.1 to increase its level of involvement in Europe. The acquisition of the Scottish manufacturing plant in 1989 and the establishment of a joint venture with a Dutch paper company reflect the organisation's growing awareness that to take advantage of the new opportunities means consolidating their 'presence' within Europe.

Similarly in the food industry, Company 3.5 (the frozen food manufacturer) commented on the importance of local sales and marketing facilities to support local brand development and to combat the growing concentration of power in the retailing sector, where strict delivery schedules, proximity to the market and visible commitment (in the form of locally established facilities) are critical to profitable market penetration for branded goods as well as the development of own-label contracts with leading customers.

Cultural divergence and the growing need for local presence to support activities within individual Member States appears to work against the potential for rationalisation and the exploitation of scale economies which lies at the heart of improved efficiency within economic unions. Developing strategies on a market-by-market basis implicitly involves a degree of duplication of effort, diluting economic advantages which accrue from centralisation. While this suggests little potential for the exploitation of scale economies, a closer analysis of the nature of strategic development reveals a certain duality in the approach to European expansion by some of the companies in the sample.

For example, Company 6.3 (the mainframe computer manufacturer), Company 3.5 (the frozen food producer) and Company 6.2 (the telecommunications equipment manufacturer) are all attempting to rationalise their European facilities, taking advantage of the greater freedoms offered by the opening up of markets in Europe. Company 6.3, through the centralisation of production in Ireland (taking advantage of investment inducements and tax breaks and thus the potential for more competitive bids) and the establishment of a centralised distribution centre in Amsterdam (located in the economic 'core' of the Community), has split out the sales and marketing function as the critical element for decentralisation and local market presence. Alternatively, Company 3.5, which has a number of EU manufacturing units acquired through acquisition to extend the company's portfolio, has taken advantage of the new border freedoms and has reorganised EU production on the basis of product specialisation – eradicating duplication of effort in individual plants. EU markets are therefore now served through a combination of indigenous production and exports from other Member States.

Product specialisation also features in the strategy of Company 6.2, although here such reorganisation has taken place on a global scale with a number of components, telecom systems and ancillary equipment (such as telephone sets) being produced in England, Wales, Northern Ireland, the Republic of Ireland and France, with others being sold through Europe being sourced from Canada and the United States. This kind of global product organisation, facilitated by trading bloc freedoms, is however more a reflection of the global character of the industry rather than economic union *per se* (a theme which will be returned to later).

To conclude, it would appear that Canadian firms operating within the EU are subject to the same freedoms (and barriers) as their European counterparts, with no evident discrimination once established. This supports the proposition by the Canadian government that full exploitation of Single European Market opportunities means establishing a local presence, a proposition which is reinforced by competitive intensity and the need to 'act local' to support sales growth at the Member State level. Inevitably this demands a degree of duplication of effort, although there is scope, either by splitting up the value chain into its constituent functions (and deriving a balance between the gains accruing from local responsiveness and those relating to centralisation), or reorganising production on a product-specific basis (facilitated by greater border freedoms) to improve business efficiency. These findings are reminiscent of earlier research on the competitiveness of UK firms in Continental Europe (Buckley, Pass and Prescott, 1992) which reinforces the notion that, once established within the Union, Canadian firms may compete on a par with other European competitors.

FREE MARKETS AND COMPETITION – NORTH AMERICA

The situation for UK firms in Canada differs quite significantly from that for Canadian firms in the UK. The only real similarities which emerged were in respect of procurement bias induced 'presence', highlighted by Company 1.1 (the ethical pharmaceutical producer), and potential for greater pan-American business rationalisation being alluded to by Companies 1.1 and 7.1 (the producer of fluid power systems) both in terms of product specialisation and locally dedicated sales and marketing concerns. Overall, however, greater freedoms created by NAFTA are likely to see UK firms creating or consolidating their presence in the USA, with Canadian activities being treated more as a 'satellite' of the US operation. However, in the short term at least, continued 'barriers' between the two markets are slowing down the development of such pan-American business activities.

With the US market being approximately ten times the size of the Canadian market, it is perhaps not surprising that UK firms' primary concern in relation to North American expansion is consolidating efforts in the United States. Many examples of this kind of thinking emerged from the sample, running the gamut from multinational firms to those entering the North American market for the first time. For example, Company 6.1 (the telecommunications service producer) having made the decision to pull out of its early forays into the telecommunications equipment industry and focus on its core business strength (telecommunications services) recently divested the Canadian company it had acquired in 1989. Its North American focus is now on accessing national service networks, particularly in areas of new technology (such as cordless – mobile – telephones and voicemail). For this it feels that it is better served by developing business linkages in the US market (the critical hub), retaining only a sales/marketing office in Canada which serves as a 'spoke' in the operation, ready to take advantage of planned deregulation by the Canadian government and the potential offered by NAFTA through greater integration of user company's pan-American business.

The story for Company 8.1 (the gas distribution company) is similar in many respects: the Canadian gas distribution business, acquired in 1990, was divested in 1993 as a result of the failure of NAFTA to provide greater impetus for deregulation, and the continuance of tight price and service controls by the Canadian government. The company is now focusing its North American efforts on the development of new energy sources in the USA, where it has acquired a number of oil and gas exploration companies and established joint exploration ventures with US companies to develop oil fields in the Gulf of Mexico. As a result, Canadian concerns have been sidelined in favour of greater concentration on the US market.

The financial service sector and power equipment also feature developments of this kind. Company 5.2 (the commercial banking division of a major UK Clearing Bank) has closed down two of its four offices in Canada (without damaging overall business levels) as part of the process of integrating the Canadian operation into their wider North American strategy. In time, they hope that legislative harmonisation between the two markets will remove the requirement for Canadian subsidiaries, with the market being served through a local office – a 'satellite' of the US operation. Company 3.2 (the speciality tea producer) whose products have, following the firm's takeover by a UK food group, been handled in the USA by their parent company's sales subsidiary, hope that NAFTA will allow greater potential for cross-border trade such that this subsidiary may replace the distributorship currently employed to service the Canadian market.

No less significant were the comments of two of the financial service firms expanding into North America for the first time. Recognising that true encroachment on the market may demand replacing direct sales effort with a company dedicated sales subsidiary, they suggested that the preferred location for such a subsidiary would inevitably be the United States. Company 5.1 (the UK insurer focusing on investment trusts) and Company 5.3 (the investment trust specialist), both of which are currently 'exploring' market opportunities by sending out head office personnel to the market to build links with potential customers, expressed tentative plans (dependent on generating enough market volume) for the establishment of a US-based sales office in the future. Some problems were, however, expressed with regard to servicing the Canadian market from the USA as a result of Canadians' reluctance to deal with a firm with no market presence, and thus no visible sign of local commitment:

> Xenophobia may mean such an operation would be a disservice to the Canadian business as Canadians may similarly reject doing business with a US-based Scottish operation. (A spokesman for Company 5.3)

While such evidence suggests that Canadian activities are overshadowed by the dominance of US concerns, this is not the case for all firms. Company 3.1, for example, (the UK food group) is using its experience in Canada as the impetus for further expansion into the USA where the company's record has been 'patchy'. As in Europe, however, integration serves as the spur for further encroachment, but fails to afford real advantages for cross-border trade flows – excepting market testing opportunities in the early stages of development. Alliances with major US producers/distributors and acquisitions are being sought in order for the company to make a bigger impact on the US market. Alternatively, Company 7.1 (the producer of fluid power systems) displays an equally complex array of activities in both Canada and North America which has been developed through both greenfield and acquisition FDI in production and sales/marketing/servicing. With the development of close customer linkages being critical, proximity to the market (particularly in relation to service centres), is fundamental to business success.

A further barrier to cross-border expansion emerged for a number of firms currently operating via locally based intermediaries. This is encapsulated by the experiences of Company 1.1 (the 'over-the-counter' pharmaceutical producer) which, eager to explore new business potential in the USA, is being forced to look for new US distributors as a result of the nationally constrained nature of Canadian intermediaries. Company 4.1 (the producer of hydraulic tipping hoists) which has, as a result of similar barriers, had to develop linkages with distributors in both Canada and the USA, expressed its hope that NAFTA will break down traditional 'spheres of influence' and permit greater expansion opportunities for indigenous North American distributors.

Relating back to the idea that continued barriers between the USA and Canada are stifling the potential for pan-American strategic development, a number of Canadian firms referred to continued US protectionism despite the efforts of the NAFTA agreement. The financial services, transportation services, communications, and wood, paper and pulp sectors all came under attack. For example, taxation on monies transferred out of the USA makes it difficult for insurance companies to move money between the two markets, making the extension of US operations out of Canada unfeasible and creating a need for the development of a separate business entity. As shipping services are excluded from the GATT agreement, no additional freedoms have emerged which means the powerful shipping lobby in the US makes it a very difficult market to penetrate. Subsidies and duties remain in US soft-wood lumber – again frustrating the efforts of Canadian firms to further penetrate the market. Finally, a recent US space project open to international tender was awarded exclusively to US organisations which resulted in an industry backlash, firms endeavouring to protect constituent technologies, highly damaging in an industry which relies heavily on intra-firm cooperation.

As many of these barriers are not specific to UK firms, it would be tempting to conclude that such restrictions are likely to have little impact on the dealings of the firms in the sample. However, many industry observers have recently focused on the continuance of protectionism between Canada and the USA, and the failure of existing provisions to fully eradicate the scope for the individual governments to seek preferential treatment for their indigenous firms. To this extent, there is now concern that the NAFTA be further extended in much the same way as the Single Market initiative, to include a more comprehensive competition policy which will allow the development of a 'level playing field'. This would, undoubtedly, assist the objectives of many of the UK firms in the sample which are hoping for greater freedoms as a means of rationalising and consolidating their North American business.

To conclude, it would appear that trade and investment flows between the UK and Canada are set to change in the future. The attractiveness of Canada as a target for foreign investment, built out of colonial links and cultural affinity, is giving way to greater concerns over 'North American expansion' in which Canadian operations will be managed as satellites of US business operations. Canadian government fears over the possibility of US business retrenchment out of Canada in the wake of the North American Free Trade Agreement may well be compounded by loss of business from other countries keen to locate activities in the economic 'hub' of the USA. Talk of Canada becoming a peripheral 'state' in the wider United States of America is being confirmed by the activities of UK firms. Such a shift in activity, which will inevitably intensify competition in the USA, is also likely to act as a spur for greater FDI in the USA as firms attempt to combat growing pressures, further diverting investment flows away from the Canadian market.

TECHNOLOGICAL ADVANCE

A number of firms across the sample may be described as 'technology dominant'; these include the pharmaceuticals, communication and transportation equipment sectors. These industries obviously display wide disparities in terms of supply and demand conditions which implicitly includes the nature of products and services, the nature of competition and technologies and the changing legislative environments which are shaping their development. However, there are certain common elements which can be seen to be shaping similar attitudes towards, and responses to, global integration in terms of technology development.

The rise in research and development costs has, for many years, outpaced inflation rates in most of the world's developed markets, which means that to survive, firms have been forced to develop global distribution networks through which they may maximise the potential from their technological developments (and thus profits for re-investment in R&D). They have also begun to develop strategic alliances with major competitors for the purposes of sharing costs (and risks) in R&D, and alliances with customers to ensure that new technologies are customised to the increasingly exacting needs of clients.

The European Commission, through the targeting of research grants at joint development projects, is actively encouraging intra-EU technology development, although as the evidence from the firms in this sample demonstrates, the emergence of new technologies is more a global than regional concern.

Company 6.2 (the Canadian telecommunications equipment supplier), in its 1990 company report, described the developments in the industry in the following terms:

> In fact, major developments in computer and telecommunications technologies and their integration into worldwide networks have resulted in something closer to a 'global village' than anything we have ever seen before. Businesses are facing changes more extensive, more far-reaching in their implications, and more fundamental in their transforming quality than at any time since the modern industrial system was established.

This attitude is reflected in the company's global strategy, with subsidiaries established in the European Union and the United States of America not only serving as production facilities for local market servicing, but centres of business development from which the firm may develop strategic alliances with competitors. Indeed, Company 6.4 (the Canadian aerospace manufacturer), commenting on its production facility in the UK, stressed that the importance of this venture to the company had little to do with adding capacity or extending the firm's product portfolio, but was seen as an essential means of raising the company's profile in the European market (a local persona above and beyond its more nebulous and anonymous involvement in strategic alliances) and a vehicle for coordinating the company's strategic alliances on a pan-European scale.

Similarly, Company 4.2 (the UK car components manufacturer) has established manufacturing facilities in the USA and 'service' companies in Canada to support the development of business linkages with leading global car producers for whom international success increasingly hinges on reducing product lead-times and introducing reliable, high-performance vehicles which demands interaction with component suppliers for customised design and construction of component parts. Recently developed business linkages in the USA by Company 6.1 (the telecommunications systems supplier), also reflect the thinking that to remain globally competitive means establishing alliances with firms to either access, or jointly develop, new technologies.

As a result, these sectors now feature an array of increasingly complex international networks of firms, tenuously linked through their common desire to remain abreast of global technological developments. Foreign direct investment in emerging trading blocs, therefore, facilitates the development of such linkages, although the trading blocs are unable, as a result of the global character of these emerging sectors, to retain technologies within their borders. The implication is that technological developments are set to traverse artificially developed economic unions as inter-firm alliances override the importance of trading blocs in their contribution to product development and innovation. Consequently, dynamic efficiency is likely to emanate more from global competition and international strategic groupings, rather than internal policies to promote technology on a regional basis.

CONCLUSIONS

The experiences and attitudes of the firms in the sample, discussed in the light of the original propositions outlined, clearly demonstrate that there are now evident changes in bilateral trade and investment flows between Canada and the UK as a result of regionalisation.

In terms of trade creation and diversion, it is apparent that the threat of 'Fortress Europe' was overstated: little evidence emerged of renewed European protection, either tariff or non-tariff. Where barriers were alluded to, the focus was mainly on remaining barriers between the EU markets as opposed to trade barriers with non-members which challenges the proposition that regionalisation results in free trade on the inside and protectionism on the outside. Nevertheless, the potential threat of renewed protectionism, possibly engendered by the 'hype' connected with the establishment of the Single European Market rather than the reality of firms' experiences, has initiated a growing belief that to take full advantage of the freedoms being offered by the Single Market means establishing a position on the inside.

From a UK firm perspective, experiences in Canada are rather different. The Canadian market which has historically been viewed as protectionist, while bowing to certain international pressures, liberalising markets and opening up borders to foreign trade and investment, is seen to retain a nationalistic character in the eyes of many UK firms. Both UK and Canadian managers referred to the continuance of policy and regulation differences between Canada and the USA, partly resulting from the Canadian government's fear that Canada will be 'sidelined' in the economic developments which are now taking place in North America, and the fact that NAFTA has failed to create a common agenda for business – specifically a common competition policy. Such national protectionism, rather than enabling economic benefits, may result in European institutions seeking to further develop their activities in the USA rather than Canada which will reinforce the economic shift towards the North American 'hub' – the USA.

Relating to free trade and competition, the shift away from Canada in favour of the USA was given further emphasis. With the US market being ten times the size of Canada, giving rise to greater opportunities (and more intense competitive activity), the potential for business reorganisation in the wake of NAFTA appears to favour deepening involvement in the US market, with regional offices in Canada. This will, undoubtedly, result in a shift in UK FDI away from Canada in the future, adding to the burden of the Canadian economy which is witnessing growing unemployment rates and the closure of American branch plants. As a result, the proposition that UK firms may use their Canadian base as a 'platform' for further North American business encroachment can be rejected.

For Canadian firms operating in the UK, there was some belief that the UK may act as an important 'doorway' to Europe – at least in the sense of being a strong starting point and a position from where firms can observe changes taking place within the EU. However, the extent of cultural diversity (involving 15 separate Member States compared to only three in the NAFTA agreement) and the growing intensity of competition at an individual market level, means that the potential for exploiting the advantages of the Single Market from a single UK centre is limited. In turn, this appears to suggest limited scope for business rationalisation and the pursuit of pan-European scale economies, although firms are increasingly splitting up their businesses into constituent functions, enabling scale economies to be achieved in some areas of the business – local market sensitivity and adaptation in others. Equally, with the realisation of greater border freedoms, there are growing opportunities for manufacturing reorganisation on a product basis, removing the necessity to duplicate effort in different business centres.

Finally, in relation to technology, there is clear evidence that technological developments are taking place outside of economic unions. High levels of intra-bloc FDI now mean that leading global players have investment presence within the main economic regions of the world, facilities which allow them to foster alliances with customers and competitors to develop technologies which may then be exploited on a global scale. From this point of view, while there is a tendency when discussing the issue of regionalisation to view the world as a number of disparate economic centres, it is perhaps more pertinent to view the world along the same lines as multinational companies: a 'global village' of competitors or industrial customers wherein strategic alliances are linking organisations together, and a regionalised market place of end users which demands local adaptation and sensitivity.

Notes

1. This chapter is part of a wider project, sponsored by the Canadian High Commission, on Bilateral Trade and Investment between Canada and the UK.
2. This firm has been included in the sample as typifiying the complex ownership patterns of many Canadian-based firms.

4 Internationalisation of Service Firms: Strategic Considerations

Niklas Arvidsson

INTRODUCTION

Research on the internationalisation of firms has traditionally been focused on manufacturing firms. This focus has been natural, since these types of firms have had significant historical importance in international trade and national development. Today, there is an increasing attention on service firms, which can be explained by the growing importance service industries have in industrialised countries.

The international investments by service firms have increased significantly during the 1980s, and the importance the sector has had on international trade has grown accordingly. The service sector's share of international investment flows grew rapidly during the 1980s. The investment flows accounted for around 50 to 55 per cent of total outflows from the largest investing nations during the latter part of the 1980s. Furthermore, the service sector's share of the economy of the largest nations increased quite drastically (UNCTC, 1992).

Even though one reason for the importance of service firms is the reduction of legal restrictions on international trade and investments, there are still significant artificial international trade and investment restrictions in many service industries. This text, however, will ignore these barriers and focus on what influence specific characteristics of service production have on international investment opportunities and strategies.

As a result of increased international activity in service industries, there is a need to develop the understanding of internationalisation of service firms. Using research on manufacturing firms as a base, this text will discuss internationalisation of manufacturing and service operations, with the aim of developing the understanding of the most influential factors in the internationalisation process of service firms. The discussion leads to a new, alternative definition of 'service firms'.

The chapter begins with a discussion of theoretical findings about the internationalisation of service and manufacturing firms, as well as how the two generic types of firms, that is manufacturing and service, are related.

The internationalisation of service firms, and the effects that the most commonly cited characteristics of such firms have on the internationalisation process is then focused on; concentrating on the most crucial and obvious issues that a service-providing firm must deal with during its internationalisation. This is followed by an outline of strategic considerations for service firms, exemplifying different aspects of the internationalisation process by studying some Swedish service-providing firms. The final section summarises the previous discussion and formulates the final conclusions.

THEORETICAL AND CONCEPTUAL DISCUSSION OF INTERNATIONALISATION IN MANUFACTURING AND SERVICE FIRMS

Theoretical Models

One of the most well-known models on foreign direct investment has been provided by Dunning (see, for example, Dunning, 1988a). This model, often called the eclectic paradigm or the OLI-framework, explains foreign direct investments by a framework that incorporates trade theory (for a lengthy discussion see Hood and Young, 1979) and transaction cost theory (for example, Teece, 1986). Foreign direct investment is believed to be caused by ownership-specific advantages, location-specific advantages and internalisation ability. The main idea behind the model is that firms willing to operate in a foreign market are facing a disadvantage since they do not know the market or its local competitors. This disadvantage must be compensated with an owner-specific advantage. In other words, location-specific advantages, such as inexpensive labour or a large market, provide incentives for foreign direct investments. The ownership-advantages, e.g. process or product advantages, compensate for foreign market disadvantages. Furthermore, it is beneficial to internalise the function, which may be caused by high transaction costs in the market for this specific function, instead of selling it to a local firm via a market.

Another widely quoted model on internationalisation is the Uppsala-model, which originated in the 1970s (Johanson and Vahlne, 1977; Johanson and Wiedersheim-Paul, 1975). There has been additional research based on ideas from the Uppsala-school (for example, Luostarinen, 1978; Cavusgil, 1980), and there has also been critique (Hedlund and Kverneland, 1985; Turnbull, 1987; and Sullivan and Bauerschmidt, 1990). The Uppsala-model has its roots in Cyert and March (1963) in the sense that uncertainty is dealt with by the use of negotiated environments, for example, by using contractual arrangements with agents as local sales people. Moreover, the firm is assumed to adapt to a new environment as uncertainty is reduced through organisational learning.

The Uppsala-model rests on the assumption that firms are facing high uncertainty when starting operations outside the domestic market. They are consequently reluctant to make large capital investments. One way to overcome this uncertainty is to build the internationalisation of the firm gradually. Initial, small capital investments will increase the knowledge of the foreign market, and of overseas operations *per se*, through incremental investments in the foreign market. The internationalisation is seen as a process where firms gain knowledge about the foreign business environment gradually, which results in gradually increased investments (Johanson and Vahlne, 1992, 1990).

The idea of incremental investments has been exemplified by an establishment chain. This chain of sequentially increased investments abroad starts when a firm initiates foreign operations through exports from the domestic factories. The firm then gradually increases efforts to internationalise its activities and contact a local sales agent. As long as the experience is successful, this evolution will continue, which may result in opening a local sales subsidiary and eventually a manufacturing subsidiary (Johanson and Vahlne, 1977).

In other words, this model describes the internationalisation process as having several distinct stages. This text, however, argues that the stages are linked in a continuously evolving process without clear distinctions between them, and that it is only the manifestations[1] of these phases that develop stage-wise. In other words, attitudes and cognition are assumed to develop continuously, while behaviour, which in this case would be investment patterns, is assumed to develop stage-wise.

Thus, a general description of the characteristics of the internationalisation process may be as follows. At first, the firm or its managers are not interested in, or are unaware of, any internationalisation possibilities, which in the initial stage usually is exports. Exports may then be initiated after intentional or unintentional action by external or internal actors. In a third phase, managers are more actively evaluating and considering the possibilities to export its products, but they are still acting on an experimental basis. Later, exports become more common and the efforts are likely to expand. However, unsuccessful initial attempts may limit expansion.

In a fifth phase, the firm is seen as an experienced exporter and will often continue its internationalisation through agents, sales subsidiaries and, finally, manufacturing subsidiaries. In other words, the process involves continuously increased degrees of foreign direct investments (see Bilkey and Tesar, 1977; Cavusgil, 1980; Czinkota, 1982; and Reid, 1981).

One can distinguish three stages in the internationalisation process: initiation, expansion and consolidation. These three stages of resource commitment constitute the basic parts in the internationalisation life-cycle dimension.

The initiation phase is characterised by high uncertainty and indecisiveness, since the idea of becoming an international competitor is likely to be unfamiliar and new to most firms. The expansion phase occurs when the firm has attained some experience of foreign markets, with satisfactorily successful results. The uncertainty is gradually reduced as familiarity and knowledge are gathered and the foreign activities grow.

Consolidation occurs when the firm is experienced internationally, and usually involves slowed growth. The consolidation phase is also likely to result in attempts to coordinate international activities on a cross-national basis. In other words, operations are coordinated globally in an attempt to reap economies of scale and/or scope (for further discussion see, for example, Bartlett and Ghoshal, 1987a; Bartlett and Ghoshal, 1987a; Porter, 1986).

The Theoretical Models and Service Firms

The discussion of internationalisation thus far has been quite general, and most of the research has been based on the behaviour of manufacturing firms. Consequently, there is a need for further research on service firms.

One example of such research was presented in an article by Li and Guisinger (1992). They conducted a statistical study of determinants to the globalisation of service multinationals in Japan, Western Europe and North America. To summarise, the study shows that foreign direct investments by service firms were positively affected by factors such as large host markets, small cultural distance between home and host country, the openness of the host market, the foreign direct investment by a global oligopolistic competitor, high growth of the firm itself and the desire to service clients globally. These findings are similar to conclusions concerning the internationalisation of manufacturing firms (see, for example, Caves, 1982; or Hood and Young, 1979).

In publications about the internationalisation of service firms (Löwendahl, 1992; Walter, 1988), there are four commonly cited factors that are assumed to stimulate service firms toward internationalisation:

1. Clients that have internationalised their activities may demand that the service supplier provide a global network and/or global experience.
2. Economies of scale may lower the costs per unit of sales for the service firm and consequently provide an incentive for globalisation.
3. Economies of scope may provide incentives for the service firm to use the experience gained from one specific activity worldwide. This will lower the costs for each new performance of the activity.
4. If a major competitor globalises its activities, the service firm may have to become global itself if it wants to keep its position in the competitive race.

How does research on service firms relate to that on manufacturing firms? A common feature of studies on internationalisation is the separation between manufacturing and service firms. These two categories of firms are often treated as having widely different characteristics of their production and sales processes, which is assumed to cause different types of internationalisation processes. Each internationalisation process is treated as being a separate and unrelated phenomenon.

This text does not agree with the treatment presented in the previous paragraph, however. It is too simplistic to separate manufacturing of physical goods from production of services in general terms. And it is consequently extremely important to go beyond this superficial treatment; that is, beyond a dichotomous view of the world. The production and sales processes contain both elements that are similar in nature as well as those that are highly different. Furthermore, each category of firms contains a great variety of firms and products. It is not sensible to categorise all firms as being either a physical good producer having specified characteristics, or a service producer having other specified characteristics.

In this text, a service is seen as 'a product, the main purpose of which is to provide a service'. A physical good is 'a product, the main purpose of which is to supply tangible goods' (Dunning, 1989). Consequently, products are hereafter defined as being either services, physical goods or combinations of the two.

The texts that want to separate the two types of firms, based on these general terms, mention three characteristics of services as the reasons to differentiate the production of services from that of physical goods. These three characteristics are *simultaneity*, *perishability* and *intangibility* (see, for example, Löwendahl, 1992; Normann, 1992).

Simultaneity means that the buyer consumes the service at the same moment it is produced by interacting with the producer; that is, simultaneous production and consumption. Perishability means that the service cannot be prefabricated, stored and delivered to the consumer at a later moment. The perishability factor is consequently closely related to the simultaneity factor. Intangibility means that the consumer may have difficulties of knowing what the producer really is offering, which is caused by asymmetrical information between the buyer and the seller.

A clear-cut distinction between services and physical goods is given by Edvardsson and Gummesson (1988): 'A service is something that can be bought and sold, but which you cannot drop on your foot'. This definition is humorous but misguiding since it emphasises a dichotomous standpoint.

Thus, this text argues that it is too simplistic to separate the production of services and physical goods on a general basis. Still, the previous discussion of characteristics of services may nevertheless be helpful when one wants to characterise different types of manufacturing and service providing firms. The characteristics called simultaneity, perishability and intangibility are regarded to constitute the main causal variables to the outcome of the operations of a firm.

A Modified View on Service and Manufacturing Firms

Most, if not all, products contain some elements of service features and some elements of physical goods. Accordingly, the degrees of service content, or physical good content, can be an insightful component when one tries to understand the effects on the internationalisation process based on the specific characteristics of the product. But the main issue to concentrate on is where is it in the total process of delivering a product to a final consumer that the physical good and/or service-contents are performed. Traditionally, it is whether the consumer experiences the service or physical good content most intensely that has been the determinant of whether a product is considered to be a physical good or a service.

Consequently, one can characterise products, including both goods and services, as well as their production and sales processes by the service intensity (see, for example, Hirsch and Meshulach, 1991). Products contain different degrees of mechanical or man-made service offering as well as different degrees of reliance on physical goods. Products can be said to be goods-embodied, that is, the final product is supplied in the form of a physical good, or service-embodied, that is, the final product is supplied in the form of a service.

Goods-embodied services are services that require physical goods to be at hand. This type of product can be exemplified by an automated teller machine – a machine that provides the service of cash withdrawal – a service that bank personnel used to provide. On the other hand, physical goods may also be provided through services, that is, service-embodied goods. This may be exemplified by a restaurant dinner. In general, services always contain elements sourced from either people or a product, and/or contain a technology-embodied feature (Dunning, 1989; Maister, 1982; Aharoni and Sticht, 1990b).

A physical good can consequently be seen as a manifestation of performed services. For instance, an auto-manufacturer can be seen as selling the services of sourcing inputs, modifying these inputs, assembling and styling the parts, and distributing the manifestation of these services – the car – to the consumer. The manufacturing firms provide services, and the physical good is a result of performed service and manufacturing processes.

A comparison can be made between the lease of a car, which traditionally has been defined as supply of a service, and the purchase of a car, which traditionally has been defined as supply of a physical good. From the customer's user-perspective these two different types of transactions are very similar. The customer gets to use a car when and how much he or she wants. The difference appears when the question of risk is approached. Who stands the risk of a stolen or crashed car? Who has to account for the car in the balance sheet? Without making the comparison too detailed, one can state that the differences between the two alternatives are basically of a financial and risk-related nature.

Figure 4.1 The relation between customisation, physical goods, services and interaction between seller and buyer during the production process

	Standardised products – little interaction	**Customised products – much interaction**
Examples of a physical good	A Volvo 740	A Formula One racing car
Examples of a service	A fund for investments in a portfolio of stocks that is managed and offered by bank	A stock depot that includes management of a stock portfolio as well as investment a advice

On the basis of the previous discussion, this text will relate the characteristics of products to the internationalisation process. This means, for instance, that some types of service firms may have more characteristics in common with some types of manufacturing firms than with other types of service firms, and the other way around.

To exemplify, the degree of interaction or the degree of simultaneity between the producer and the customer is determined by the need for a customised product. It does not matter whether the product is a service or a physical good. If the customer wants a customised physical good, the degree of interaction is likely to be higher than if the customer wants a standardised service. This reasoning is contrary to the idea that the degree of simultaneity is always higher in service firms than in manufacturing firms (see Figure 4.1).

INTERNATIONALISATION OF SERVICE FIRMS

To facilitate the discussion on internationalisation of service firms, a new, alternative definition of a service firm will be given. The term 'service firm' will in the remainder of this text be defined as a firm providing products supplied through production and sales processes that are characterised by high degrees of simultaneity, perishability and/or intangibility.

The Establishment Chain and Entry Strategies for Service Firms

The general argument in this text is that firms characterised by high degrees of simultaneity, intangibility and perishability in the production process do not face the same investment alternatives in their internationalisation process as a firm characterised by low degrees of simultaneity, intangibility and perishability. Thus, the establishment chain presented earlier must be modified.

A hypothetical establishment chain for a service firm may be that the firm starts its internationalisation by performing project-type customer-ordered studies or work abroad by temporarily placing employees with the client. These types of projects may be done on an *ad hoc* or long-term basis, and can perhaps be performed at the home country office. A second step may be to open an office abroad, which can be operated by travelling domestic employees or by locally recruited personnel. A third step may be to open several offices abroad and to recruit a larger share of local personnel. This step is comparable to a foreign manufacturing subsidiary for a manufacturing firm.

Thus, there are generally three modes of international involvement that are connected with service firms. One mode is the export of final services, which can be said to involve a situation where, for instance, a bank sells a financial solution to a customer based in a foreign country. A second mode is contractual agreements on intermediate services, which can be exemplified by a management consultant firm that analyses the operations of a firm in a foreign country. A third mode is service provision directly by a foreign establishment (for a lengthy discussion see Dunning, 1989).

A classification of the three most obvious foreign country entry strategies for service firms is also provided by Dunning (1989). These strategies are:

- internal development;[2]
- acquisitions of local firms; and
- licensing a service concept to a local firm.

Other strategies are to develop internal ventures, which is a situation where an individual department within the firm operates internationally. Or the firm may seek internationalisation via joint ventures or alliances.

To explain the main features of the internationalisation process of service firms, the eclectic paradigm, or the OLI-framework, will be used. The ownership-specific advantage for service firms is usually almost entirely resting within the employees and within firm-specific concepts, or service delivery systems, that can be kept proprietary at least to some extent. These two parts' historical performance constitutes the firm's reputation on the market.

The long-term possibilities to maintain an ownership-specific advantage can be argued to be higher if the firm's conceptual service system is the major factor behind the firm's success. If an advantage is based only on the abilities of the employees themselves, the firm is in a more risky situation since these people are able to leave the firm overnight. Furthermore, it is likely to be easier to signal a quality signal to customers if the system is the important part of a firm's offering. On the other hand, a system, in the sense of standardised work routines and models for analysis and product design, can be easier to imitate by competitors.

Manufacturing firms that establish operations abroad are often seeking advantages from inexpensive factors of production, large markets or reduced transportation costs (for a lengthy discussion see Caves, 1982; Hood and Young, 1979). As stated previously, the service firm is usually also seeking customer closeness and is thus highly influenced by cultural differences. The location-specific advantages that the service firms seek can perhaps be argued to be more of an intangible nature than those that manufacturing firms seek or are influenced by. For instance, local customers originating from the same country as the service firm may be likely to select this firm as the supplier to their local operations. On the other hand, cultural differences between the international service firm and local customers may make it difficult to provide excellent service.

The internalisation aspect of the OLI-paradigm is highly applicable when discussing service firms and internationalisation. Internalisation is almost by definition done in service firms that start up activities abroad. But there are factors both working in favour of and against internalising the foreign operations. Native employees can be a crucial asset when the service firm wants to approach local customers, since these employees know the culture. They may also have an already developed experience record that the firm can use as the bridge to a new market. Cooperation with local firms may, on the other hand, provide opportunities to develop crucial relations with customers or other actors rapidly, and may also provide legitimacy and a good reputation.

Accordingly, a truly fundamental issue that faces an internationalising firm is the meeting with new cultures and new values. This issue has in research about internationalisation been addressed under the term *psychic distance*. Psychic distance has been defined as 'the sum of factors preventing the flow of information from and to the market' (Johanson and Vahlne, 1977). Thus, this concept includes such disparate factors as language barriers, differences in taste among consumers, and differences in values, behaviour and attitudes.

When discussing psychic distance in relation to service providing firms, there is one important factor that must be addressed. One of the most crucial assets for a service firm is its reputation. In fact, the reputation, or the experience record, of a service firm may be the main, or perhaps the only, source for a customer to control the quality of the service offered before the actual transaction (see, for example, Löwendahl, 1992). The experience record has been described as a curriculum vitae for the service firm.

Consequently, a large psychic distance between the service firm and its customer is likely to increase the probability that the experience record is not assessed to its full value by the client. There may be several reasons for this. First, the experience record does not appear as valuable for the customer as the firm would like, since the customer may have alternative views on manners in which business should be done. Secondly, a large psychic distance is likely to increase the possibility that the service firm does a less than satisfactory job due to communication problems.

Figure 4.2 The internationalisation of a firm in relation to the internationalisation of its business environment

		Degree of internationalisation of the business environment	
		Low	*High*
Degree of internationalisation of the firm	*Low*	The early starter	The late starter
	High	The lonely international	The international among others

Source: Johanson and Mattsson (1988)

Internationalisation via Network Growth

The very nature of the characteristics simultaneity and intangibility point to the value and need for a service firm to have relevant personal contacts with other firms that are important to the industry. A study on Swedish service firms (Johanson and Sharma, 1987) found that the evolution of service firms is usually highly influenced by networks, which is consistent with studies on the internationalisation processes within manufacturing firms. Networks, cooperative arrangements and personal relationships are often very important factors for possibilities to perform, and results of, foreign operations (Aharoni and Sticht, 1990a; Johanson and Mattsson, 1988).

There is reason to believe that networks are relatively more important for service firms than for manufacturing firms in buyer–seller relationships, since the service often is produced through personal interaction between seller and buyer. This implies that the surrounding network to a service firm, and its resulting opportunities, are main factors influencing the internationalisation of service firms.

The network's role in the internationalisation process depends on, for instance, the degree of a firm's internationalisation in comparison with its business environment (Johanson and Mattsson, 1988). This reasoning is summarised in Figure 4.2. The early starter operates in a business environment with few and relatively insignificant international relationships. The firm consequently has little knowledge and experience of foreign markets, and does not hold international contacts that can be used to attain such knowledge. As a result, the firm is likely to be influenced by initiatives from familiar or unfamiliar external actors in the internationalisation process. The internationalisation is often initiated by spontaneously emerging opportunities. Relying on external actors, such as agents or middle men, is a common way to overcome the lack of experience. However filled with risk, acquisitions of local firms and their personnel are other ways to overcome the lack of knowledge. The early starter also faces the problem of reaching a position built on trust from its international counterparts, since the local firms often have not dealt with foreign firms previously.

The lonely international is characterised by a firm that has become a successful international actor in a business that is domestic in its nature; that is, a successful early starter. In this new situation, the early starter has succeeded in becoming international and holds a major advantage over competitors that have not internationalised their operations. The advantage will come from the experience and knowledge of relationships in international business, and from possibilities to attain new types of resources. The firm has, for instance, access to networks in several countries and may initiate new types of business ventures. The firm is more likely to affect the internationalisation of others rather than being affected by others. One of the most important tasks of the lonely international is to pursue international integration of its activities.

The late starter is a firm that is domestic in its operations, but is active in a highly international industry. This means that the firm is likely to face difficulties when it wants to internationalise its activities. Distribution channels may be occupied, its lack of international experience will create difficulties, or international competitors may have become large and unwilling to let new firms enter the global scene. A large late starter can often make rapid steps in its internationalisation through acquisitions, even though this may cause risks due to lack of international experience as compared to other large internationalised firms. The smaller firms are more dependent on other firms and their relations, but are on the other hand usually quite flexible to find a niche position in the international market.

The international among others is an international firm that operates in an international industry. Here, further internationalisation will be marginal, and dependent on how the firm's entire global operations perform and act in a complementary manner. These types of firms are likely to be able to rely on external sourcing to a greater extent than other firms, since they are likely to be located in large, international networks. In this situation, the firm is likely to gain heavily from effective global coordination of its activities, and is consequently often focused on this matter. The international among others is often operating in a global and oligopolistic market.

As seen above, the service firm can attempt to enter global networks with foreign counterparts in order to reap gains from efficiency in scale and scope. The internationalisation can be attained through multi-firm collaboration or networking. The internationalisation of a Swedish firm, Upplysningscentralen, follows this pattern. The firm sells financial company-related data to be used as credit-related information. The internationalisation of Upplysningscentralen has been pursued through an information network with similar organisations in other countries. The mutually beneficial goal of this cooperation has been to develop the ability to trade information internationally (Edvardsson, Edvinsson and Nyström, 1992).

An important issue during the internationalisation process of a firm is the selection of distribution channels. The exporter of physical goods is dependent on finding economically efficient and effective distribution channels. However, the most effective and efficient channels are often occupied. The exporter of products characterised by high simultaneity and perishability do not face this problem. These firms are not dependent on existing distribution channels. They are able to create their own distribution channel(s) through interacting with the customer during production and consumption of the product. The network contacts are not needed for intermediation between the seller and the buyer, but the need for network contacts to develop customer relationships are still crucial.

Consequently, the internationalisation process of firms is highly affected by the personal experience and characteristics of leading managers. These persons' international outlooks, personal and business experience and their relations with important actors in the industry will have significant influence over the internationalisation process. Thus, the process will, for instance, depend on visionary management, spontaneous decision-making and a desire to meet challenges.

INTERNATIONALISATION STRATEGIES IN SERVICE FIRMS

Strategic Thinking in Service Firms

Löwendahl (1992) found that much of the research on strategy formulation in professional service firms came to the conclusion that firms often had neglected their strategic thinking. Questions as in which competitive domain the firm was operating, which clients they served and did not serve, which core services they offered and did not offer, and how the firms could expand their business operation had not been analysed properly, or at all. A conclusion that can be drawn from these findings is that service firms to a large extent have done their strategic decisions in an *ad hoc* manner based on emerging tendencies and spontaneous opportunities.

Obviously, one effect of high degrees of simultaneity between the buyer and the seller during the production process is that the internationalisation becomes closely tied to each customer relation, and is not altogether under the control of the service firm itself. The service firm must tailor-make its operations to the demands of each customer. For instance, if an accountant firm wishes to serve a Swedish-based multinational firm in Sweden as well as in France, it must know and provide service related to tax laws in each country in addition to industry-specific knowledge. This forces the service provider to be flexible towards each customer during the internationalisation process.

Furthermore, the simultaneity factor relates closely to the issue of customer selection for service firms in their internationalisation process. It may be tempting to merely supply services to foreign operations of domestic customers, since the close interaction between seller and buyer in combination with a large psychic distance will make it more difficult to sell to foreign firms.

This can be described as a passive internationalisation process, since the firm follows its existing customers. This strategy can be a good way to internationalise one's operations while holding down the risk level. Once the firm has become successful in providing services to familiar customers in an unfamiliar country, it may try to take another step.

The most obvious disadvantage with the passive internationalisation strategy is the potential dependency on old customers, which may result in a lack of control over customer focus and product offerings. To a very large extent, it is likely to be the customers that decide the goals and focus of the specific activities. Furthermore, due to the passive strategy the service firm may not be able to learn about and understand the specific environment – that is, the local country in which business is done – which is dangerous for a long-term competitive position.

A high degree of perishability for service-based products implies that there may be benefits from internationalisation *per se*. Due to perishability, the service firm is always pressed to schedule tasks as efficiently as possible, avoiding periods with lack of work in-between projects. In other words, economies of scope are likely to be quite substantial due to the perishability factor, since the activities characterised by perishability can become infrequently used if there are not complementary operations that can employ these resources.

Being present on a larger number of geographical markets should consequently decrease the risk of being out of projects, and can result in better capacity utilisation. As long as employees hold the relevant competence, it is possible to move people to projects in other countries if business is slow in the domestic country. Since the largest cost for these types of firms most often consists of wages and salaries, the potential benefit from high capacity utilisation is substantial. This reasoning rests on the assumption that employee costs, that is wages and salaries, are treated as fixed costs.

The intangibility of products is likely to result in increased necessity of being physically located in the local market if the firm is to receive orders. If the firm is not located in the market, it may be difficult for the customers to understand the firm's abilities. In fact, being located on the specific market may be the only way to overcome the intangibility problem, unless the firm's experience record speaks for itself. That is, the firm is so well reputed that customers believe in its quality even before it starts to sell its products on the market in question.

Two Examples of Internationalisation Strategies

To illustrate some of the ideas discussed above, the following section will present two examples from internationalisation processes within Swedish service. The examples, Securitas and WM-Data, as well as conclusions are taken from Edvardsson, Edvinsson and Nyström (1992).

Securitas is a firm in the security industry, where it sells alarm systems, both manual and mechanical, and different types of locking devices. The firm's sales during 1992 reached 6537 million SEK, and was based on operations in 11 countries with almost 25 000 employees.

The firm has not had the goal of following domestic customers to foreign markets during its internationalisation, but has instead always been focused on meeting local demand. The most critical issues during the internationalisation process are said to have been to find qualified personnel, and to grow with maintained profitability and equity ratio.

Initially, the internationalisation followed a similar path as described by the establishment chain. The originally Danish firm started a small subsidiary in Sweden, which later become an individual firm. The firm then expanded in Sweden, and started to aim at becoming an international firm. Later, the international growth of Securitas has mainly been done by starting foreign subsidiaries through acquisitions or joint-ventures. The success of the firm's internationalisation is said to lie in local recruitment and local adaptation of its security system concept that was developed for the Swedish market. As an effect, the firm has worked hard to control cultural differences between managers, customers and employees.

The main causes of the firm's successful internationalisation are said to have been four. First, it has been able to systemise and market its knowledge advantage over competitors. Second, it has built substantial local involvement and influence in the business operations. Third, its employees have been highly qualified and motivated. Fourth, there has been an international customer need for its products.

WM-Data is a consulting firm focused on developing computer systems for administration purposes. The firm's sales in 1988 approximated 365 million SEK with about 600 employees. Its internationalisation, as well as all its operations, has been built mostly with internally generated capital, since a low-risk profile is wanted. The ambition has been that each new activity should finance itself. Furthermore, the internationalisation is under the control and responsibility of one of the two founders of the firm. There are also special budgets for new attempts to enter a foreign market.

The firm officially started its internationalisation when it stated that the Nordic countries constituted its home market. The idea behind this was to create advantages through transfer of knowledge between the countries, larger size that could be used in negotiations with knowledge or system suppliers and to have a larger market.

WM-Data has been intensively focused on maintaining and developing the customers it already has, instead of trying to find new customers. This has resulted in a reputation of trustworthiness and long-term care of customers. The firm has three major goals for its operations. First, customers must be comfortable with the relation to WM-Data and always feel that supplied quality is at least as high as expected quality. Second, the profitability of the activities must be higher than the industry average. Third, WM-Data should be the leading supplier of computer-based administration systems in the Nordic countries. The strong position in the Nordic countries is then to be used as a gate-opener to other European markets.

The internationalisation of WM-Data started through an order from a foreign division to a domestic customer. This led to additional orders from other geographically dispersed business areas in the multinational firm, and soon the first foreign subsidiary was started in Denmark. The orders built network contacts for WM-Data that became the key to new foreign markets and a good reputation abroad. WM-Data's internationalisation is said to be based on building competence locally and selling products; that is, systems that are developed in Sweden. References from earlier customers are seen as crucial factors for receiving orders from new customers.

The conclusions that may be drawn from the examples above are that issues that are very important during internationalisation are the development of conceptual service delivery systems, attempts to closely connect with customers' needs and to adapt to local standards.

The 'Intermingling' Internationalisation Strategy

As seen in the previous examples, a service firm has a good opportunity to connect its offer to the specific needs and interests of each customer. This behaviour, if successful, also increases the possibilities that the service firm is able to hold a long-term relationship with the customer, since the offering is highly customised and thus valuable for the customer. These ideas are connected to a discussion by Normann and Ramírez (1993; see also Porter, 1985).

Normann and Ramírez discuss how firms can increase the customer's value of their offerings through knowledge about customer behaviour and innovative ability to redesign the roles of sellers and buyers. Firms' key strategic tasks today are said to be 'the reconfiguration of roles and relationships among this constellation of actors (that is, suppliers, business partners, allies and customers) in order to mobilise the creation of value in new forms and by new players' (p. 66). Their ideas are supported by several examples.

The Swedish furniture and interior decoration seller IKEA is one of these examples. IKEA managed to redesign the entire furniture industry when they introduced knocked-down furniture that customers buy at the store, transport home and then assemble at their own expense. This new behaviour in the furniture industry created increased value both for IKEA, who could concentrate its efforts on inbound logistics and design, and for the customer, who found IKEA's less expensive but still attractive furniture highly valuable. The main idea put forward in Normann and Ramírez' article is that the goal of firms ought not be to create value for customers, but to mobilise customers to create their own value from the company's offerings.

The idea of redesigning value for customers is closely connected to simultaneity; that is, the simultaneous production and consumption of products. The supplier of products with high degrees of simultaneity will receive unique understanding of and plentiful information about the customer's operations and sources of competitive advantage. This understanding can be used to develop an offering that results in high value for the customer and that, due to its intangibility, may be difficult to match for competitors.

This results in the proposition that competitive advantages can be gained through value-sharing with customers due to redesigned product offerings. In other words, the firm will strive to intermingle its own value-chain with one or several value-chains of customers. This strategy is apparent for service firms since they often are forced to become internationalised by their customers.

CONCLUSIONS AND MANAGERIAL IMPLICATIONS

As discussed previously, there are significant opportunities for service firms to grow internationally with limited financial risk-taking. The possibilities to provide services from domestic offices or through temporary offices abroad staffed with domestic personnel require low financial investments, which increases the flexibility of the entire internationalisation process.

At the same time, there is a crucial risk to consider. The internationalising service-providing firm risks a deteriorated reputation due to its inability to maintain a quality standard in a new and culturally different market. The internationalisation process can be seen as an interplay between the high risk of a reduced experience record, and the relatively low financial risks that a service firm must take.

Main Considerations during Initiation

Another critical conclusion on the internationalisation of service firms concerns the initial steps towards a foreign market. The initiation of internationalisation is described as a phase highly influenced by network contacts and one's own abilities to become international. Thus, one important issue to deal with is the development of a potentially valuable and rich system of network contacts at an early stage in the internationalisation.

Even though it may at the time be less obvious which role and value that each contact ultimately may have, it is still important to nurture relations carefully. Furthermore, as the first steps towards internationalisation often are taken by an external actor, usually a customer, it is important to select customers, if at all possible, in order to facilitate and improve the internationalisation process. By following a customer to a new and unfamiliar market, the firm may achieve its internationalisation through a low-risk mode. This strategy yields a possibility to develop an understanding of the specific market and of internationalisation *per se* gradually, without having to face a high risk of a deteriorated reputation.

Johanson and Sharma (1987) suggest that if managers of service firms want to be successful in their investments outside the domestic market, they should map their initial network, analyse how the present relations have been developed, and analyse how the present network can be utilised to provide bridges into new markets. This idea also appears in a study by Aharoni and Sticht (1990a). A network is seen as an important factor when discussing and explaining how service firms approach foreign markets.

Aharoni and Sticht (1990a) argue that since business in the service industry is to a large extent done through interactive project work, the key to success lies in network contacts. Another important step towards internationalisation may be to recruit personnel with earlier experience of international operations and a rich international network of contacts.

Main Considerations during Expansion

The second phase of internationalisation, the expansion, is to a high extent influenced by new experience, knowledge and confidence gained through the international operations. Consequently, new relationships will yield additional opportunities, and virtuous or vicious circles are likely to occur during this phase. Initial success may lead to increased desire and ability to expand, and the other way around. However, even if the firm is successful at first, it should develop a system of elements that control growth! Rapid international growth may result in problems to maintain a high quality standard of provided services.

One way to overcome the quality problem is to systemise the entire service-providing concept. A well-developed system for service production is more likely to result in an even production of high quality service, than if the service production operations are based entirely on the individual's performance. Newly recruited personnel are also likely to need substantial time to develop the skills necessary to provide the quality standard that the firm currently sells, and customers are likely to notice the difference immediately.

In line with the previous reasoning, the sales of intangible products will benefit if the firm is able to develop system concepts that can be sold or perhaps licensed to the customer. This will be especially valuable when there is a significant psychic distance between the seller and the buyer, or between the firm and its newly recruited personnel in the foreign country.

Main Considerations during Consolidation

The implication for firms offering products with high perishability is to start operating in several activities with substantial economies of scope. In this way, the activities can complement each other in times of slow demand. This will result in a higher capacity utilisation, and consequently a better economy of production.

The simultaneous production and consumption of products imply an opportunity to customise one's own activity closely to the activities of the customer. This will consequently increase the value of one's offer for the customer. In this sense, the switching cost for the customer to select a new supplier can be increased if the customisation is successful. Learning from customers will be facilitated, which in turn will enhance opportunities to pursue continuous change. Both these factors are crucial for long-term survival and growth.

In other words, by redesigning the products that are offered to the market, a firm may be able to interrelate the customers' value-creating activities to one's own. This strategy has as its potential results a redefinition of responsibilities and roles, and increased total value for both seller and buyer. The goal is then to share this newly created value with the customer to the benefit of both. Consequently, the service firm should aim at integrating knowledge and relationships, or competence and customers, during its internationalisation.

Two General Conclusions

To conclude, the success of different strategic choices for internationalising firms offering products characterised by high degrees of simultaneity, perishability and intangibility will be influenced by two main categories of abilities.

First, is the potential to build relationship-driven product offerings to the customers. These will be based on the connection between the firm's value-creating activities and those of the customers. In other words, the opportunity to customise, or integrate, one's own value-chain with that of customers is obvious due to the simultaneity factor.

Secondly, the ability to select effectively from numerous investment alternatives where the selection is based on the risk of a reduced experience record and the ability to handle this risk. One of the most important trade-offs for these types of firms is that between the risk of a deteriorated experience record and the benefits of increased economies of scale and scope. In order to minimise the risk of a deteriorated experience record, the firm should strive to develop service systems or concepts.

Notes

1. That is, for example, exports, a local sales agent, a sales subsidiary and a manufacturing subsidiary.
2. When majority-owned foreign offices are started and operated by the internationalising firm: that is, greenfield investments.

5 Industrial Restructuring and the Control of 'Concentrations' in the European Market

Eleanor J. Morgan

INTRODUCTION

Common competition rules were introduced when the EEC was founded, to help ensure that anti-competitive behaviour by firms and governments did not thwart the establishment of a unified market and that the potential consumer benefits of integration could be realised. The Treaty of Rome provides a system to ensure that 'competition in the common market is not distorted'. Among the main provisions, cartels and other restrictive practices can be prohibited under Article 85; Article 86 allows the control of monopolistic practices by dominant firms; Article 90 brings public enterprises and state monopolies within the control of competition rules and Articles 92–94 allow the European Commission power to restrict state aids. These powers have been applied more rigorously as the barriers to trade have been dismantled. For excellent general reviews of European competition policy see, for example, Swann (1992), and George and Jacquemin (1990).

No mention was made of mergers in the Treaty of Rome, largely because few cross-border mergers were taking place, and those that were had little impact on trade between member states. As the barriers to trade were dismantled, however, the importance of such mergers increased. European Commission statistics suggest a threefold increase in the total number of mergers involving the largest EC firms between 1983 and 1987. Table 5.1 charts the subsequent increases in merger activity since 1986/7 in manufacturing, distribution, banking and insurance taken together, and highlights the growing importance of cross-border mergers among large firms, especially international mergers between EC firms and firms from third countries.

The Cecchini Report (1988) pointed to the potential importance of mergers in allowing firms within the EC to reap the benefits of the single market and to acquire the industrial strength needed to compete internationally on a more equal footing against Japanese and American rivals. This type of restructuring was expected to account for a large part of the estimated welfare

Table 5.1 National, community and international majority acquisitions (including mergers), number and increases in annual activity[1]

Year	*Total*		*National*[2]		*Community*[3]		*International*[4]	
	No	*Index*[5]	*No*	*Index*[5]	*No*	*Index*[5]	*No*	*Index*[5]
86/87	151	100	94	100	46	100	11	100
87/88	240	159	110	117	80	174	50	454
88/89	350	232	155	165	123	267	72	655
89/90	439	291	147	156	176	383	116	1 054
90/91	367	243	145	154	127	276	95	864
91/92	291	193	142	151	103	224	46	418

Notes:
[1] Includes those with a combined turnover of greater than ECU 2 billion
[2] Operations of firms from the same Member State
[3] Operations of firms from different Member States
[4] Operations of firms from Member States and third countries with effect on the Community market
[5] 1986/87 = 100

Source: Derived from Commission of the European Communities, XXII Report on Competition Policy, Annex IV

gains from further integration. The majority of mergers were expected to be pro-competitive in nature, but it was also recognised that firms might use them defensively to protect their market positions.

Some countries, most notably Germany and the UK and to a lesser extent France, had well-developed systems of merger control by the mid-1980's, but other countries had no provisions. In any case, the European Commission did not regard merger regulation by purely national authorities on the basis of domestic self-interest as sufficient in view of the potential spill-over effects of such transactions into other countries; it first proposed a European merger regulation as early as 1973. After 16 years of negotiation a merger control regulation was finally agreed in December 1989 and introduced in September 1990 (Council Regulation 4064/89).

This chapter briefly examines the operation of Articles 85 and 86, both of which were used by the Commission to control mergers prior to the introduction of a specific merger regulation. It then outlines the main features of the new regulation and examines certain aspects of its operation up to the end of February 1993. During this period, 145 cases were notified to the Commission; these provide a considerable body of case material to examine the application of the regulation in practice, and the evolution of policy. This research was primarily based on the evidence provided by both the decisions taken after full proceedings, which appear in the Official Journal, and the unpublished decisions provided by the European Commission.

EXISTING POWERS UNDER ARTICLES 85 AND 86

Before the merger regulation was introduced, Article 85 was the only available EC competition policy instrument to reach transactions involving no pre-existing dominant position. This prohibits

> as incompatible with the common market all agreements . . . which may affect trade between Member States and which have as their object or effect the prevention, restriction or distortion of competition within the common market.

The wording might appear to cover agreements to buy stock or assets which would result in the combination of two or more parties into a single entity. In 1966, however, the European Commission published a memorandum which distinguished between cartels, which were deemed to be subject to Article 85, and concentrations, which were not. The distinction rested on the fact that cartels are contractual agreements relating to firms' behaviour while concentrations are structural, resulting in a new organic unit with permanent loss of economic independence of the parties. Cartels and behavioural types of joint venture, now known as 'cooperative' joint ventures, were therefore covered by Article 85, but mergers and merger-like arrangements, such as 'concentrative' joint ventures, were ruled out.[1] The criteria on which distinctions are currently made between these two types of joint venture are discussed towards the end of the chapter.

Article 85 does not completely prohibit cartels and cooperative joint ventures. Under Article 85(3), an agreement which limits competition may be exempted if it contributes to 'improving the production or distribution of goods or to promoting technical or economic progress.' Exemption is subject to various conditions: the agreement should allow consumers 'a fair share of the resulting benefits'; restrictions on competition must be limited to those which are indispensable to achieve the aims of the agreement, and the agreement must not eliminate competition entirely from a substantial section of the industry.

In addition, block exemptions have been granted for certain types of arrangements where it is expected that cooperative behaviour, although restricting competition, might lead to efficiency and other social benefits. These include arrangements relating to R&D, patent licensing, the development or application of standards and specialisation in the manufacture of products involving small and medium sized enterprises.

The simplest form of cooperation is collusion to fix prices and outputs, and the Commission has taken an increasingly hard line on these types of arrangements. Such cartels have generally been prohibited; as well as banning the arrangements, the Commission has the power to impose fines of up to 10 per cent of total turnover of each company involved, and there has been a marked increase in the level of fines imposed recently.

In contrast to the firm stance taken against cartels, recent policy towards collaborative joint ventures has been relatively relaxed and the trend has been to facilitate joint ventures as long as they do not contain unreasonable terms. The maintenance of competition is virtually the only consideration in assessing collusion, whereas industrial policy considerations have been given considerable weight in assessing joint ventures. The Commission has avoided clear contradictions between its treatment of joint ventures and cartels, by not allowing joint ventures to explicitly enter into price fixing and market-sharing agreements. However, the distinction between cartels and some collaborative joint ventures has been a fine one, and critics have pointed to examples of cases where a price fixing cartel has been declared illegal but a joint venture formed subsequently to achieve many of the same benefits for the firms involved has been allowed by the Commission (Cutler *et al.*, 1992).

While joint ventures involving behavioural arrangements were within the scope of the Commission's powers, there was difficulty in exercising satisfactory control over mergers and merger-like transactions in the absence of a specific merger regulation. In *Philip Morris* (1987), the Commission extended its interpretation of Article 85 by applying it to a minority acquisition, and this controversial move was upheld by the Court of Justice.[2] However the main attempts at control were through the application of Article 86.

Article 86 states that

> any abuse by one or more undertakings of a dominant position within the common market or in a substantial part of it shall be prohibited as incompatible with the common market insofar as it may affect trade between Member States.

Article 86, which unlike Article 85 does not allow for an efficiency defence, was first applied in 1971. There have been comparatively few formal Article 86 decisions; 25 had been officially published by 1992, compared with 340 formal Article 85 decisions.

The wording of Article 86 allows the Commission to regulate the 'abuse' of an existing dominant position, but it is difficult to regulate the creation or strengthening of a dominant position which might result from a merger under this provision. Article 86 was first interpreted as applying to mergers in 1972 when Continental Can sought to merge with a Dutch can producer, Thomassen Drijver.[3] Although the case was overturned in the Court of Justice largely because of problems in the way the market had been defined, it was an important landmark in the Commission's struggle to exercise some control over mergers.

Despite a number of notable cases in the years that followed, the system of informal merger control which emerged had a number of drawbacks (see Bishop, 1990). There was no requirement for firms to obtain Commission approval in advance, so if the Commission decided against the merger it could be very costly for the companies concerned. The criteria for referral were not clear; the standard of appraisal in the large number of informal decisions appeared inconsistent, and there was no time limit on the Commission's investigation. The appraisals leading to the informal decisions did not appear to be based on a consistent standard of assessment. As well as the uncertainties in the Commission's approach, firms faced the risk of parallel investigation by two or more authorities, national and European; although a national authority could not approve a merger which had been banned by the Commission, a merger which the Commission had approved could be banned by the national authorities.

THE 1989 MERGER REGULATION

The increased number of mergers and merger-like activities across Europe highlighted the inadequacies of existing policy and the need for a formal system of prior control at EC level. The new merger regulation was introduced in 1990 to fill this policy gap. It gives the European Commission exclusive power to control the largest mergers and certain types of joint ventures, subject to limited exceptions which are at the Commission's discretion. The regulation has two main aims. One is to facilitate mergers by reducing transactions costs; the other is to control the minority of transactions which the Commission felt were likely to have adverse effects on competition.

The Scope of the Regulation

The first step in the Commission's investigation of any case is to establish whether it falls within the scope of the regulation. This covers 'concentrations with a Community dimension'. 'Concentrations' are defined as covering mergers or merger-like transactions which lead to a lasting change in the structure of the undertakings concerned through the acquisition of sole or joint control. This broad definition includes full function joint ventures known as 'concentrative' joint ventures; 'cooperative' joint ventures are excluded but can still be dealt with as restrictive practices under Article 85. In practice, the distinction between these two types is rather blurred, a point which will be discussed towards the end of the chapter.

Whether a particular 'concentration' has a 'community dimension' is defined by reference to the dual criteria of turnover and its geographical distribution. A merger is considered to have a Community dimension if:

1. The combined aggregate worldwide turnover of all the undertakings concerned is more than ECU 5 billion (then £3.5 billion);
2. The aggregate Community-wide turnover of each of at least two of the undertakings concerned is more than ECU 250 million; and
3. Each of the parties concerned has no more than two-thirds of its aggregate Community-wide turnover within one and the same member state.

These thresholds mean that the regulation is confined to large firms; the ECU 250 million criterion is designed to exclude relatively unimportant transactions where large firms acquire minnows. The two-thirds rule was introduced to rule out mergers which are primarily of national concern.

The use of absolute size as the qualifying criterion for investigation was expected to reduce the uncertainty about when the regulation would apply, while allowing attention to be focused on substantial mergers. The Commission originally proposed much lower turnover thresholds but was forced to confine the scope of the regulation to relatively large transactions in order to obtain agreement from the countries with well-established merger controls of their own. Evidence on the operation of these thresholds is discussed later in the chapter.

Mergers within the scope of the regulation have to be notified to the Commission not more than a week after the agreement is concluded or a public bid announced. The Commission has a month to decide whether there are 'serious doubts' about compatibility with the common market on the basis of a competition test and, if so, a full enquiry is opened.[4] The Commission then has a further four months to reach a decision and, meanwhile, the merger is suspended. Investigations are conducted for the European Commission by a Mergers Task Force which was created for this purpose. For a useful insight into the internal procedures adopted by the Mergers Task Force, see Overbury (1992).

The merger regulation was intended to introduce a 'one-stop shop', with the EC having sole jurisdiction over transactions of Community dimensions and other mergers being dealt with by the national authorities (unless the European Commission was specifically requested by a member state to intervene in its territory). Two main exceptions were included: Article 9 allows a member state to ask the Commission to refer transactions with competition effects in a distinct market to the national authority and was introduced in response to pressure from the Germans, who feared that there might otherwise be a deterioration in competition in its domestic markets; and Article 21(3) allows member states to intervene to protect legitimate non-competition interests such as public security, plurality of the media and prudential rules and was requested primarily by the UK authorities.

An Overview of the Cases

It was estimated that some fifty to sixty mergers a year would be notified to the Commission. This estimate has proved reasonably accurate and 145 mergers were notified by the end of February 1993 (Commission of the European Communities, 1993). The most common type of notification was majority acquisition (69 notifications, including three contested bids). Joint ventures were the next most common (66 notifications) and the other categories were relatively unimportant – mergers (6), minority acquisitions (2), cross shareholdings (1) and demerger (1).

Cross-border transactions have been the most important form of transaction considered, accounting for 114 of the cases. Nineteen have involved non-EC firms alone, reflecting the broad geographical reach of the regulation. Merger activity as a whole during the period was heavily concentrated in the larger member states and this is reflected in the cases examined under the regulation. Analysis by member state shows France involved in 75 cases out of the 145 (52 per cent), UK next (40 per cent), Germany (34 per cent), Italy (17 per cent), Spain (12 per cent), the Netherlands (8 per cent), Belgium (6 per cent) and Denmark and Portugal represented in two cases each, with firms in Greece and Ireland not involved in this initial period.

It was expected that the exceptions to the 'one-stop shop' approach of the regulation would be rarely invoked, and so far they have been little used. No exceptions had been made under Article 21(3) by the end of February 1993, and there were only five requests for referral under Article 9 of which four were by the German authorities. One case was refused *(Alcatel/AEG*

Kabel).[5] In three cases, viz. *Varta/Bosch*, *Mannesmann/Hoesch* and *Siemens/Philips*, the Commission decided to open full proceedings itself.[6] The only successful request was *Steetley/Tarmac*, a joint venture in the building materials industry involving a regional market for bricks and clay tiles in the UK; this case was referred back to the Monopolies and Mergers Commission for investigation.[7]

Of the 136 cases on which decisions had been taken at the end of February 1993, 17 were found to be outside the scope of the regulation so investigation was terminated. One hundred and eight did not raise serious doubts about compatibility with the Common Market after initial scrutiny, and were cleared within one month. Full proceedings were opened in 11 cases and, of these, two have been cleared unconditionally, seven have had conditions attached to clearance, one has been banned and one case was withdrawn by the participants (see Table 5.2).

The fact that 91 per cent of the first cases considered within the scope of the regulation were cleared after initial scrutiny, and only one merger to date has been banned, seems somewhat surprising, particularly in view of the force with which the Commission had argued the need for an effective merger control at European level. Some indications of activity in other merger control regimes presented in Overbury (1992) are helpful to put these statistics in context, although, as the author himself acknowledges, one must be wary of making too much of such comparisons.

The approach does appear rather lenient by UK standards; of the 541 cases investigated by the Office of Fair Trading over the last three years, 41 were referred to the Monopolies and Mergers Commission, of which 16 were found to be against the public interest. In contrast, the German Bundeskartellamt prohibited only one of more than 2000 mergers it investigated during 1991. The system of regulation in France makes it difficult to obtain statistics showing the number of cases scrutinised but, over the last three years, four of the eight cases subject to fuller investigation were approved subject to conditions.

Such statistics suggest that, in general, mergers tend only to be banned as a last resort and certainly the approach taken by the Commission appears to be to reach a compromise solution with the parties wherever possible, by agreeing structural changes to the proposed transactions to allow clearance. According to Overbury (1992), there has been a strong resistance to taking cases into a full enquiry on the part of all concerned. Structural modifications have sometimes been agreed to conclude the case after the first stage but, as the Commission has no power under the regulation to enforce these (unlike the undertakings agreed after full proceedings), they have to be irrevocable by the parties concerned.

Table 5.2 Decisions after full proceedings (to 1 March 1993)

Date received	*Companies (nationality)*	*Product*	*Result*	*Date of final decision*
11 Dec. 1990	Alcatel (NL)/Telettra (Italy)	Telecommunication and microwave equipment	Cleared*	12 April 1991
11 Dec. 1990	Sicind (Fr)/CEAC (Fr) subsid. of Fiat	Starter batteries	Cleared*	30 May 1991
6 Feb. 1991 reinstated	Tetra Pak (Switz)/Alfa Laval (Sweden)	Food processing and packaging machinery	Cleared	19 July 1991
18 Feb. 1991				
25 Feb. 1991	Varta (Ger)/Bosch (Ger)	Starter batteries	Cleared*	31 July 1991
13 May 1991	Aerospatiale (Fr)/Alenia (Italy)/de Havilland (Can)	Regional turbo-prop aircraft	Banned	2 Oct. 1991
14 November 1991	Accor (Fr)/Wagons Lits (Belgium)	Hotel chains Motorway catering	Cleared*	28 April 1992
25 Feb. 1992	Nestlé (Switz)/Perrier (Fr)	Bottled water	Cleared*	22 July 1992
30 April 1992	Du Pont (USA)/ICI (UK)	Nylon fibres	Cleared*	30 Sept. 1992
12 May 1992	Mannesmann (Ger)/ Hoesch (Ger)	Steel pipes	Cleared	12 Nov. 1992
26 Aug. 1992	Siemens AG (Ger)/Philips (Neth)	Cables and optical fibres	Withdrawn	
8 Dec. 1992	NV Koninklijke (Neth)/ VRG (Neth)	Paper and printing and equipment	Cleared*	(4 May 1993)

Note: * cleared conditionally
Source: Merger decisions

The Standard of Assessment

There was much discussion before the regulation was finally adopted about the criteria which the Commission should use to decide whether or not a particular merger should be allowed to proceed. Should the assessment be solely competition-based, or should effects on competition be weighed against possible cost savings resulting from the merger, as well as wider effects on industrial, regional and social policy? This question is part of the broader debate among member states about the appropriate role for government to play in encouraging industrial competitiveness, and the respective places of competition policy and other types of industrial policy (see Neumann, 1990; and Sawyer, 1992).

Although the Commission placed considerable emphasis on the role of merger activity in improving industrial performance and assumed that most mergers would have beneficial effects, theoretical arguments about the likely effects of mergers suggest a range of possible outcomes and do not support any general presumption about their desirability either in a domestic or European context (see Jacquemin, Buigues and Ilzkovitz, 1989; and Jacquemin, 1990). The empirical research has shown that domestic mergers have been far from a panacea to improve competitiveness; they have clearly contributed to increases in concentration and numerous studies suggest the frequent absence of efficiency gains. Many mergers have apparently failed because of the premium prices being paid, because of overestimation of the potential of the acquired business in terms of synergies and market position, and the unsatisfactory management of the integration process after acquisition. For a useful review of the recent evidence, see Department of Trade and Industry (1988, Annex E).

The empirical studies have usually been based on the effects of mergers and acquisitions within national economies but, as Table 5.1 shows, cross-border mergers have become more important recently in the EC. Many have questioned whether the potential benefit from scale economies through merger in the European market would be as great as suggested by Cecchini (see, for example, Geroski, 1989; and Cutler *et al.*, 1992). The motives for cross-border mergers may be somewhat different from those involved in purely domestic mergers (see, for example, Davis, 1990; and Markides and Oyon, 1992), but whatever the motives, coordination and integration problems which have bedevilled domestic mergers may be particularly severe in the case of foreign acquisitions, limiting their chances of success.

It is too early for the actual effects of mergers within the dynamic market conditions created by the 1992 programme to be fully assessed. However, a pathbreaking study by Kitching (1974) suggested that US acquisitions in Europe only had a 50 per cent chance of success, and what later evidence there is also indicates that a large number of cross-border acquisitions fail (see Bleeke and Ernst, 1993, and a useful review by Hamill, 1992). This evidence casts doubt on the official view that mergers will be a major source of efficiency gains in the single market, and suggests that a permissive merger policy may decrease both efficiency and competitiveness.

The regulation makes no presumption for or against mergers; it takes a neutral stance, and each merger is examined on its merits using a competition test. The substantive test for appraisal is whether 'a concentration creates or strengthens a dominant position as a result of which effective competition would be significantly impeded in the common market or in a substantial part of it'. If so, it can be banned, or conditions for clearance imposed to alter the effects of the merger so that it is no longer regarded as having a serious effect on competition. This approach represents an intermediate position between a strict *per se* approach, and the more lenient cost–benefit assessment which was incorporated in an earlier draft of the regulation.

In assessing the effect on competition, the regulation requires a wide range of considerations to be taken into account. These include market structure, actual and potential competition from firms both inside and outside the Community, the opportunities available to suppliers and users, access to supplies and markets, barriers to entry, supply and demand trends for the relevant goods and services, the interests of consumers and, finally, the development of technical and economic progress, 'provided it is to the consumers' advantage and does not form an obstacle to competition.'

Although the final criterion refers to efficiency, it suggests little scope for efficiency arguments as, when there is a conflict between competition and efficiency, competition effects are to be the dominant consideration. However, there were still concerns that the wording of the regulation as a whole is somewhat ambiguous and that, irrespective of its precise wording, there is a risk of non-competition considerations influencing the actual decisions (see Jacquemin, 1990, for example).

Such concerns arose partly because of the institutional framework within which the regulation operates. There is no separation of power, and members of the Commission act as prosecutor, judge and executioner in merger cases. It is both an administrative and a political body; the 17 members are political appointees, some of whom are responsible for industrial, regional or social policy, and this was one reason for the fears that considerations other than the effects on competition might play a role in the decisions. In addition, as the decisions involve large-scale mergers, sensitive national interests were likely to be involved and substantial lobbying was expected.

When the regulation was being debated, attention was focused (particularly by the German and UK governments) on ensuring that it was drafted to limit the Commission's power to use it as an instrument of industrial policy or other wider concerns. Much less attention was paid to making sure that the wording of the regulation would provide the Commission with the means of preventing the build-up or strengthening of oligopolistic market structures.

The thresholds for investigation are based on absolute size, with no reference to industrial concentration or market share. The appraisal criteria make no reference to relative firm size. The regulation simply refers to the creation or strengthening of a dominant position, but the term 'dominant' is not defined. There is a presumption in the recitals to the regulation that a market share of no more than 25 per cent will raise no serious competition concerns despite the fact that it could form an important share in the context of an oligopoly market. Under Article 86, which regulates the abuse of dominant positions, dominance is usually defined with reference to the power of a single firm position, and it was this definition of dominance which was apparently to apply in the merger regulation (see Brittan, 1990).

When the regulation was introduced, there was considerable uncertainty about how strict the approach would be and how the list of criteria would be applied in the assessment (see Langeheine, 1991; and Venit, 1991). The Commission's approach is becoming clearer as the case law evolves.[8] This chapter continues by discussing the treatment of oligopoly with particular reference to the *Nestlé/Perrier* case, and the role of non-competition concerns in the decisions, before examining possible changes in the scope of the regulation and the difficulties of distinguishing different types of joint ventures.

THE ASSESSMENT IN PRACTICE

The first step in assessing the effect of a proposed merger on competition is to define the relevant market in terms of the products involved and territorial scope. Defining the market is a perennial problem in anti-trust policy, and made more difficult when market boundaries are in the process of change (see Fishwick, 1989); the Commission has tended to leave the definition open when this is not crucial to the outcome of the case.

Once the market has been defined, the Commission's next step is to investigate whether a dominant position has been created or strengthened by the transaction by examining the likely effects on competition in horizontal, vertical and unrelated markets.

The market shares of the merging companies are quantified as the first step. Initially, it was assumed (in accordance with the presumption in the regulation's recitals) that where market shares were 25 per cent or less, no serious competition concerns existed. Where higher market shares are involved, other features of the case were examined in more detail to see if the high market shares would be likely to lead to dominance on the part of a single firm. The number, size and strength of the remaining competitors have played a central role in this analysis.

In some of the early cases (for example, *Renault/Volvo* and *Varta/Bosch*), the existence of companies with similar shares to the merged firm was regarded as an indication of their ability to influence its behaviour and prevent independence of action; the possibility of collusive behaviour resulting in higher profitability to the detriment of the consumer was ignored.[9] Dominance was treated as characteristic of a single firm, in line with existing practice under Article 86, and market concentration and the implications of oligopoly structures were rarely mentioned.

The existence of this oligopoly loophole seems to have weakened the potential power of the merger regulation as an instrument of competition policy in a number of the early cases. However, in view of the likely difficulties of modifying the regulation itself, the Commission appears to have decided to wait for a suitable case to test whether its powers could be interpreted as extending to the control of multifirm or joint dominance.

Nestlé/Perrier presented an ideal test case both from an economic and a legal point of view and, as the decision of 22 July 1992 appears to be a landmark decision in the development of policy towards oligopolies, it is worth discussing in some detail. This case will also serve to illustrate how the other features of the market, apart from market share and actual competition, are taken into account in the decisions.[10]

On 25 February 1992, the Commission was notified of a public bid by Nestlé, the large Swiss food multinational, to acquire 100 per cent of the shares of Source Perrier, a French company which manufactures and distributes bottled water. Nestlé had previously agreed with the French food manufacturer, BSN, that one of the main Perrier brands, Volvic, would be sold to BSN if Nestlé successfully acquired Perrier. The merger was challenged on the grounds that it would give Nestlé and BSN a duopoly position in the French bottled water market, which was likely to harm the interests of consumers. Even if the Volvic agreement was not implemented, the Commission concluded that the proposed merger would still create a dominant position for the new entity which would prevent effective competition in this market.

Both the product and geographical market definitions were controversial. Nestlé argued that the relevant product market should include both bottled water and soft drinks. However, the evidence of differences in demand conditions and in production and marketing on the supply side supports the Commission's conclusion that the relevant product market was bottled still and sparkling water, both mineral and spring. The most telling part of the argument was that, over the past five years, the national suppliers of bottled waters had been able to increase their prices (both nominal and real) substantially and enjoy increased demand in spite of the decreasing trend of soft drinks prices over the same period. The Commission also seems justified in concentrating on France as a separate geographic market, excluding Belgium and certain parts of German Lander which Nestlé wished to be included.

Once the market had been defined, the analysis of competition within it was more straightforward. The French bottled water market was highly concentrated before the merger with the only three national producers, Perrier, the leading firm, BSN and Nestlé between them accounting for 76 per cent of total volume and an even higher share of mineral water sales of nearly 95 per cent. The Commission stopped short of claiming that the market was jointly dominated by Nestlé, Perrier and BSN before the merger, although the evidence does suggest the leading suppliers were already exercising substantial market power.

The proposed bid would increase concentration because it would eliminate the largest operator in terms of sales and capacity, with two suppliers instead of three having 75 per cent of the market volume (82 per cent by value) and 95 per cent of still mineral water. A number of conditions suggested the likelihood of coordinated behaviour between the duopolists.

Nestlé and BSN would have similar market shares and capacity as well as similar cost structures, and so their interests might be expected to be similar. Differences in nationality of the firms and geographical spread of activity might affect the likelihood of their interests coinciding, but this was not discussed, perhaps a reflection of the Commission's general tendency to disregard the impact of multinationality in its policies. It was felt that coordination of their activities would be easier because they were both long-established in the French bottled water market; both were active in the wider food industry and they already had experience of cooperation in some parts of that industry. In the bottled water industry they supplied the same customers, and pricing and sales data were readily available to each of them. Although they were selling differentiated, rather than standardised products, competition would be weakened by the fact that the two companies' strengths were in different segments of the market.

Actual competition was limited to a number of independent fringe suppliers, of which the largest two each had only about 9 per cent of sales volume and 4 per cent of the market by value. These local competitors have smaller sources, less developed distribution systems and less well-known brands, and lacked the resources to invest heavily in marketing and promotion, unlike the would-be duopolists who themselves also owned a number of local spring water sources.

In previous cases, the Commission had relied on the buying power of customers to constrain monopoly power on the selling side. However, although the ten largest buyers represented 70 per cent of the turnover of the largest firms, none had more than 15 per cent of the custom. The Commission concluded that the buyers would, if anything, be weakened by the merger, as it increased the number of major brands held by BSN and Nestlé and reduced the choice of retailers from three to two sources of supply. Concentrating on local spring waters could not be considered a realistic alternative for the retailers to stocking the well-known brands.

The threat of new entry seemed unlikely to act as a disciplining force from the supply side. The market is relatively mature in terms of the proliferation of products and the degree of product differentiation, and there appears to be little scope for technical innovation. It would take time for a new firm to be able to establish a significant operation from scratch and, with the acquisition of Perrier, the possibility of buying an existing major water source had been effectively foreclosed. New entry would be risky because of the heavy sunk costs required to advertise and promote new products. After the merger, there would be no other firm in the EC of a size, range of products and reputation of either Nestlé or BSN. In addition to the structural entry barriers, there was a danger of joint action to deter entry, signalled by the previous combined opposition of Nestlé and BSN to a bid by Ifint (controlled by the Italian family, Agnelli) for Exor (a French holding company which held nearly 29 per cent of Perrier), which had threatened to upset the existing market structure.

The evidence points to the existence of many of the classic conditions facilitating oligopolistic (or in this case duopolistic) coordination (see Scherer and Ross, 1990). The Commission also highlighted the weakness of competition in the market pre-merger concluding:

> The maintenance or development of whatever competition there remains on that market therefore requires particular protection. Any structural operation restricting even more the scope for competition in such a situation has to be judged severely. (Para. 118)

In practice, the Commission appears to have been far from severe in its remedies. Instead of banning the merger outright, the merger was cleared in July 1992 subject to some complex conditions which appeared more interventionist in terms of dictating the future structure of the market than the conditions agreed in other cases. Nestlé agreed to sell a number of brands and water sources, representing about 20 per cent of the total capacity previously held by the three national suppliers, to a suitable buyer in order to create a viable competitor and prevent Nestlé and BSN having a position of collective dominance.[11] However, it is questionable whether their market power would be satisfactorily curbed by the presence of the 'third force' the Commission wished to create. Indeed, in view of the difficulties the Commission had identified of building up a market position in this market, it is not at all certain that the attempt to introduce such a force will be successful. If the new company does not succeed (which will only become clear after several years), the French market will revert to being dominated by two suppliers.

Various aspects of the decision attracted criticism both from a minority of the Advisory Committee and more widely.[12] Some of the criticisms centred on the leniency of the decision. The power of the Commission to apply the regulation to situations of collective dominance was also challenged by a minority in the Advisory Committee, and another minority felt that it could only have been applicable if there had been proven economic links between undertakings (in the light of the recent *Flat Glass* case).[13] However Nestlé agreed to the conditions negotiated with the Commission, and the merger was cleared. The decision establishes for the first time that the EC will take into account the impact of duopolies and oligopolies in its investigations, although these powers have yet to be tested in the Courts.[14]

The second issue in the appraisal of mergers which has attracted more attention than the existence of an oligopoly loophole is the role of non-competition considerations, and this aspect will now be discussed. Although the debate about the appropriate role of such wider considerations continues, the decisions have all ostensibly been taken on competition grounds. The Commission has taken a fairly permissive stance towards high market shares in rapidly growing markets involving modern technology (for example, *Digital/Kienzle* and *Digital/Philips*) where strong market positions tend to be transient.[15] Relatively little detail is generally given about cost structures, although this would help in assessing entry barriers, and there are few references to efficiency considerations, benefits to the economy and economic progress.

It has recently been suggested on the basis of the early cases where technical or economic progress was explicitly discussed, that 'not only is there no efficiency defence in the EEC Merger Regulation but that there can be cases of "efficiency attack"' (Jenny, 1993, p. 597). Jenny cites the *AT&T/NCR* merger, for example, where the Commission noted that there were potential synergies both on the technical side and in the marketing of work stations and communication products, which might give the combined firms the opportunity of developing more advanced communications features at lower cost. Instead of making the merger more attractive, the Commission appears to have viewed it as a negative feature of the proposal, commenting, 'it is not excluded that the potential advantages flowing from synergies may create or strengthen a dominant position' (Para. 30).[16] The merger was not blocked, but this seems to have been partly because the Commission did not expect the potential synergies to be realised, as similar attempts to combine computer and telecommunications activities (for example, *Siemens/Nixdorf*) had failed or had not yet realised the benefits the participants expected.

Similar reasoning was applied in *Drager/IBM/HMP* and *Delta Airlines / Pan Am*, suggesting that if a merger is likely to allow the merging firms to develop services or products that competitors could not provide, it could be a reason for disallowing the merger.[17] Fortunately this approach, which is reminiscent of the approach taken to mergers in the US in the 1960s, has not proved decisive in any of the merger cases considered by the Commission.[18]

The *ATR/de Havilland* merger is the best known case which dealt with questions of efficiency and technical progress.[19] It concerned a proposed bid by two state-owned aircraft manufacturers, Aerospatiale of France and Alenia of Italy, for de Havilland which was a Canadian division of Boeing. Through their joint venture, ATR, the bidders, were the world and leading European manufacturer of regional turbo-prop (commuter) aircraft, and de Havilland was second largest. Undertakings had been given to the Canadian government to run de Havilland as a full function aircraft manufacturer and not to combine R&D effort.

The merger was banned on the grounds that a dominant position would be created both in the EC and the world, and the high market shares of the joint venture would not be counter-balanced by other factors. The market was defined according to seat capacity and, as a result of the bid, ATR would be the only manufacturer to compete across the range. ATR's share of the mid-range would be raised from 45 to 64 per cent in the world market (72 per cent in the EC) and de Havilland eliminated as a potential competitor in the market for larger capacity aircraft. The Commission judged that the potential increase in monopoly power would not be counterbalanced by the remaining competitors and the strength of buyers, and new entry was felt unlikely because of the expected downturn in the market by the time new competitors would be able to move in. Possible efficiency and marketing gains were again viewed as likely to be detrimental to the consumer in the long term, because of their likely effect on industrial structure; existing competitors were expected to find it harder to compete than previously, perhaps being driven out of the market, resulting in a monopoly for ATR.

The decision to block the acquisition of de Havilland (which was eventually bought by the Canadian company, Bombardier, and the Ontario government), the only transaction to be banned to date, attracted widespread criticism. Some of these concerned the narrowness of the market definitions and the possibility that the potential power of the joint venture had been exaggerated. The major objection concerned the industrial policy aspects of the decision which it was felt had been given insufficient weight. The fact that the decision was firmly based on the competition test in this sensitive case involving two state-owned companies, was cited by the Commission as evidence of its determination to protect competition. However, the decision also highlighted the pressures to widen the basis of assessment.

A minority of the Commission apparently supported the merger as a means of strengthening the European aerospace industry, despite the possible anticompetitive effects, and the decision was reportedly adopted by only a single vote.[20] The French and Italian Ministers of Transport demanded that the case be re-examined by the Commission but, as any appeal would have to be to the European Court, this was not granted. The EC Industry Commissioner suggested to the Commission President that, in future, the approval of the industrial policy department concerned should be obtained before full proceedings on a merger could be opened, but this was also resisted.

REVIEWING THE SCOPE OF THE REGULATION

Distinguishing 'Concentrative' and 'Cooperative' Joint Ventures

It is generally agreed that one of the most problematic aspects of the regulation, in practice, has been in distinguishing between 'concentrative' joint ventures which fall under the regulation, and 'cooperative' joint ventures which can be examined under Article 85. The Commission's original guidelines on the definition of a concentrative joint venture were fairly restrictive, perhaps to reduce the number of cases falling outside EC competition rules altogether; if a joint venture is judged concentrative but beneath the thresholds, it escapes EC scrutiny. However, in practice, the Commission has interpreted the term 'concentrative' fairly broadly, bringing more joint ventures than otherwise within the regulation's scope.

Three main aspects in the official policy development towards this issue can be distinguished (Commission of the European Communities, 1993). First, under the so-called doctrine of 'industrial leadership', the joint venture is normally considered to be concentrative where only one parent stays in the joint venture's market while the other parent is either inactive or withdraws completely on a long-term basis from that market. In this situation, the joint venture and the parent company remaining in the market usually form an economic entity, so there is no room for the coordination of independent undertakings. Second, a '*de minimis*' rule means that, even if there are cooperative elements, the joint venture can be treated as concentrative if the cooperative elements are of limited significance. Finally, if the parent companies coordinate their behaviour but this only has a limited effect inside the Community, the joint venture is still considered concentrative.

The treatment of collaborative joint ventures under Article 85 has been less favourable than the treatment of concentrative joint ventures under the merger regulation, especially in terms of the longer period which firms have to wait for a decision and the degree of uncertainty about treatment. This creates strong incentives for firms to restructure their joint venture to be concentrative rather than cooperative. In December 1992, the Commission decided to introduce measures aimed at providing a more favourable environment for firms wishing to create cooperative joint ventures. Guidelines were published outlining how such joint ventures would be assessed, the group exemptions under Article 85 were broadened and the proceedings for dealing with certain types of structural joint ventures were speeded up. However, there is still considerable dissatisfaction with these reforms which are felt not to address the fundamental problems inherent in the cooperative/concentrative joint venture distinction (see Hawk and Huser, 1993; and Hampton, 1993).

The Thresholds

The merger regulation was initially confined to relatively large transactions, in order to gain agreement from countries with well-established merger policies of their own. There is a danger that wherever the size thresholds dividing jurisdiction are set, some mergers with effects in only one country will be included and some mergers with effects going beyond a single country excluded. The referral clauses in the regulation were introduced as a mechanism to deal with this problem, but provision was made for the thresholds to be reviewed by December 1993. The European Commission had originally proposed lower thresholds for the merger regulation of ECU 2 billion rather than 5 billion, and ECU 100 instead of 250 million (Brittan, 1990).

The published data do not allow an easy assessment of the effects which lowering the thresholds would have (see Morgan, 1994). The European Commission recently conducted a survey which aimed to establish how many additional operations would have fallen under the merger regulation in 1991 and 1992 if the thresholds had been relaxed in the way originally proposed. 276 non-financial EC companies with turnovers greater than ECU 2 billion were contacted, with a 63 per cent response by May 1993. The survey found that an additional 33 cases would have fallen under the regulation if the thresholds were lowered and an additional 20 if the two-thirds rule was also abolished (Commission of the European Communities, 1993).

Any lowering of the size thresholds is bound to increase the number of mergers with purely national effects falling within the scope of the regulation. The Commission's survey found that of the additional 33 cases resulting from a lowering of the thresholds, 9 would have had an effect in only a single country, and a further 9 of the additional 20 which would have resulted from the abolition of the two-thirds rule had a local or regional rather than a cross-border effect. One way of dealing with this would have been to adopt a more liberal policy of referral back to the member states, and this had been proposed by the Commission. Many countries are now in a better position to deal with mergers nationally, having recently introduced merger controls of their own (for example, Belgium, Italy and Portugal). However, more liberal referral would be at the expense of jurisdictional uncertainty and would detract from the 'one stop shop' which the regulation was intended to provide.

A reduction of the thresholds was generally favoured by industry because of the speed of decision-making and the benefits of the 'one stop shop', as well as perhaps because of the relatively lenient approach. However, growing concern about the further centralisation of power in Brussels, as well as unease about some of the merger decisions (for example, *ATR /de Havilland* and *Nestlé/Perrier*), meant that the Commission's attempt to increase the scope of its powers over mergers was successfully resisted by some of the larger countries, especially by the French who would have favoured an increase in the thresholds for EC investigation, and by the German and UK competition authorities.

As markets extend beyond EC borders with the increased internationalisation of business, it is likely that there will be increased emphasis by policy makers on trying to secure a more level playing field for business at an international level. Some advances are already being made in this direction through multinational agreement (GATT for example), regional agreement (for example, EFTA) and bilateral moves (as recently between the US and EC).

CONCLUSION

Common competition rules are a key feature of the European Community's policy. On the one hand they are designed to remove obstacles to the Europeanisation of firms' activities by ensuring that anti-competitive behaviour does not keep the 'internal' market divided. On the other hand, they are intended to ensure that consumers enjoy the potential benefits from market integration. The basic tools of competition policy are given in the Rome Treaty and through two landmark cases, *Continental Can* and *Philip Morris*; the Court confirmed that Articles 85 and 86 could be applied to mergers, although there were important weaknesses in the informal system of control which developed in the absence of a specific merger regulation.

The progressive removal of barriers to trade, as part of the single market programme, encouraged corporate reorganisation through mergers and merger-like transactions and threw the inadequacies of the EC controls into sharp relief, increasing the pressure for a new merger regulation at EC level. The introduction of the EC merger regulation in 1990 represented an important development in European competition policy, intended both to facilitate mergers by reducing transactions costs and to give the Commission specific power to control those which appeared anti-competitive. The scope of the regulation has been limited by the high thresholds for investigation and, with the onset of recession in the late 1980's, the pace of merger activity slowed. Despite this, 145 mergers were notified by the end of February 1993.

The regulation has been relatively successful in reducing the costs firms face in seeking regulatory approval, although there are still some uncertainties about jurisdiction. Firms tend to consult both the national and EC authorities at the outset if there is any doubt about whether the proposed transaction falls within the scope of the regulation and any possibility of referral. Procedures are streamlined and all the decisions up to the end of February 1993 were reached within the comparatively short deadlines. Indeed, there is some evidence of firms structuring their transactions to ensure that they would be dealt with under the regulation rather than under Article 85 (in the case of joint ventures) and national provisions. This may be both because of the speed of decision-taking and because the approach has appeared relatively lenient, with the Commission willing to try to reach an agreement with the parties over conditions for clearance in cases of doubt about the compatibility of the proposal with the common market.

Although the regulation was based on a competition test, the early decisions suggested a potentially serious weakness in the Commission's ability to tackle mergers in highly concentrated markets where there was no single market leader. The decision to challenge *Nestlé/Perrier* on the basis that it would result in a duopoly structure marked an important change in the interpretation of the term 'dominance' to include collective or joint dominance and, although untested in the Courts, is likely to mark a major development in Community law. This brings its coverage nearer to that of other merger control regimes.

The adoption of the merger regulation was delayed by differing views of the aims of competition policy – whether to try to safeguard workably competitive market structures as the best means of ensuring international competitiveness, or to view it as a means of achieving the objectives of a broader industrial policy. Although the day was apparently won by those advocating a strict competition approach and it is arguable that there is even some evidence of potential efficiency gains being regarded as an 'offence' under the regulation, the Commission has been under considerable pressure to allow broader considerations to influence merger policy.

In the *ATR/De Havilland* case, the main test of its resolution to stick to the competition test, the Commission resisted the introduction of industrial policy considerations. However, the conditions for clearance of *Nestlé/Perrier* represented a move towards interventionism not seen previously, and the decision to allow the merger to proceed seems at variance both with the earlier approach and the requirement to maintain and develop effective competition. A further move away from strict competition based assessment seems likely under the present Competition Commissioner, Mr Karel Van Miert, who has stated an intention to broaden the scope of anti-trust analysis.[21] Whether this will, in practice, mark a new phase in the Commission's evolving policy remains to be seen from the evidence provided by future decisions.

Notes

I wish to thank Graham Atkinson, formerly at the Office of Fair Trading, for his encouragement in the early stages of this work, and members of the Mergers Task Force for their help with my enquiries. I am also grateful to two anonymous referees for helpful comments. Any errors or omissions are my responsibility. The research has benefited from a grant from the University of Bath.

1. The term 'merger' is used throughout to refer to all 'concentrations' unless otherwise specified.
2. This case is usefully discussed in Korah and Lasok (1988).

3. *Europemballage and Continental Can* v. *Commission*, 6/72 (1973), ECR 215, *Common Market Law Review*, 199.
4. Under the recent European Economic Area (EEA) agreement, the Commission will examine the effect within any substantial part of the EEA as well as the Community in assessing compatibility, although the scope of the regulation is unaltered.
5. *Alcatel/AEG Kabel*, decision of 18 Dec. 1991, OJ 10 Jan. 1992.
6. *Varta/Bosch*, decision of 31 July 1991, OJ L320, pp. 26–34.
   Mannesmann/Hoesch, decision of 12 Nov. 1992.
   Siemens/Philips was withdrawn by the parties concerned.
7. *Steetley/Tarmac*, decision of 12 Feb. 1992.
8. For a useful review which has appeared since this paper was first written, see Neven, Nuttall and Seabright (1993).
9. *Renault/Volvo*, decision of 6 Jan. 1991.
   Varta Bosch, see above, note 6.
10. *Nestlé/Perrier*, decision of 22 July 1992, OJ L356, pp. 1–31.
11. In February 1993, Nestlé announced that it had reached agreement to divest assets to Castel, a French brewing company owned by Société d'Investissement d'Aquitaine. This company was already in the mineral water market as one of the two larger fringe suppliers (GCES) named in the decision.
12. Opinion of the Advisory Committee, *Nestlé/Perrier* (1992), OJ C319, p. 3.
13. *Italian Flat Glass*, Judgement of the Court of First Instance in Cases T 68,77,78/79, 10 March 1992 (mimeo).
14. The Perrier workforce has asked for a judicial review mainly because of alleged infringements of the procedural rights of recognised employee representatives of the companies concerned, and the failure of the Commission to respect fundamental social rights recognised by Community law.
15. *Digital/Kienzle*, decision of 22 Feb. 1991.
    Digital/Philips, decision of 2 Sept. 1991.
16. *AT&T/NCR*, decision of 18 Jan. 1991.
17. *Drager/IBM/HMP*, decision of 28 June 1991.
    Delta Airlines/Pan Am, decision of 13 Sept. 1991.
18. See Utton (1993) for comparisons between the US approach and EC merger policy.
19. *ATR/de Havilland*, decision of 2 Oct. 1991, OJ L334, pp. 42–61.
20. Opinion of the Advisory Committee, *ATR/ De Havilland* (1991) OJ, C 314, p. 7.
21. *Financial Times*, 19 Jan. 1993.

6 National Culture, Corporate Culture and Economic Performance: An Interdisciplinary Synthesis and Implications for Internationalisation Strategy

Christos Nicolaidis and Carla Millar

INTRODUCTION

This chapter highlights the important role of the external – cultural – environment for company performance, nationally and internationally. The theoretical synthesis combines selected aspects from the well-articulated (economic) theory of the entrepreneur, and from recent developments in social psychology and sociology. It emphasises the different cultural values which exist between nations, and the fact that entrepreneurs may draw upon the general cultural values of their nation-state in order to increase performance in their organisations. The synthesis forms a suitable theoretical framework for suggesting specific propositions concerning the significance of national and corporate culture on the internationalisation-related strategic decision-making in the pursuit of firms' economic performance. The chapter argues that harmonising corporate culture with both nation and industry-specific environmental factors promotes excellence in corporate performance. This, in turn, implies that a nation's culture may be integral to the process of creating and developing a distinct competitive advantage for a culture's domestic firm. MNEs will tend to reproduce significant features of their national cultures in their internal structuring and functioning.

Corporate culture enjoyed a prominent position in business literature during the eighties. It was identified as a distinct source of competitive advantage – a glue that held organisations together. However, despite the considerable gains in knowledge during the last decade, literature still approaches cultural phenomena and their influence on organisational performance in a rather atheoretical perspective. On the one hand, most research has been directed towards testing the so called 'culture free' (Child and Kieser, 1979; Haire *et al.*, 1966; Hickson *et al.*, 1974, 1979) or 'convergence' (Cole, 1973; Form, 1979) hypothesis in comparative management. On the other hand, organisation theories, so far, are mainly concerned with the inside of an organisation and subsequently fail to treat organisations as if they were integrated in their societal environment (Adler and Jelinek, 1986).

Yet scholars generally recognise a shortfall in the development of clear distinctions, discriminating causes and effects and the processes connecting them (Rose, 1985, pp. 77–82). Nor has the newly emerging field of economic psychology benefited the discussion on corporate culture – the individualistic tradition in psychology has encouraged extensive study of intra-individual phenomena. Consequently, it has ignored the social nature of human behaviour and the need for a synthesis of the individual and the collective in explaining everyday behaviour (Forgas, 1981a). With the notable exception of consumer behaviour, social psychology has had even less influence on the study of economic behaviour (Warneryd, 1988).

Economics has also been reluctant to study corporate culture. The utilitarian and contractarian philosophical foundations of neoclassical economics influence economists towards placing too much emphasis on hedonistic motivation and pecuniary reward, and economists overlook emotional satisfactions derived from social life (Casson, 1992a; Etzioni, 1988). The core assumptions of economics are of much wider validity within the social sciences than is usually argued (Buckley and Casson, 1992).

Overall, research has been hampered by the absence of a comprehensive theoretical framework relating managers' perceptions of strategic issues to their cultural predispositions on the one hand, and to the outcomes of their actions on the other (Millar, 1989). Furthermore, theories on corporate culture fail to address explicitly the impact of national and societal culture on corporate culture and performance.

The present chapter develops an interdisciplinary theoretical synthesis for the study of corporate culture, internationalisation strategic decision-making and economic performance. In particular, it combines recent developments in social psychology (which emphasises the importance of societal values in determining how knowledge and perceptions of reality arise and are communicated within a social group) with elements from the well-articulated economic theory of the entrepreneur (which emphasises the importance of judgement and coordination in complex situations).

The synthesis emphasises the different cultural values which exist between nations, and the fact that business leaders can draw upon the general cultural values of their nation-state when addressing internationalisation issues for increased performance in their organisations. The two theoretical disciplines are developed on the basis of the framework of organisational culture proposed by E. Schein (1985). The entrepreneur is viewed as the main operator in shaping organisational culture. The personality of the entrepreneur and the qualities that make him effective within the institutional context of his organisation are, therefore, emphasised.

This chapter contributes to the study of corporate culture in certain distinct ways:

1. It advances international business theory by defining psychological processes through which social factors may shape organisational strategic action, internationalisation decisions and condition firm's economic performance. It is relevant to company competence, national prosperity and the relative competitive advantages among different national cultures; subjects which attract great concern in international business literature (Lodge and Vogel, 1987).
2. It encompasses both the economic and behavioural perspectives in the study of corporate culture. Organisational culture is shaped by both contingency factors (such as group history, industrial environment, or phase of industry development), and organisation members' value systems and basic beliefs which permit them to interpret their experience and adapt to their domestic, cross-border or international environment. In this respect, the chapter also contributes a psychological perspective on economic and strategic decision-making with respect to internationalisation phenomena. Social cognition theory sheds light on how meaning is socially constructed and elucidates the role of values in constructing reality, guiding action, and preserving and differentiating the members of a social group. Psychological factors are therefore designated to explain variation in economic and strategic behaviour.
3. The analysis complies with the neo-institutional economic and sociological paradigm in organisational analysis, which emphasises the cognitive dimension of human action and the significance of institutional arrangements in influencing human exchanges. Hence, the paper may contribute useful insights both for economists and for sociologists, but also strategists concerned with organisation theory and internationalisation phenomena.

Through the combination within a single framework of economics, social psychology and sociology, international business is provided with a more systematic and broad view of corporate culture as a factor influencing internationalisation strategy.

The following section critically examines the concept of organisational culture in organisation literature; introduces recent developments in social psychology and outlines the economic theory of entrepreneurship. In the next section, an articulation is given to an integrated synthetic view for the study of corporate culture and company performance. Implications and conclusions are drawn at the end.

LITERATURE FOUNDATIONS

Organisational Culture and Organisation Theory: A Critical Appraisal

The concept of organisational culture has been given many and different interpretations within organisation literature. Borrowing from anthropology and psychology, different schools of thought place emphasis on society's values, organisation history, leadership and contingency factors on the one hand (the sociocultural approach), and on cognitive and symbolic phenomena such as values, beliefs and symbolic actions of actors within organisations on the other (the prevalent, ideational approach) (Allaire and Firsirotu, 1984).

In the symbolic view of cultural phenomena in organisations, culture has taken the different names of paradigms (Pfeffer, 1981; Johnson, 1987), rituals (Deal and Kennedy, 1982), stories (Mitroff and Kilman 1976), legends (Wilkings and Martin, 1980), specialised language (Donnelon, 1986; Evered, 1983; Hirsch and Andrews, 1983; Huff, 1983) and myths (Boje *et al.*, 1982; Pondy, 1983). When shared, symbols and beliefs are primary ways through which organisation members are drawn together and given a sense of belonging (Pfeffer, 1981; Smirich, 1983). Symbols also determine the way managers perceive their environment and the reality upon which their decisions are made. Environments are 'enacted' since they do not really exist, but are rather created by organisation members in a process where symbolic interactions and beliefs play a crucial role in interpreting what the organisation perceives (Smirich and Stubbart, 1985).

The symbolic school, however, does not reveal much about the modes of integration of organisational members and symbols in the organisational setting, or about the nature of mechanisms through which symbols and beliefs are shared and generated among group members. The analysis is also silent about how these shared meanings and symbols are originated and generated in the first place. By considering organisational belief systems as relatively closed systems, the school gives insufficient weight to the fact that organisational beliefs may be influenced by beliefs prevailing in the business community or in society. Furthermore, in the case of 'enacted' environments, leading psychologists (for example, Rosch *et al.*, 1976) argue that individuals' perception is both subjected to the particular knowledge of the people and the potential structure of the world. Human knowledge cannot provide correlational structure where there is none: people can only ignore or exaggerate correlational structures. Meaningful interpretations of the world are more likely to be imported from the environment than to be manufactured from within (Brown, 1978).

In the cognitive approach to cultural phenomena in organisations, culture is seen as a shared cognitive construct of members, a system of knowledge consisting of standards of perceiving, evaluating and acting. Organisations exist largely in the mind of individual members, and their existence takes the form of schemata and cognitive maps. Emphasis is placed on managerial categories, semantic networks and expert systems (Stubbart, 1989), concepts, beliefs and assumptions (Dutton *et al.*, 1983), interpretative schemata (Bartunek, 1984), cognitive heuristics and cognitive biases (Duhaime and Schwenk, 1985; Hogarth and Makridakis, 1981), strategic assumptions, strategic schemata, analogies and metaphors (Huff, 1982; Schwenk, 1988) and cognitive maps (Weick, 1979; Weick and Bougon, 1986).

The proponents of the cognitive view, however, fail to consider fully the impact of culture as a shared property of groups. In their perspective, the organisation becomes an artefact of shared cognitive maps, a sort of collective mind which has cognitive systems, memories and develops world views. These world views, however, are different from, yet also related to, the individuals' minds – though not in a clear and consistent way. Their analysis focuses mainly on the individual strategist. It does not explain how cognition might evolve from an individual's idiosyncratic thought process into some form of shared aggregate that is useful for collective and purposeful action. However, to study cognitive systems at the level of the individual only is an abstraction (Doise and Mackie, 1981). Individual decision-making involves processes which are social in nature too. Indeed, individual learning and experience is insufficient to account for many of the schemata that people hold. Societal culture and communal systems of meanings affect the way schemata are acquired from other people and shared with other people (Eiser, 1986). The crucial problem is not how to process the information once given, but rather how to decide what the information is in an immensely complex, confusing and subtle social environment (Forgas, 1981a, p. 266).

Overall, in organisation theory the significance of the immediate social, national and subsequently international environment is often subordinated to the concern for internal organisational phenomena. Despite the fact that symbolic and cognitive schools are based on an open systems framework, they both fail to address explicitly the influence of the environment and of societal culture on corporate culture.

Recent Developments in Social Psychology

The Principles of Cognitive Categorisation

Categorisation is probably the most important element in the analysis of cultural phenomena in groups (Triadis, 1972), since all cultural groups employ categories (Kluckhohn, 1954). Categorisation systematises the environment for the purposes of action by segmenting and ordering it in terms of groups of people, events or objects which are considered as being equivalent (Tajfel and Forgas, 1981). Besides being a tool for the systematisation of the environment, categories are also active constructions imposed on the environment which affect the perception and the interpretation of incoming information (Rosch *et al.*, 1976; Tajfel and Forgas, 1981). Categorisation, therefore, is both a condition for survival of the group and a prerequisite for action. It stems from the human propensity to create order out of chaos.

Categories appear to be organised hierarchically according to the different levels of information they contain (Rosch, 1978; Triandis, 1972). Abstract categories include members of less abstract categories so that they form cognitive taxonomies. According to Rosch (1978), a cognitive taxonomy

> is a system by which categories are related to one another by means of class inclusion. The greater the inclusiveness of a category within a taxonomy, the higher the level of abstraction. Each category within a taxonomy is entirely included within one other category (unless it is the highest level category) but is not exhaustive of that more inclusive category. Thus the term level of abstraction within a taxonomy refers to a particular level of inclusiveness. (p. 30)

In this hierarchy, a basic level of abstraction exists in which categories carry most information; the other levels display an ordering from richer to poorer in information. At the basic level of abstraction, categories possess the maximum proportion of unique attributes relative to people, events or objects and thus it is argued are most differentiated from other categories (Rosch *et al.*, 1976).

Literature suggests that though the principle of category formation is claimed to be universal, the content of categories is not. This is due to cultural differences emanating from differences in the structure of the environment in different parts of the world, and the differing knowledge and interest in attributes. Categorisations result from the interaction between the potential structure of the world and the particular emphasis and state of knowledge of the people who are categorising (Rosch *et al.*, 1976).

Recent theoretical and empirical developments in cognitive psychology such as social categorisation (Tajfel and Forgas, 1981) and the theory of social representations (Moscovici, 1981, 1984), emphasise the interaction between individual cognition and the moral character of social life. They assert that phenomena such as reasoning and understanding can only be studied within their proper sociocultural context (Forgas, 1988b). They further argue that it is not only individuals but also societies, collectivities and groups who are engaged in the creation, processing and definition of knowledge. In these collectivities, decision-making embodies aspects of social reasoning. This is because the processing of information is also itself a social creation which selectively embodies the dominant metaphors of the culture of the period (Forgas, 1981a). Indeed, the social nature of individual thinking has been well recognised by the classics in sociology (Durkheim, 1938; Weber, 1947).

Recent Developments in Social Cognition: Social Representation

More specifically, Tajfel and Forgas (1981) argue that 'social categorisation entails much more than the cognitive classification of events, objects or people as being similar, equivalent or different to an individual's' (p. 114). Social categorisation is also linked to social identity. Insofar as social categorisation affects group differences and is related to an individual's social identity, individuals can be drawn together on the basis of the positive differentiation which exists between their own group and others. A social group may contribute to an individual's moral worth by preserving its positively-valued distinctiveness from other groups. In this process, values play an important role in the formation, maintenance and presentation of existing categories. Values act as filters or active modifiers of incoming information, enhancing, therefore, the clarity and distinctiveness of the categories (Tajfel and Forgas, 1981). This view points to the significance of both the economic (objective) and behavioural (subjective) factors of group membership. It stresses the importance of moral considerations along with materialistic principles in determining group membership. This is often reflected in the importance of social myths, movements and thought which guide the behaviour of certain social groups.

The theory of social representations, on the basis of empirical evidence, asserts that two main sets of processes are central in the process in which memory and pre-established experiences dominate the formation of categories. These are 'anchoring' and 'objectification'. Anchoring refers to a human inner-directed process which allows something unfamiliar to be attached or compared with a recognisable reference point and, therefore, to be incorporated into the human network of categories. Anchoring depends on classification and naming. Moscovici (1984) argues that classifying is not merely a denotative system but an evaluative one. Each individual or each thought is assigned a positive or negative value and is given a positive in an hierarchic order. This is essentially a judgmental process which reveals the theory about society and human nature.

Objectification refers to a hypothesised process whereby initially abstract ideas come to be treated as if they were objective facts and reality. Objectification combines and reproduces already existing concepts and images from memory in order to create something new for one to see with the help of what is already known. Under objectification, the group, firstly, reproduces a visual image of the unfamiliar concept, a figurative nucleus so as to synthesise its features. By comparing God to a father, for instance, group members may replace an invisible abstract idea with a visible person and associate it with certain concrete characteristics. Secondly, when the unfamiliar concept has been processed and its distance from the reality has been eliminated, the perceived concept replaces the conceived and the unfamiliar, therefore becoming familiar. Objectification is a group-dependent rather than an inner-directed process, and is other-directed by a main operator in each group or culture.

Overall, social categorisation and social representation processes do not merely allow humans to interpret their experience, they also condition their social identity and define the reality that they experience. Further, social categorisations and social representations act upon both the human experience and the pattern of social relationships present in the external environment.

The Theory of Entrepreneurship

The economic theory of entrepreneurship emphasises the importance of taking judgmental decisions about the coordination of scarce resources in the face of highly complex situations (Casson, 1982). The theory assumes that there are psychological costs of being fully rational, and that the process of adjustment towards an economic equilibrium involves the acquisition and communication of knowledge. It also emphasises the value of foresight and the personal psychological qualities of the entrepreneur.

The theory provides a vision of the firm as a coalition of individuals who have contracted to fill prescribed roles within an institutional structure. The firm functions as a nexus of contractual arrangements designed to promote the problem-solving activities of the entrepreneurs. These arrangements establish relatively stable relations between the individual members and the entrepreneurial team. The approach reveals the firm as a specialised institution geared to problem-solving activity where, due to economies of specialisation in problem solving, the mental division of labour and the distinction between leader and follower are of foremost importance. The creative activity of the firm stems from the judgmental capabilities of the entrepreneurs and the cooperative creativity of the individuals within (Casson, 1990, Chapter 3).

In the above mental division of labour, the entrepreneurs are the persons who are able to use judgement and make choices in highly complex situations where the environment cannot be fully specified. Unlike the rational economic man who operates in a basically well-specified environment, entrepreneurs cannot normally optimise using a fully specified model of their environment. They are likely to rely on their idiosyncratic view of the environment and their feedback on outcomes of their actions.

One of the entrepreneurial decisions with greatest effectiveness in enhancing the efficiency of the group, is the decision to set up the appropriate norms for problem solving and members' behavioural interactions. In taking this decision, the entrepreneur first identifies those objectives to which members of the group are supposed to be committed. Second, he (or she) restricts the incidence of the technical and moral failings of the group by establishing norms for performance and manipulating individual preferences. The established norms may act as a justification mechanism for action and define acceptable behaviour within the group by setting the boundaries which mark behaviour as deviant (Triandis, 1972). Further, they can be used not only to identify problems but also to identify information which makes it worthwhile to reconsider problems later.

However, an important feature of norms is that like objectives they are subject to social influence. Norms are subjective and socially determined by social and ethical factors. At the societal level, thus, different cultural systems support specific values and moral principles by arguing that they are instrumental in the pursuit of some more general material or moral objective. Indeed, human activities and responses are also moral performances and demonstrations of a social character (Harr, 1981). This, in turn, implies that moral objectives must be shared or at least minimally affirmed by all members of the group including the leader.

At the firm level, therefore, the entrepreneur intermediates between group members in order to manipulate individuals' norms towards an increased performance, an atmosphere of shared trust, commitment and cooperation directed towards specific goals. This achieves a measure of consensus regarding objectives and ultimately fosters group cooperation (Casson, 1990, Chapter 2). Hence, it fosters members' problem-solving capabilities and economises on the transaction costs of negotiating, monitoring and enforcing the exchanges between members (Ouchi, 1980). The entrepreneurs are able to manipulate individuals' norms and assert moral persuasion due to their judgmental abilities and their confidence in backing their own judgement. Entrepreneurs teach their followers the norms through both deliberate and unintended mechanisms such as expressions of approval or disapproval, through role-modelling, through what they pay attention to and reward, through the manner in which they deal with critical incidents, and through the criteria they use for recruitment selection, promotion and communication (Bandura, 1977; Casson, 1990, chapter 2; Schein, 1985; Wilkins, 1983). Learning by doing is thus the social mechanism through which knowledge of norms is usually imparted. Ethical rhetoric and ritualisation can also play an important role in transmitting knowledge of social practices.

Overall, the theory of entrepreneurship provides an important link between corporate culture and strategy. The theory emphasises the interaction of the entrepreneur and his or her followers as well as the attempt of the entrepreneur to increase commitment, purpose and performance of his organisation. Corporate, business and subsequently internationalisation strategy may be seen as an artefact of the cultural assumptions underlying the entrepreneur's view (Hofer and Schendel, 1978; Pennings and Gresov, 1986). This is in line with the literature's suggestions that top management views have a significant impact on strategy formulation, organisational culture and organisational performance (Bamberger, 1986; Davis, 1984; Goil and Zeitz, 1991; Guth and Tagiuri, 1965; Hambrick and Mason, 1984; Hofer and Schendel, 1978; Lorsch, 1986; Shrivastave, 1985, Stonch, 1982; Sturdivant *et al.*, 1985).

CORPORATE CULTURE AND CORPORATE PERFORMANCE: A SYNTHETIC VIEW

For the purposes of a synthesis, this section follows the operational framework for the study of corporate culture proposed by E. Schein (1985).

Schein's Framework of Organisational Culture

Schein (1985) suggests that:

> The . . . culture of any group or social unit is . . . the total of the collective or shared learning of that unit as it develops its capacity to survive in its external environment and to manage its own internal affairs. Culture is . . . taught to new members as the correct way to perceive, think about, and feel in relation to (internal and external) problems . . . The power of culture is derived from the fact that it operates as a set of assumptions that are unconscious and taken for granted. (pp. 19–20)

According to Schein, organisational culture consists of three interconnected levels arranged according to their visibility. Organisational culture is made visible in the artefacts and creations produced – like technology, stratification or a status system. These manifestations of culture are the reflection of a more primary and underlying set of values which make up the second level of organisational culture. This set of values, which are the stated operating principles of the culture, condition how people communicate, explain, rationalise and justify what they say and do as a group. However, they derive from an even deeper, invisible and more abstract level which consists of a few basic assumptions that are the essence of culture. These basic assumptions, taken for granted among members of the group, and the group orientation towards time and space prescribe ways of perceiving, thinking and evaluating the world, self and others. Figure 6.1 summarises Schein's framework for organisational culture.

Schein's framework is well-suited for the purposes of a synthetic view:

1. Culture is defined in ways which correspond to the two central dimensions of strategic planning; namely, adaption to the external environment and integration in terms of internal commitments. The definition, therefore, conceptually links corporate culture with corporate performance. The competitiveness of a firm depends on its capacity to identify and understand the competitive forces in its external environment, and to mobilise and manage the necessary resources so as to respond to the opportunities and threats of the external environment (Hofer and Schendel, 1978; Porter, 1980; Whipp, Rosenfeld and Pettigrew, 1989). The definition also shares many common elements with the theory of management which

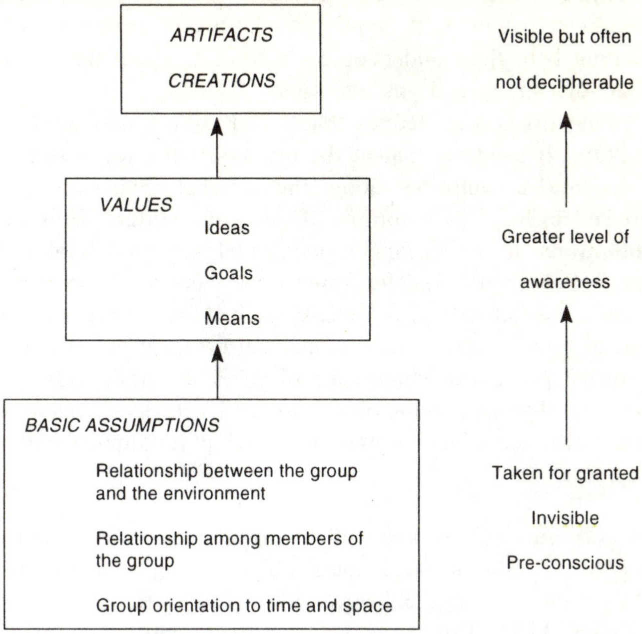

Figure 6.1 Schein's framework of organisational culture

possesses underlying assumptions about human nature. These assumptions are clear in the works of McGregor (1960), Likert (1967), Herzberg *et al.* (1959) and other classic writers.

2. By stressing the importance of learning mechanisms, the framework emphasises both the elements of prevalence of accepted solutions and their evolution in successive generations. Therefore, it provides for the existence of some degree of moulding of values which, through learning mechanisms, are recognised and become acceptable patterns of behaviour in a given organisation; a sort of personality at the institutional level. The framework, therefore, emphasises intra-group processes which are important, since many groups facing similar environments and socioeconomic backgrounds exhibit cultural variations. It stresses the fact that interacting members of a group selectively attend to their environments and constantly alter the collective understanding with which they work. The above aspects match suggestions from strategic management and organisation theory (Argyris and Schon, 1978; Daft and Weick, 1984; Levitt and March, 1988; Prahalad and Bettis, 1986; Smirich and Stubbart, 1985).
3. The framework synthesises the different views on organisational culture found in the literature. It describes both conscious processes and beliefs, and unconscious values and assumptions which serve to relate human

communities to given environments. The framework is also both structuralist and interactionist in intent. It emphasises both the importance of structure in shaping behaviour and people's actions to enact these structures through symbols, interpretations and signs.

4. Schein's framework acknowledges that social culture may affect organisational culture. It suggests that at the organisational level, organisation members' cultural assumptions about the external environment and human nature reflect basic assumptions of the wider culture. However, cultural assumptions at the organisational level are more elaborate and differentiated (Schein, 1985). The framework, therefore, emphasises cognitive processes which are also socially embedded. The connection between societal culture and organisational culture suggests that there are active cognitive processes which take place in the translation from the wider societal level to the specific organisational level. Hence, the framework stresses the existence of an important social psychological element in organisation culture.

Features of corporate culture may reflect (a) broader national cultural assumptions and (b) specific sectoral, industrial or group-related cultural assumptions. This, in turn, echoes the theoretical suggestions from social cognition theory (Moscovici, 1984; Tajfel and Forgas, 1981) and sociology (Powell and DiMaggio, 1991). This may facilitate theoretical synthesis.

The Synthetic View

The three levels of group culture suggested by Schein (1985), namely, artefacts, values and underlying assumptions, can be seen as a cognitive taxonomy. As theory suggests, though the formation of categories will be universal, the content of categories in this taxonomy will differ across cultures due to the different structure of the environment in different parts of the world and the different emphases placed on aspects thereof.

In this taxonomy the deepest level of organisational culture, the level of underlying assumptions, will consist of categories at higher levels of abstraction. These categories will include universal values and unconscious moral principles mostly inherited from the social environment. These moral principles and values, thus, will differ across cultures. The second level of organisational culture, the level of values and ideas, will consist of categories at the basic level of abstraction. These categories will carry the most information and will possess high cue-validity relative to categories at higher and lower levels of abstraction. Therefore, they will be attended to more frequently during the course of everyday action. At this level, most of all the attributes will be learned rather than inherited, and will be collective since they will be shared with people who went through the same learning process. Further, they will positively differentiate the particular group from others by providing it with a distinct social identity. Finally, the first level of organisational culture, the level of artefacts, will consist of categories with more specific attributes towards the nature of products, the use of technology and the use of regulatory, planning and power systems.

The above view distinguishes corporate culture at the national and organisational levels. National culture influences corporate culture by providing the universal values and moral principles which condition the deepest and most abstract levels of organisational culture, and determine the formation and the maintenance of categories which prescribe primary ways of perceiving and evaluating the world. National culture provides the values against which other values are compared; it is the basis for the classification process of any event, object or people (Moscovici, 1981, 1984; Tajfel and Forgas, 1981). It, therefore, conditions the judgement process of any national group by prescribing the 'default' unconscious values about society and human nature.

At the firm level, the entrepreneur's assumptions and behaviour provide the values which condition the group's specific goals and behaviour, the upper two levels of organisational culture. These values condition the formation and maintenance of categories at the intermediate (that is, industry) and lower levels of abstraction. These categories include views or attributes towards the goals of the group, its mission, its ideology, its values and the employees' specific goals. The views afford the group with a positive social identity which differentiates it from other groups (Hogg and Abrams, 1988; Tajfel and Forgas, 1981). Categories at this level are attended to most frequently in the course of everyday organisational activities, since they possess higher cue validity. Further, they are subject to the influence of the higher in abstraction categories, that is the values and moral principles prescribed by the industrial and national culture. The above view is supported by evidence on the categorisation theory which has shown that relatively commonly held sets of beliefs and assumptions which are organisational or industry specific exist in many organisations (Huff, 1982; Porac *et al.*, 1987). These beliefs and assumptions constitute received wisdom and tacit knowledge, and act to define reality for the particular organisation. The view is also well represented in research treating industry as consisting of strategic groups pursuing generic strategies (Porter, 1980).

The entrepreneur's ability to manipulate goals stems from an apparent competence in making judgmental decisions in highly complex situations where the environment cannot be fully specified (Casson, 1990, Chapter 3). The entrepreneur is able to condition the categorisation of group schemata due to his (or her) capability of perceiving the potential correlational structure of the world and the emphases placed on it. Emerging as a leader, the entrepreneur provides (objectifies in psychological terms) the vision (the figurative nucleus) for a group to attain specific goals or create something new. Due to his (or her) comparative advantage in making judgmental decisions, the entrepreneur interprets followers' experience and legitimates followers'

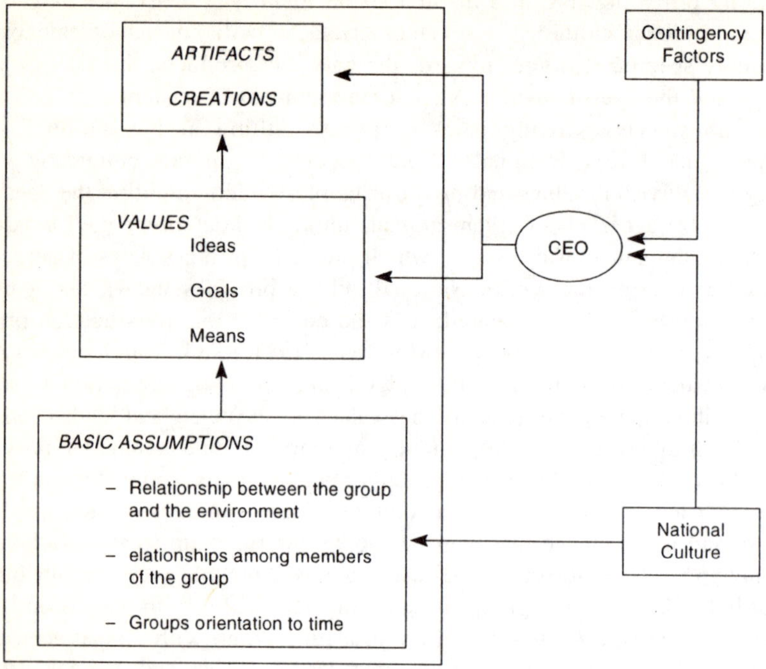

Figure 6.2 Corporate culture: a synthetic view

preferences in such a way as to make them technically and morally plausible. This vision is communicated with the help of norms as discussed earlier. The actions of the entrepreneur, however, are culturally bound by the values that national culture prescribes.

The synthetic view is represented schematically in Figure 6.2. The Chief Executive Officer (CEO) conditions the upper levels of corporate culture due to his (or her) personal predispositions and qualities. Situational and firm-specific factors are also important in influencing this process. National culture influences the CEO's assumptions as well as the deepest level of corporate culture by prescribing the dominant values regarding the nature of the environment, human nature, nature of truth, space and time.

Implications of the Synthetic View: Five Propositions

The synthetic view and its implications for company culture, company performance and the internationalisation process of the firm can be summarised in five main propositions:

Proposition 1
CEOs may be able to engineer an optimal culture that is appropriate for the specifics of the situation. The content of this optimal culture will differ across countries, however. While CEOs can introduce important norms that may result in significant behavioural adjustments, they will leave intact the deep-rooted cultural assumptions their national culture prescribes. Corporate cultures will reflect national cultural differences.

The synthetic view implies that skilful entrepreneurs may be able to engineer cultures specifically adapted to the industrial and social environment within which their firms operate. These cultures may borrow eclectically from various sources. They may draw on certain cultural themes of the entrepreneur's national culture, or they may draw upon his or her own personal values and commitments. While the entrepreneur can modify employees' specific goals, the upper two levels of organisational culture, the general values derived from national culture cannot be overturned.

The proposition is supported by suggestions in the literature that leadership qualities are crucial in mobilising cultural resources towards the attainment of corporate goals (Casson, 1992b; Pettigrew, 1979; Schein, 1985). Both theoretical (Gagliardi, 1986; Schein, 1985; Selznick, 1957) and empirical (Bennis, 1985; Hofstede *et al.*, 1990; Kotter and Heskett, 1992; Noel, 1988; Pettigrew, 1979; Sapienza, 1986; Whipp, Rosenfeld and Pettigrew, 1989) studies suggest that the leader may affect organisational culture. It is likely that CEOs can influence aspects of their organisational culture through the decisions they take (Gagliardi, 1986), their role-model behaviour (Bandura, 1977; Casson, 1992b; Schein, 1985), the symbols, stories, myths, rituals (Mitroff and Kilman, 1976; Pettigrew, 1979; Pfeffer, 1981) and language (Huff, 1983; Pondy, 1978) that they promote, the management practices (Schwatz and Davis, 1981) and the formal system they create (Payne, 1990; Schein, 1985; Sethia and Glinow, 1985; Wilkins, 1983). But some other aspects of organisational culture such as professional cultures (Barley, 1983; Wilkins and Ouchi, 1983), industrial cultures (Fombrun and Zajac, 1987; Huff, 1982; Pennings and Gresov, 1986; Spender, 1989) and national cultures (Hofstede, 1980; Laurent, 1983; Tayeb, 1988) are much more difficult to change.

The proposition is supported by evidence derived from comparative management studies. The evidence suggests that nationality is a significant predictor of organisational practices and individuals' attitudes towards organisations in both domestic (Graves, 1973; Hofstede, 1980; Millar, 1989; Hofstede *et al.*, 1990; Laurent, 1983; Maurice, 1979, Nicolaidis, 1992a) and expatriate (Nicolaidis, 1992b) enterprises.

Proposition 1, in turn, implies that CEOs may use corporate culture to influence the successful implementation of internationalisation strategies in the pursuit of organisational performance by increasing both the technical and moral efficiency of their organisations. To the extent that national culture conditions corporate culture, its influence should also extend to not only the characteristics of internationalisation action adopted, but also to implementation matters and its subsequent effects upon performance of the companies. Companies which possess national and corporate cultures which are compatible with the critical managerial practices in their industrial sector or the international market place will demonstrate a higher performance. These companies will economise on transaction costs in coordinating human resources, and will further establish finer problem-solving capacities by adjusting appropriate norms (see the discussion earlier in this chapter, p. 121).

The above analysis also parallels the isomorphic argument of institutionalised organisations proposed by Meyer and Rowan (1977) in modern sociological theory. These authors argue that organisations structurally reflect socially constructed reality (Berger and Luckmann, 1967) and within their boundaries imitate environmental elements. Organisations whose structuring (that is policies, procedures, technologies, functions or language) becomes isomorphic with the myths of their institutional environment (that is public opinion, view of important constituents, knowledge legitimated through the educational system, social prestige or laws) gain legitimacy, attract resources and enhance their survival prospects.

Organisational performance, including internationalisation strategy, will, therefore, be contingent to national culture, and national cultural characteristics will emerge as predictors of strategies and processes of internationalisation as well as company performance. Where these characteristics are pronounced, company's performance (controlled for firm-specific and industry-specific non-cultural factors) will excel. Two additional propositions are, therefore, suggested from the preceding discussion.

Proposition 2

Since overall economic performance and internationalisation strategy depends on the capacity of a firm to innovate and on the level of transaction costs, the success of a firm depends on the 'quality' of its culture, and its compatibility with the internationalisation aims of the company. The long-run performance of the firm will be conditional on the strength of the corporate culture created and its suitability to the interactions created in an international environment.

Proposition 3

Within each country, the firms which adopt managerial practices compatible with their national culture will be the best performers. Controlling for non-cultural industry-specific and firm-specific characteristics, national and cultural characteristics will emerge as key determinants of corporate excellence. However, these may have a different effect when decisions to internationalise occur.

The relation between organisational culture and organisational performance has been widely embraced and elaborated by scholars (Deal and Kennedy, 1982; Pascale and Athos, 1981; Peters and Waterman, 1982; Schwartz and Davis, 1982; Ouchi, 1981). However, lacking an appropriate theoretical framework, cultural theories of corporate excellence so far overlook the importance of national and firm-specific cultural factors in motivating corporate excellence. No substantiated evidence either supports the view of a unique and universal management culture which may be used as a sort of managerial lever to increase managerial performance: for instance, initiation or development of international activities. By contrast, it is now clear that social influences positively differentiate economic actors from each other (De Bettignies, 1973; Maurice, 1979; Smith 1984) and social systems impose different economic rationalities across countries (Powell and DiMaggio, 1991; Whitley, 1989, 1991).

Evidence supporting proposition 3 comes from a study conducted by Nicolaidis (1992a) on 105 British and 99 Greek companies. The study indicated that the most profitable companies adapt their organisational culture to the idiosyncrasies of their national culture: for example, individualistic attitudes linked to objective measurements promote profitability in the UK; familism and intolerance of dissent enhance profitability in Greece.

With respect to internationalisation strategies, proposition 3 in turn suggests that internationalising companies should also recognise that the importance of their home base extends beyond the significance of traditional cost factors of production. Strategic analysis, decision and implementation will be affected by the home-base cultural features, and will facilitate or constrain the creation and maintenance of competitive advantages of the internationalising enterprise in its international setting. For instance, management techniques such as management by objectives (MBO) developed in individualistic countries may well be applied in other individualistic countries too. However, since they presuppose some form of negotiation between subordinates and superiors, they may not offer competitive advantages for international firms operating in a collective culture (Hofstede, 1980). Innovation characteristics and entrepreneurial behaviour are also mediated by the home culture. More interestingly, these cultural features cannot be easily imitated by outsiders. This view highlights another important set of speculations. An internationalisation strategy may not be successful if based upon an incompatible and weak national culture since:

Proposition 4

Multinational enterprises, in their internal structuring and functioning, will tend to reproduce significant features of their national culture. Sustaining competitive advantage in the long run, therefore, may be difficult unless most of the underpinning of innovation and entrepreneurial behaviour is present at home. And,

Proposition 5
National culture may be integral to the process of creating and developing a distinct competitive advantage for the domestic as well as the internationalising firm. National culture may provide the firm with competitive advantages over international rivals by providing new bases for competition and better means to compete in old ways.

The above propositions match suggestions that national wealth is not only inherited but also created (Casson, 1990; Porter, 1990). Therefore, they can go beyond conventional economic factors such as wages, interest rates and resource endowments in explaining why some firms from some nations are systematically better than others in creating advantages based on quality and innovation. Indeed, national economic prosperity depends on a continuous upgrading of industries mediated by the entrepreneurial elite. In this process, key aspects of source-country culture may be synergised with industry-specific factors through the activities of a country's entrepreneurial elite to generate national-level competitive advantages. This competitive advantage, first, derives from the capacity of national culture to condition the process of perceiving opportunities for innovation. Second, it derives from the importance of culture in shaping the institutional structures available for managing technological innovations and subsequent systems operation (Casson, 1990, chapter 2). Third, it derives from the influence cultural factors exert on transaction costs by prescribing levels of trust within the economy.

Accordingly, some national cultures may be better than others in competing in particular industries and in sustaining and upgrading competitive advantages over international rivals and adoption of adequate internationalisation strategies. This is supported by both theoretical and empirical suggestions. Casson (1992) suggested that the high-trust cultures of Sweden and Japan may have contributed to the capacity of these countries to respond effectively to changing world markets. He also pointed to the fact that Western countries are currently imitating the Japanese industrial culture in the hope of raising productivity through better industrial relations. Dunning and Pearce (1985) suggested that the UK industrial culture, in comparison with the German industrial culture, may not facilitate the development of high-technology firms. The UK, therefore, may lack a competitive advantage in high-technology international industrial sectors. Cultural characteristics may also help to explain differences in innovation characteristics and patterns of technological change. Kagono *et al.* (1985) argued that cultural factors may explain the product v. process innovation found in the USA and Japan respectively. Different time orientations were found to influence the priority given to product quality v. delivery goals (Ferdows *et al.*, 1985).

CONCLUSIONS AND IMPLICATIONS FOR FURTHER RESEARCH

This chapter has outlined a synthetic view for the study of corporate culture and company performance, with an application to internationalisation strategies. The synthetic view, by combining elements from social cognition theory and the economic theory of the entrepreneur, suggested a theoretical framework and a research agenda regarding organisational practices and effectiveness across national and societal boundaries. However, because the attempted synthesis has embraced economic, sociological and psychological theories, it has been guided by wider but less detailed facts than those addressed by the above theories themselves. The novelty and the proliferation of theories of corporate culture has, arguably, made the task of synthesis even more difficult. Different scientific 'subcultures' will surely require more specific, detailed and analytically tractable frameworks.

Research is needed to identify the relation between corporate culture and the competitive domain (nationally and internationally) of the firm (that is its technological capacity, degree of differentiation and diversification, market concentration and homogeneity of management practices), in the pursuit of corporate performance. Economics of culture should specifically measure and distinguish cultural and material determinants of economic and strategic behaviour. It is also vital to link internationalisation strategies of the firm to established cultural values and determinants, both at national and corporate level.

Overall, it is suggested that besides economic ones, sociological and psychological forms of analysis are needed to investigate new organisational boundaries and to clarify cultural phenomena applied to international companies and their strategic decisions and internationalisation processes.

Part Two

Internationalisation Methods

7 International Franchising: Market versus Hierarchy

Fred Burton and Adam R. Cross

INTRODUCTION

A substantial body of literature has accumulated in recent years on one of the so-called 'frontier issues' of international business: the selection, by a firm, of an appropriate organisational structure which enables it to service a foreign market in a manner most likely to achieve premeditated objectives. Scholars of this foreign market entry and development literature (surveyed, for example, by Young *et al.*, 1989) describe, individually, the advantages and disadvantages of many of these entry modes, including (in rough order of increasing resource commitment to the local market): exporting; the so-called 'new forms of investment' (a range of contractual arrangements falling significantly short of majority entrant ownership and which include, for example, licensing, strategic alliances and management contracts, Oman, 1984); equity joint ventures; and wholly-owned subsidiaries.

More recently, attention has been turned to the rigorous and systematic analysis of the factors contributing to the optimality of one of these entry mechanisms versus the others (Anderson and Gatignon, 1986; Hill, Hwang and Kim, 1990; Contractor, 1990; Erramilli, 1990, amongst others). However, despite being increasingly deployed in the internationalisation of firms during the last three decades (Kaynak, 1988; Falbe and Dandridge, 1992; McCosker, 1992), one particular 'new form of investment' – cross-border franchising – has received only scant coverage within this literature. What is more, scholars of foreign market entry often presume, both implicitly and explicitly, that international franchising involves arm's-length transactions between independent parties homologous to those of the licensing entry mode. This, we feel, misrepresents the franchise entry method as it is used today.

First, we outline what we mean by the term 'international franchising'. We illustrate, by describing the different ways firms structure entries into non-domestic markets using franchising, the somewhat simplistic manner in which this entry mode has been treated to date in the international marketing literature. It is argued that international franchising is a separate entry method in the general schema of foreign market entry, which should be distinguished from, and not confused with, the licensing method.[1] A framework is also presented for more appropriate analyses of the franchise entry method. In the second half of the chapter, we follow the general theme of this book (that the nature of a firm's internationalisation strategy is determined by combinations of constraining and enabling circumstances) by discussing, in the context of our framework, some of the factors that can affect how cross-border franchising techniques are used to extend a firm's operations to non-domestic markets.[2]

INTERNATIONAL FRANCHISING: TOWARDS A DEFINITION

The concept of franchising defies definition. Although literally meaning 'freedom from servitude', the term now has many different interpretations and connotations; while numerous and often contradictory categorisation schemes exist, depending on what is being franchised or the nature of the relationship between contracting parties (see, for example, Euromonitor, 1987; Bradley, 1991; Hoffman and Preble, 1991). Here, we concentrate on business format franchising (often referred to as second generation franchising) because this 'seems to be the basis of all successful [international] franchising operations during the last three decades' (Götberg, 1989, but confirmed by Welch, 1989; Sanghavi, 1990), and because the foreign market entry analysis literature almost universally presupposes a reference to this form.[3]

As an entry mode, business format franchising (henceforth franchising) involves a relationship between an entrant, the franchisor, and a host-country entity, in which the former transfers, in a controlled manner, a business package (or format) to the latter. This contains most, if not all, the elements needed by the recipient to establish and replicate the business and run it profitably in the host country, including, amongst other things, intellectual property rights (encapsulated in, for example, trade names, marks, copyright and business know-how), managerial assistance and geographic exclusivity. It can also include the right for purchasers to develop their own sub-system of franchised outlets. The franchisor is usually compensated by an initial fee up-front and/or continuing franchise fees (based typically on a percentage of annual turnover) and by a mark-up on any goods supplied.

THE TRADITIONAL VIEW OF INTERNATIONAL FRANCHISING

The origin of the traditional view of cross-border franchising in the market entry literature seems to have two roots: the managerial economist's view of franchise contracts, and the notion that franchising is merely a special form of licensing.

Managerial Economists' View of Franchising

Managerial economists see franchising as a hybrid organisational form, located somewhere between the extremes of vertical integration on the one hand and completely independent operations on the other. They hold that, although the parties to the franchise arrangement are independent (Caves and Murphy, 1976; Rubin, 1978; Adams and Mendelsohn, 1986), transactions which take place between them resemble those of intra-firm vertical integration, because features of the contract encourage the agent (the franchisee) to act in the interests of the principal (the franchisor) and to maximise sales and profits over and above levels which company employees might generate. This inducement derives from the franchisee's residual claimant status (that is, their right to appropriate a substantial share of the profit generated by activities under their control), and 'bonding effects' arising from both their investment in the initial franchise fee and any purchase of assets specific to the franchise format. Additional franchisee–franchisor bonding occurs with unilateral termination clauses in the franchise contract; restrictions in the use of trademarks and other franchisor-owned property rights; and the franchisee's dependency on technical improvements, on-going training, sub-supply deliveries and/or tied purchases from the franchisor.[4]

Managerial economists thus assert that the franchise contract provides the franchisor with greater control over operations than would occur in fully market-located transactions, whilst avoiding complete integration and its associated costs. Perhaps not surprisingly, many scholars simply extrapolate this perspective, based as it is on the experience of domestic-only franchising, to the international environment, by presuming that non-domestic franchise operations are independent of the entrant in respect of ownership (Oman, 1984; Kaynak, 1988; Götberg, 1989; Hoffman and Preble, 1991, amongst others), and that franchise contracts are negotiated with each franchisee on an individual basis.

Licensing versus Franchising

Oman, in outlining his taxonomy of international market entry modes, is typical of many scholars of international business when he states that 'franchising may be regarded as a particular type of licensing' (1984, p. 15). For example, Root insists that, 'franchising is a form of licensing in which a company (franchisor) licenses a business system as well as other property rights to an *independent* company or person (franchisee)' (1987, p. 109, emphasis added). Those few researchers of foreign market entry analysis that recognise the franchising entry option also explicitly concur with this (for example, Anderson and Gatignon, 1986; Erramilli, 1990; Hill, Hwang and Kim, 1990), while Boddewyn, Halbrich and Perry demonstrate the possibility that this perception of franchising as a licence arrangement has adversely affected the academic appreciation of this option when they write, 'since franchising is a form of licensing, it will *not be discussed* as a separate type of foreign business involvement' (1986 p. 55, emphasis added).

In as much as 'licensing' is a generic term used to describe a variety of contractual arrangements in which the entrant offers a local entity access to (that is, a permission to use) one, or a set, of its proprietary technologies or know-how in return for financial compensation (Young *et al.*, 1989), we accept that a similarity between franchising and licensing does exist: franchising clearly involves a comparable, albeit often a more comprehensive, technology transfer between entrant and host-country entity. However, in the foreign market entry analysis literature, the term 'licensing' has a very specific connotation: it is an arm's-length transaction that occurs in the marketplace between independent parties, and which is, therefore, a zero-equity form of international association involving low resource commitment, low risk and limited capital outlays on the part of the entrant (Contractor, 1985, 1990). We do accept that equity participation by licensors in licensee firms is a growing phenomenon (in one international survey around one in seven licensing firms questioned indicated that they had an equity stake in companies to which they licensed, OECD, 1987), but this possibility has been largely overlooked by scholars of foreign entry.

Categorising franchising as a variant of licensing promotes the traditional view that, in the context of foreign market entry, franchising is also a purely contractual, non-equity, non-direct method of international association (Anderson and Gatignon, 1986; Root, 1987; Czinkota and Ronkainen, 1988; Young *et al.*, 1989; Contractor, 1990; Erramilli, 1990; amongst others). The managerial economists' perspective of the franchise contract merely reinforces this notion. The characteristics of international franchising commonly cited in the literature reflect these views (see Table 7.1).

Present day international franchising activity, as reported in accounts of the legal aspects of international franchising (Abell, 1990; Mendelsohn, 1992) and descriptions of inward and outward franchising in the UK press and franchise trade journals (for example, *Franchise World* and *The Franchise Magazine*) does not fully corroborate this traditional view, as the following section demonstrates.

DIFFERENT ORGANISATIONAL FORMS OF INTERNATIONAL FRANCHISING AS AN ENTRY MODE

Clearly, the principal aim of a profit-maximising franchising entrant is to establish a network, or sub-system, of sales outlets and production facilities (termed 'units') to operate the franchise format and generate income in the target country or territory. When the franchise format has been sold to independent operators, these units are external to the franchisor, and transactions take place between parties at 'arm's-length'. However, and as recorded in

Table 7.1 Characteristics of international franchising cited in the literature

Advantages	*Suggested by (amongst others)*
Low-risk, low-cost entry mode	Brooke (1986); Götberg (1989)
Ability to develop new and distant international markets, relatively quickly and on a larger scale than otherwise possible	Root (1987); Young *et al.* (1989); Bradley (1991)
Using highly motivated business contacts with local market knowledge and experience	Root (1987); Götberg (1989); Bradley (1991)
Creating additional turn-over with small investments in, e.g. personnel, capital outlays, production and distribution	Young *et al.* (1989); Bradley (1991)
Disadvantages	
Lack of full control over franchisee's operations	Root (1987); Götberg (1989); Young *et al.* (1989)
Limitations on franchisor's profit	Root (1987); Götberg (1989)
Costs in protecting goodwill and brand-name	Götberg (1989)
Disclosing internal business secrets and knowledge may create potential future competitor	Root (1987); Götberg (1989); Young *et al.* (1989)

domestic-only franchising (for example, Norton, 1988), franchising companies also choose to own units they establish. These are internal to the franchisor: transactions take place hierarchically and revenues which they generate can be fully appropriated by the franchising entrant.

This sub-system of internal and external units is developed in a number of different ways (see Figure 7.1). In direct international franchising, the franchisor sets up services (that is to say, provides on-going back-up and support), polices and monitors the activities of each host-country unit individually, direct from its home-country base. Units established in this manner are called franchisees.

However, franchising firms also incorporate 'intermediary' parties (sub-franchisors) between themselves and host-country units. These have the exclusive right to exploit the franchisor's business package within a designated region, developing and servicing a sub-system of units which themselves are either owned by the sub-franchisor or are sub-franchised out to independent parties. Sub-franchisors can be wholly-owned by the franchisor (when the arrangement is termed 'subsidiary international franchising'); they can be jointly owned with a local partner (joint-venture international franchising);

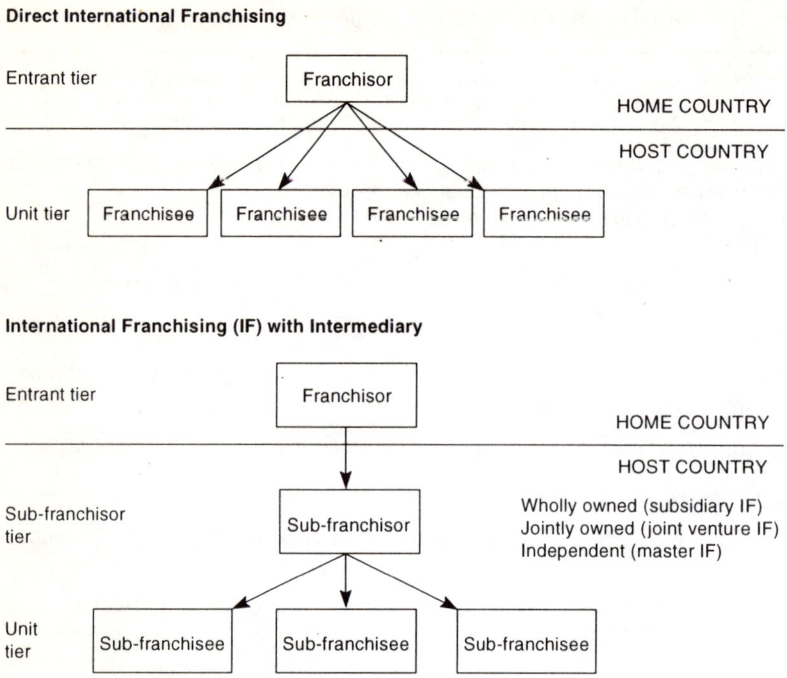

Figure 7.1 Various structures of international franchise entries

or they can be totally independent entities (master international franchising). All units developed by sub-franchisors are called sub-franchisees.[5]

Franchising entrants may invest equity in foreign markets in one of two 'tiers': in the unit tier (as internal franchisees and sub-franchisees) and in the sub-franchisor tier (as subsidiaries and joint ventures). What is more, depending on (i) the proportion of internal to external units established, and (ii) the type of international franchise arrangement used, each franchising entry can be located on a continuum, illustrated in Figure 7.2. This shows the percentage of the total equity value of a local operation that can be owned by the franchising entrant using each franchise arrangement. It ranges from zero (when the franchisor has made no equity investment in the sub-franchisor tier and where all units established are external), through to 100 per cent (when the franchisor owns all of the local units together with support facilities at the sub-franchisor tier). For expositional purposes, which will become clearer later, we divide this continuum, somewhat subjectively, into five different 'types' of franchise entry, which relate directly to the scale at which entry is made: Scale One (zero to very low levels of entrant ownership of local operations), Scale Two (low), Scale Three (moderate), Scale Four (high) and Scale Five (very high to 100 per cent franchisor owned).[6]

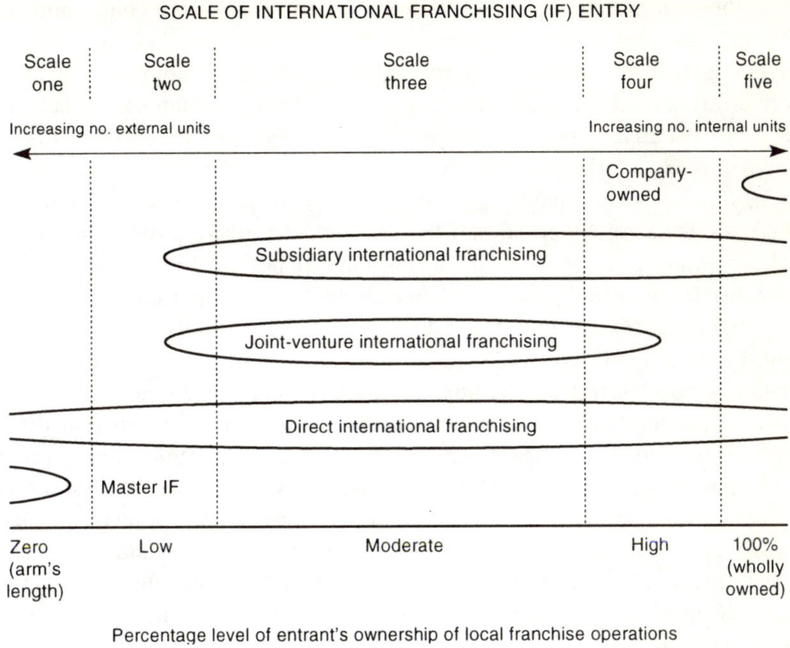

Figure 7.2 Continuum of resource commitment to the local market

The continuum shows, for example, that the full spectrum of investment levels only occurs in direct international franchising, when the location of a particular entry is simply determined by the proportion of internal to external units established. In both joint-venture and subsidiary international franchising the equity invested by the franchisor at the sub-franchisor tier precludes Scale One entries, while in joint-venture international franchising the equity invested at the sub-franchisor tier by an independent local partner precludes Scale Five entries. Similarly, all master international franchising entries are Scale One since, as the sub-franchisor is an independent local entity, all sub-franchisees established must be, by definition, external to the franchising entrant, irrespective of their ownership relation with the sub-franchisor.

The equity which franchising entrants can potentially invest in host-country operations, at both the sub-franchisor tier and the unit tier, must challenge the presumption that international franchising is always an arm's-length, contractual, non-equity, non-direct form of international association between entrants and independent host-country concerns. This only occurs in Scale One franchise entries (when international franchising most conforms to the traditionally-held perspective).

As the level of franchisor's equity participation at the sub-franchisor tier and/or the unit tier increases from left to right across the continuum, the low-risk, low-cost characteristics traditionally presumed of cross-border franchising become increasingly invalidated. Indeed, a moment will arrive where a foreign market entrance using several of the international franchising forms can effectively be regarded as foreign direct investment. As this approaches, many of the assumptions traditionally held regarding the use of franchising as an international growth strategy need to be re-assessed.

Even so, the term 'international franchising', we assert, still applies across this continuum, even at the point when most, if not all, local operations are owned by the entrant, because it is merely the institutional mode of transfer of the business format to foreign operatives which differs between arm's-length (open market) and hierarchical (intra-firm) transactions. The elements which make up the transferred business package are, for the most part, unaffected by the mode of transfer, and consumers perceive no apparent difference between internal and external operatives (Sanghavi, 1990). Furthermore, the same package can be transferred to internal units in one sub-system and external units in another, while, equally, operations in one country can easily be converted from being independent to franchisor-owned and vice versa, through, respectively, acquisition and divestment. The concept of the 'international franchise entry mode', we suggest, embraces all these scenarios.

OTHER RESPECTS IN WHICH FRANCHISING IS DISTINCT FROM LICENSING

Lawyers and other practitioners of international franchising have also argued that the terms 'licensing' and 'franchising' 'actually refer to two distinct legal concepts' (Konigsburg, 1987, p. 59) and are not synonymous in any context, let alone foreign market entry analysis. Although, as with many areas of international business, generalisations are problematic, this legal distinction is based on various observations.[7]

Firstly, in licensing the licensee only acquires a portion of the licensor's total business function, typically via the transfer of a right to manufacture and/or to distribute a single product or process using a combination of the licensee's skill and operation together with the benefit of the licensor's patents, know-how, trade marks and reputation (Baillie, 1987). Franchising, on the other hand, involves the transfer of a complete business package (the format) which includes, if not all, then most of the elements of the franchisor's *modus operandi* needed to establish non-domestic operations. As Perkins states, 'franchising is all-encompassing, whereas licensing concerns just one part of the business' (1987, p. 15).

Secondly, under a licence agreement, the licensor can have some control over the manner in which the independent licensee uses the licensor's transferred technology, know-how and trademarks, but frequently has little or no

Table 7.2 Principal differences between the licensing and franchising entry modes

Franchising entry mode	*Licensing entry mode*
Can and, often does, involve significant equity investment in the host country	Generally regarded as a low to zero equity form of international association
Most, if not all, of the entrant's business function transferred to local recipients	Only part of the entrant's business function transferred to local recipients
Entrant exerts considerable control over independent operatives' day-to-day activities	Entrant generally has limited control over day-to-day activities of contracted parties
Chain of apparently commonly owned enterprises established	Individual enterprises established, with limited common characteristics
Intermediary parties can exist between entrant and host-country sales/production facilities	Generally involves a simpler direct relationship between entrant and local facilities

control over precisely how the licensee carries on his day-to-day business. By contrast, in franchising, the franchisor is able to exert detailed control over the activities of independent franchisees, sub-franchisors and sub-franchisees.

Furthermore, while licensing entries often only establish a series of individual enterprises with frequently limited common characteristics, in franchising, both the completeness of the business package transferred and the control exerted by the franchisor creates, in each foreign market entered, the image of a chain of 'commonly-owned' enterprises. This chain, international lawyers assert, distinguishes the franchising contract from the licence (Konigsburg, 1987).[8]

Table 7.2 summarises our argument that the terms 'franchising' and 'licensing' express two distinct and non-interchangeable foreign market entry modes. In Table 7.3 we present a recommended lexicon of terminology for international franchising (based on Konigsburg, 1987) which, if adopted universally, should help to maintain this distinction and minimise descriptive confusion.

INTERNATIONAL FRANCHISING AND RESOURCE COMMITMENT TO THE LOCAL MARKET

As a move towards a better understanding of the franchise entry method, we now discuss some of the circumstances that may affect whether a franchising entrant develops low-equity, Scale One and Two (and 'small' systems, see note 6) or high-equity, Scale Four and Five, franchise sub-systems.[9]

Table 7.3 Some recommenced terminology for international franchising

Recommended description of agreement	*Recommended description of parties to agreement*	*Alternative descriptions of agreement NOT recommended*	*Alternative descriptions of parties to agreement NOT recommended*	*Found in:*
1. Franchise agreement	Franchisor/franchisee	Licence agreement	Licensor/licensee	DIF
2. Master franchise agreement	Franchisor/sub-franchisor	• Area franchise agreement • Area licence agreement	• Franchisor/master franchisee • Master franchisor/master franchisee • Master franchisor/franchisor	MIF, JVIF, SIF
3. Two party sub-franchise agreement as part of a master franchise agreement (a sub-franchise agreement)	Sub-franchisor/sub-franchisee	• Franchise agreement • Licence agreement	• Franchisor/franchisee • Master franchisee/franchisee	MIF, JVIF, SIF
4. Three party sub-franchise agreement as part of a master franchise agreement (a sub-franchise agreement)	Franchisor/sub-franchisor/sub-franchisee	• Franchise agreement • Licence agreement	• Franchisor/master franchisee/franchisee • Owner/franchisor/franchisee • Owner/master franchisee/sub-franchisee	MIF, JVIF, SIF

Abbreviations: DIF, Direct international franchising; JVIF, Joint-venture international franchising; SIF, Subsidiary international franchising; MIF, Master international franchising

Description of agreement	*Recommended terminology*	*Terminology NOT recommended*
1. Consideration payable upon entering a franchise agreement	Initial franchise fee	Up-front fee, Franchise fee, Initial fee
2. Continuing consideration payable under the franchise agreement and expressed as a percentage of sales, etc	Continuing franchise fee	Royalties, continuing royalties, service fees

Agency Issues

Agency theory outlined earlier (pp. 136–7), suggests that bonding and other agent-motivating aspects of the franchise contract encourage those firms possessing a franchiseable business package to transact with external operatives in a host country rather than conduct transactions hierarchically. The specialist knowledge that these independent entities have of their local market can also be used to adopt and modify the franchise, if needed, and reduce cultural, language and legal barriers. The general optimality of Scale One and Two franchise entries over higher-equity, higher-cost, franchising entry methods is therefore implied.

Additional factors support this proposition. For example, the contribution that external operatives make (via initial and continuing franchise fees) to the cost of Scale One and Two franchise operations minimises the franchisor's overall expense and financial risk associated with market entry, while the franchisor's exposure, perceived or otherwise, to equity loss in target markets is also attenuated. Furthermore, fees are recouped relatively quickly following market entry. This can boost the franchisor's cash flow and reduce the burden of any special financing requirements. Cost benefits of low-equity franchising such as these may be particularly attractive to smaller franchisors and/or those with limited financial resources.[10] In addition, this type of international franchising can allow franchisors to develop individual markets and/or expand internationally at a faster rate than if higher-equity franchising were employed. It follows that low-equity franchising may be used as a low-cost, market-testing strategy (Root, 1987; Hoffman and Preble, 1991), or to develop markets perceived as being too small to warrant higher-equity investment. In economies or sectors where foreign equity involvement, or majority involvement, is not permitted, low-equity franchising may in fact be the only entry method available (Hackett, 1976), as with joint-venture international franchising when host-country laws stipulate the participation of a local national partner (Konigsburg, 1990). In these situations, therefore, franchising out using Scale One and Scale Two sub-systems gives entrants access to markets otherwise foreclosed and revenues otherwise inaccessible.

However, two potential disadvantages to Scale One and Scale Two franchise systems can be envisaged. Firstly, in franchising, the profits generated by external operatives are not fully appropriated by the franchisor: instead, they are effectively shared between the franchisor and independent purchasers of the franchise package. This implies that lower-equity (Scale One, Two, and Scale Three) franchising entries yield smaller returns for the franchisor than higher-equity franchise entries. This proposition will not hold, however, if, as agency theory predicts, external operatives can still generate more income for the franchisor, even after profit/revenue sharing, than would a full appropriation of the returns from internal operations. Furthermore, franchisors can inflate fees levied on unit-tier entities, to compensate themselves for any profit and revenue 'lost' because it is shared with a sub-franchisor entity (though this conflicts with observations that fees charged by franchising entrants to sub-franchisees in foreign markets are comparable to those levied on franchisees in the domestic market, Mendelsohn, 1992). Moreover, the profit-sharing issue is diminished if franchisors earn the majority of their income by marking up materials supplied to host-country operatives.

Secondly, the success of franchising is often dependent on a close working relationship between the franchisor and independent parties, even when their activities are constrained contractually. Several potential areas of conflict can strain this relationship, including issues of profit distribution (for example, to re-invest or repatriate in the short and long term); differing objectives regarding turnover, rate of growth and corporate image; and resentment of the franchisor's level of control over day-to-day activities. Such conflict can lead to sub-standard product and service provision by the external operatives involved.[11] Disputes become especially problematic in master and joint-venture international franchising, because the independent sub-franchisor entity owns (partially in the latter case) and controls the franchise sub-system and will consequently have most contact with unit-tier entities. After a breakdown in relations with the sub-franchisor, a franchisor will probably find it costly to regain effective control of the sub-system, in terms of both managerial time (for example, in reassuring external sub-franchisees with whom previous dealings had been limited) and financial expense (for example, when purchasing back the businesses of external operatives, perhaps at inflated prices if the franchise contract penalises this). This is a major disadvantage of Scale One, Two and Three franchising entries. The larger the sub-system involved, the more significant these difficulties become.

Transactions Costs

The second set of determinant factors which need incorporating here relate to the costs of franchising incurred by entrants. We group these (after Williamson, 1975) into four different categories:

1. *Search costs* Incurred as the franchisor solicits, evaluates, selects and contracts with suitable independent sub-franchisor and/or unit-tier candidates in the target country.[12]
2. *Servicing costs* Incurred as the franchisor's technology and expertise is transferred to these internal and external operatives. Servicing costs include, *inter alia*, the cost of codifying the franchise format appropriately, the cost of providing managerial and technical assistance, support and on-going training (if included in the franchise package) and the cost of any modification and adjustment of the format to suit local conditions.[13]
3. *Property rights protection costs* Although franchise agreements often

include clauses forbidding contracted parties from operating a similar business in a given territory and/or interval once the agreement terminates, the threat exists that, once fully conversant with the format, contracted parties (or indeed others) may establish operations in direct competition with the franchisor, before or after the contract officially ends.[14] Franchisors therefore incur costs as they take steps to safeguard, in each market entered, firm-specific advantages embodied within their franchise format.

4. *Monitoring costs* Incurred as franchisors seek to constrain opportunistic behaviour by policing and supervising the activities of independent entities. Franchisors need to ensure that external operatives declare their sales correctly and submit appropriate fees. More importantly, perhaps, they also need to obviate the possibility that sub-standard product/service provided by just some external operatives does not damage the goodwill of their franchise created through centralised marketing and advertising. Such behaviour could adversely affect sales in a particular sub-system and even throughout the entire franchise network.[15]

The franchisor's search, servicing and monitoring costs of market entry increase in proportion to the number of entities (both internal and external) present in the sub-system.[16] As these transactions costs increase, a point arrives when the franchisor can no longer monitor and service that sub-system adequately. Several factors determine when this point is reached. For example, when a home and a host country are psychically proximate (after Hofstede, 1983), the franchise package will probably require little, if any, modification to be viable in the target market (Sanghavi, 1990). Local entities will also be more likely to assimilate transferred technologies quickly and efficiently as their organisational culture converges with that of the franchisor.[17] However, as psychic distance increases, particularly in respect to cultural issues so, we suggest, will transactions costs. Servicing costs will increase as elements of the franchise package have to be tailored to suit local market conditions (Eroglu, 1992). Search and monitoring costs are likely to increase as differences in business ethics and practices between the franchising entrant and locally contracted parties become more pronounced. As psychic distance increases, franchisors will probably need to expend more resources to both identify acceptable independent franchise candidates and ensure their satisfactory performance; while franchise contracts will almost certainly need to be redrawn to make them enforceable in markets with different legislative regimes to those already encountered by the franchisor. Generally, it is easier (less costly) to export franchises to host markets which closely resemble the home market (Sanghavi, 1990).

Similarly, as the physical distance between home and host countries increases, so will communication and transportation costs associated with monitoring and servicing local operatives (Konigsburg, 1990). Certain firm-specific factors are also relevant. For example, larger franchisors, in terms of either their managerial or financial resources, should be more capable of financing the transactions costs of international expansion than smaller franchisors, while firms with greater experience (after Davidson, 1980) of domestic and international franchising should be more capable of identifying acceptable franchise candidates (reducing search costs) and effecting, efficiently, the transfer of know-how and procedures to foreign markets (reducing servicing costs) than less experienced franchisors. Similarly, opportunities for cost reductions independent of scale should also increase with firm experience, as know-how and operating procedures improve with time.

Finally, aspects of host-country legislation may also be pertinent. For example, to 'legitimise' franchising, disclosure legislation is becoming increasingly prevalent in many countries (for example, France and the US), requiring the franchising entrant to provide all parties considering the purchase of its format information regarding, for example, its history, business activities, owners, address of existing franchisees/sub-franchisors, registration of trademarks, bank references and financial statements. This legislation raises the franchising entrant's search costs. Finally, if host-country governments view franchising as a restrictive business practice, anti-trust legislation may exist to counter features commonly found in the agreement such as tied purchases, contract termination and dispute settlement clauses, restrictive pricing policies and other aspects of local entity control exerted by franchisors. Such legislation determines whether franchising-out is even practicable in these markets.

In summary, the point at which transactions costs become prohibitive and franchisors can no longer adequately control and monitor a particular sub-system as it grows will occur later, the greater the financial and/or managerial resources of the entrant and its experience of franchising; and earlier, the greater the psychic and physical distances between home and host countries and the greater the degree of disclosure legislation.

Transactions costs (especially product/service modification costs and disclosure legislation costs) are potentially the most burdensome in direct international franchising, because the number of individual entities transacting directly with the franchisor is potentially the greatest and changes needed to the franchise have to be negotiated separately with each contracted party. Therefore, this franchising arrangement will probably be observed when transactions costs are most attenuated: that is, when sub-systems are small; when home and host countries are psychically and/or physically proximate, and when disclosure legislation does not have a prohibitive effect. Sub-systems developed by direct methods are, therefore, often a simple extension of the franchisor's domestic network.

Franchisors can also reduce the transactions costs (especially search, servicing and monitoring costs) of franchising directly by negotiating a contract with a single entity (the sub-franchisor) in the host country, who then bears the costs of developing the franchise sub-system. However, whether franchisor equity is invested in this sub-franchisor introduces a third set of factors which we need to consider before proceeding.

Internalisation Issues

Foreign market entry theory suggests a number of reasons why franchising firms might substitute hierarchies for markets. Internalising non-domestic operations provides entrants with greater control (defined by Hill, Hwang and Kim, 1990, as authority in operational and strategic decision-making) over arm's-length transacting, but at the expense of governance costs associated with the cross-border coordination and administration of hierarchical organisations, such as salaries, rent and capitalisation expenditure (Anderson and Gatignon, 1986), and the expense of gaining knowledge of the foreign market (Contractor, 1990).

Using a totally independent sub-franchisor (that is, Scale One, master international franchising) to reduce transactions costs maximises the benefits that an entrant receives from transacting with an external operative (such as the agent's motivation levels and knowledge of the local market, reduced legal and cultural barriers and other advantages described earlier under the heading, Agency Issues), while governance costs are minimised (reducing the cost of market entry and the entrant's exposure to financial and equity loss). However, these benefits are offset by the high search costs frequently needed to identify an acceptable purchaser of the sub-franchise rights, while at the same time the difficulties associated with issues of profit/revenue sharing, agent under-performance, conflict resolution, competitor creation and threat of damage to the format's goodwill are most pronounced. Increasing entrant ownership at the sub-franchisor tier (and, but to a lesser extent, the unit tier) from Scale Two through to Scale Five franchising entries, through internalisation, negates these threats. It follows that, we suggest, as transactions costs increase (especially servicing, know-how protection and monitoring costs), so does internalisation at both the sub-franchisor and the unit tier (after Contractor, 1990; Hennart, 1989).

Scale Three, Four and Scale Five franchise sub-systems also provide the franchisor with greater 'hands-on' control over local operations, and increase the opportunities to appropriate profits generated. These sub-systems are therefore expected to be developed in markets regarded as strategically important or lucrative by the franchisor, and those that have equity participation incentives (for example, subsidies and tax benefits) for foreign investors (Konigsburg, 1990). Equity involvement at the sub-franchisor tier can also be used to reduce some of the franchisor's transactions costs associated with searching, servicing and monitoring external unit-tier entities, because the close proximity of the sub-franchisor to the host market lowers some transportation and communication expense.

On the negative side, however, increasing internalisation at the sub-franchisor level, from Scale Three to Scale Five franchising entries, will negate those agent-related benefits gained from dealing with external operatives, while the entrant's exposure to investment risk is also increased. High equity sub-systems may also take longer to develop than lower equity versions, which could cause market entry to be delayed and business opportunities missed.

CONCLUDING REMARKS

Central to this book is the notion that managers of internationalising firms have at their disposal several different ways of entering and developing non-domestic markets, and that, for a given situation, a set of constraining or enabling circumstances combine to optimise one of these entry methods over alternative strategies. However, most firms which have devised and own a business format franchise earn the majority of their income by either franchising-out and selling to independent parties the right to use the format (and associated activities), or by operating the format themselves using company-owned units. Consequently, the international franchise entry mode, as described here, will almost always be the only method available for such firms to expand beyond their domestic environment, limiting the franchising entrant's choice of entry strategy to one. But, as we demonstrate, the international franchise entry mode contains within it a sub-set of organisational forms which, in their relation to the sub-franchisor tier entity (if present), can be likened to the 'purer' entry modes, such as licensing (that is, master international franchising), joint-venturing (joint-venture international franchising) or foreign direct investment (subsidiary international franchising).

A lack of appropriate empirical research makes it difficult to place the international franchise entry mode in context with alternative internationalisation strategies with respect to, for example, comparative frequency of use. However, it can be inferred that many of the factors described as impacting on the optimality (or otherwise) of each of these alternative strategies will also have a non-trivial effect on the franchising entrant's choice of, for example, a low equity (Scale One) franchising entry over a high equity (Scale Five) entry. We have described some of these factors in the previous section and, in so doing, enter into the market versus hierarchy debate of international business. In this chapter, we have also made the observation that firms employing franchise contracts in their internationalisation process can, and frequently do, invest significant amounts of equity in host-country franchise sub-systems and this, we suggest, must question many of the assumptions traditionally held by scholars of foreign market entry that have arisen through the previously accepted franchising/licensing relation. Finally, by introducing a framework to reappraise international franchising, we claim to have laid down in this chapter some of the ground for a quantitative research agenda to address issues raised, such as, for example, the importance of international franchising versus other entry strategies; the relative frequency in use of each organisational form of international franchising; and the individual significance of the factors described here as determining the respective optimality of these forms.

Notes

1. Although there is merit in the view that franchising is 'an important form of strategic alliance' (for example, Hoffman and Preble 1991, p. 74), we concentrate on the franchising/licensing relation because this appears to be the source of most misunderstanding regarding the international franchising entry mode.
2. The authors gratefully acknowledge the support of the UK's Economic and Social Research Council (ESRC) in financing the research reported in this chapter.
3. Felstead (1993, p. 47 onwards) describes the principal differences between business format franchising and product/trade-name (first generation) franchising. Since both forms involve the exchange of a product/service for a fee, much of what follows here applies equally to both.
4. Thompson and Wright (1988, chapter 4), amongst others, comprehensively review these principal-agent issues.
5. These various forms of international franchising are recognised in the international business literature. For example, Welch (1989) identifies master franchising; Hoffman and Preble (1991) subsidiary and master franchising; while Hackett (1976) only excludes the subsidiary franchising option. Many, like Aydin and Kacker (1990) infer that all international franchising takes place directly. Franchisor ownership of units is also well documented, domestically (for example Norton, 1988) and, occasionally, internationally (for example Aydin and Kacker, 1990). Our broad research agenda is to explain patterns of franchisor ownership at the sub-franchisor tier and the unit tier. This has not been attempted in the international context to date.
6. This schema is merely a conceptual tool. It takes no account of the absolute financial value of a particular franchise sub-system (assuming a figure is calculable), and cannot be used to directly compare sub-systems without quantifying the scale of each in some way. More importantly, it takes no account of the precise number of units developed in any sub-system: very low numbers will always represent a limited resource commitment by the entrant, irrespective of their ownership status. In what follows, small sub-systems are treated as Scale One entries.
7. These legal arguments were originally presented for domestic-only franchising. They apply equally to international franchising.
8. It is interesting to note that practitioners of international law have in the past attempted to circumvent host-country franchise legislation and/or franchising's negative association with illegal pyramid selling by applying the term 'licensing' to contracts that in all respects are franchises (Konigsburg, 1987). Clearly such behaviour does little to clarify the legal distinction between these two contractual arrangements.
9. This section summarises Burton and Cross (1994). Much of it is hypothetical and awaits empirical substantiation. Statements are made as *ceteris paribus* arguments unless otherwise indicated.

10. It does not automatically follow that larger franchisors are more likely to make higher-equity franchising entries than smaller franchisors, because the optimality of franchising-out operations is independent of franchisor size.
11. Joint-venture international franchising also possesses those sources of conflict said to affect 'pure' joint ventures (for example, Harrigan, 1983).
12. By increasing their search costs, franchising entrants should improve the quality of the independent parties they select which, in turn, should lead to lower technology transfer costs, a lower likelihood of under-performance and lower risk to the goodwill of the franchise system (see servicing and monitoring costs). Unsolicited foreign franchise enquiries, commonly observed by some (for example Welch, 1989) reduce search costs.
13. Franchise modification costs are often incurred by the local independent operatives. In time, as the franchised technology becomes more easily codified and assimilated by recipient parties, servicing costs should decrease.
14. This threat probably increases as the degree of standardisation associated with the franchise format increases (franchised products and services, by their nature, are frequently highly standardised), and probably decreases, with contracted parties at least, as the level of bonding increases.
15. Increased bonding of independent entities to the franchisor should mitigate the likelihood of opportunistic behaviour.
16. While property-rights protection costs increase in proportion to the number of foreign markets entered.
17. When home and host countries are psychically proximate, demand conditions for the franchised product/service should be comparable; while as this distance increases, demand in the host country will probably abate.

8 A Study of EC Firms' Choice of Entry Mode into the Chinese Market: Licensing or Joint Ventures?

Wei-Ping Wu

INTRODUCTION

Since 1978, China has embarked on an 'open door' policy in order to develop its national economy, having been hampered by ideological considerations for many years. At the same time, Western firms have shown great interest in securing a profitable share of what is potentially the world's largest consumer market (of over one billion people). As a result, the trade and economic relations between China and Western countries have been greatly enhanced during the past decade.

Since the law on Chinese–Foreign Joint Ventures was promulgated in June 1979, the scale of foreign direct investment (FDI) has expanded considerably. This surge of foreign investment shows no sign of diminishing. Of the US$98.83 billion external capital utilised by China in the period 1979–1992, FDI amounted to US$38.18 billion (Qing, 1993). The EC has become one of the largest trading partners of China. In 1993, China's ten largest trading partners were, in order of trade values: Japan, Hong Kong, the USA, the EC, Taiwan, South Korea, Russia, Singapore, Australia and Canada.[1] However, though EC firms have been actively investing in China, they are well behind the other major foreign investors. In 1992, Hong Kong came on top of the list with US$7.7 billion, followed by Taiwan (US$1.05 billion), Japan (US$0.75 billion), the USA (US$0.52 billion) and the EC (US$0.25 billion).[2] When the transfer of technology through non-affiliate licensing[3] agreements and the sale of industrial equipment is considered, however, in 1991 the EC (41.9 per cent) ranked first, with Japan (7.8 per cent) and the USA (3.9 per cent) trailing behind.[4]

While there has been considerable research on entry-mode choice theories (Hill, Hwang and Kim, 1990; Contractor, 1990; Rugman, 1985; Anderson and Gatignon, 1986), together with an ever growing amount of empirical research on entry-mode choice (Agarwal and Ramaswami, 1992; Kim and Hwang, 1992; Gatignon and Anderson, 1988; Kogut and Singh, 1988), little is yet known about the determinants of Western firms' entry-mode choice into the Chinese market, either conceptually (except Simyar and Argheyd, 1986, 1987) or empirically. Literature on business in China has been heavily focused on business negotiations with the Chinese (Stewart and Keown, 1989; Kirkbride and Tang, 1990; Tung, 1982) and on foreign investment in China (Schroath *et al.*, 1993; Shan, 1991; Kemp, 1987; Campbell and Adlington, 1988).

The specific objectives of this research are (i) to identify the determinants of EC firms' choice between licensing and joint ventures in order to understand why EC firms have been more active in transferring technology to, rather than investing, in China; and (ii) to examine how successfully existing theories can be applied to the understanding of entry modes into China's socialist market economy. Some managerial implications and recommendations will be provided for EC firms wishing to expand their business in China, and for those intending to enter the Chinese market for the first time.

THEORETICAL BACKGROUND AND HYPOTHESES

This study is of an eclectic nature, but some of the variables have been deliberately left out as too many factors in a model might render the results of a statistical analysis unintelligible. Ten major factors have been selected and turned into their respective constructs.

Cost Motives

Production costs and transaction costs have been regarded as two key factors in the entry-mode choice (Anderson and Gatignon, 1986; Walker and Weber, 1984). Countries with low labour costs and/or abundant natural resources tend to have an above average inward investment because of their locational attractions (Dunning, 1979). Daniels *et al.* (1985) found that China's natural resources, high transport costs and trade barriers were among the key motives for US firms investing in China through joint ventures. In another study, Lo (1989) discovered that lower costs (such as costs of land, labour, electricity, water and so forth) were the most important motive for using investment modes in China by firms based in Hong Kong. While the point of operation for both licensing and joint venture is the same, for the host country, the cost difference is obvious. The income generated from licensing, in the form of lump sums, profits on sales and so on, will be much lower than that from a joint venture which can enjoy the extra benefits available only to FDI. For example, the majority of the benefits, such as government incentives to FDI and cheap local labour costs, will only be enjoyed by firms investing directly in China.

Hypothesis H1 The greater the motives for investing directly in China, the more EC firms are likely to employ joint ventures as opposed to licensing.

Country Risk

Casson (1979) predicted that internalisation would be least where the host country is politically hostile. Agarwal and Ramaswami (1991) found that firms were more likely to choose high control modes in countries that are characterised by lower country risk. However, Robock (1971) contended that not all political changes alter the business environment of a country, and thus may not significantly affect the inflow of FDI. This argument has been supported by some research findings (Green and Cunningham, 1975; Kobrin, 1976) that political instability did not significantly influence FDI. The host-government regulations and policies on inward FDI will also have profound impact on entry-mode choice decisions. Nevertheless, recently, it has been revealed that firms faced with high host-country risk tended to avoid wholly-owned subsidiaries or joint ventures in pursuit of lower resource commitment mode-licensing (Kim and Hwang, 1992). For this research, it can be hypothesised that:

Hypothesis H2 EC firms which consider China as a high risk country are less likely to enter China through joint ventures.

Psychic Distance

Psychic distance has long been regarded as one of the major variables which determine entry-mode choice (Dunning, 1988b; Johanson and Vahlne, 1977; Davidson, 1980; Anderson and Gatignon, 1986 and Hill *et al.*, 1990). There are two conflicting views regarding the impact of psychic distance on entry-mode choice. The Uppsala Internationalisation Model represented by Johanson and Vahlne (1977) contends that the better the knowledge about a market, the more valuable are the resources and the stronger is the commitment to the market. Agarwal and Ramaswami (1991) found that firms were more likely to choose low control modes (minority or equal joint ventures rather than wholly-owned subsidiaries) in countries that are characterised by greater sociocultural distance from the United States. Others argue that internalisation can provide more complete cross-cultural adaptation (Williamson, 1981). The sociocultural distance will lead to a greater desire for ownership in order to impose a firm's own operating methods. In studying the mode of technology transfer, Davidson and McFetridge (1985) found that the probability of internal transfer was greater if there was a greater similarity of sociocultural backgrounds between the two countries. However, the conflicting views and findings can be explained if psychic distance is divided into two subgroups: (i) cultural distance; and (ii) political and economic distance.

When the political and economic distance is relatively large, firms will perceive potential social instability. Consequently, they are reluctant to commit significant resources under these circumstances. On the contrary, for large cultural distance, internalisation may provide more complete cross-cultural adaptation, as the cultural distance can be narrowed through firms' efforts and experience with the local market. Therefore, for this study, there can be two hypotheses concerning psychic distance:

Hypothesis H3a The larger the cultural distance between EC firms' home countries and China, the more likely they are to employ joint ventures instead of licensing.

H3b The larger the political and economic distance between EC firms' home countries and China, the less likely these firms are to employ joint ventures.

Firm Experience

The theoretical explanation for a positive relationship between experience and the degree of control, centres on uncertainty and on how firms cope with it. Less-experienced firms perceive considerable uncertainty, overstate risk and understate returns (Davidson, 1980). Consequently, they shy away from making significant resource commitments and from assuming control (Johanson and Vahlne, 1977). However, firms with increasing knowledge of foreign markets perceive less uncertainty, and become more confident of their ability to correctly estimate risk and returns and to manage foreign operations (Johanson and Vahlne, 1977; Davidson, 1980). As a result, they become more aggressive in committing resources and assuming control (Anderson and Gatignon, 1986). This argument has been empirically confirmed by Gatignon and Anderson (1988), Davidson (1980) and Caves and Mehra (1986).

Hypothesis H4 The greater the international experience and business experience of EC firms in China, the more they will employ joint ventures.

Firm Size

Theoretical papers by Mirus (1980) and Dunning (1979) suggest that smaller firms lacking the managerial and financial resources to make direct investments would be more likely to favour licensing. Large firms are in a better position to make asset-specific investment as firm size is a proxy for internal resources and advantages. Evidence has been found that firm size is highly correlated with a higher degree of control and resource commitment (Terpstra and Yu, 1988). However, some research findings have shown that there is neither a positive relationship between firm size and the degree of control (Anderson, 1985) nor a negative relationship (Agarwal and Ramaswami, 1991). For this particular study of the choice between licensing and joint ventures, it can be hypothesised that:

Hypothesis H5 The larger the firm size, the more likely that firms will employ joint ventures.

Type of Technology

When 'know-how' is of a tacit nature, it is very difficult to transfer it through the contractual mode (Williamson, 1981; Kogut, 1988), because the very knowledge being transferred is organisationally and personally embedded. In the case of licensing, the inability to transfer tacit know-how and informal routines via an arm's-length licensing contract suggests that a licensee may not be able to generate the quasi-rents that the firm could get if it sets up a subsidiary in the host country. High control entry modes give multinational corporations (MNCs) an enhanced ability to structure the exchange relationship, so that tacit know-how and informal routines are transferred intact to the host market. Davies (1977) found that while 60 per cent of the licensing agreements only transferred designs, specifications and drawings, joint ventures were used to transfer a much wider range of know-how, including tacit know-how. Thus:

Hypothesis H6 When know-how is of tacit nature, it is more likely to be transferred through joint ventures.

Transaction Complexity

Transaction cost theory and internalisation theory predict that the complexity of transactions makes contracting options extremely costly (Williamson, 1979, 1985; Teece, 1981, 1986; Hennart, 1982, 1986; Buckley and Casson, 1976; Casson, 1979; Rugman, 1981, 1986; Anderson and Gatignon, 1986). When the technologies to be transferred are unstructured and poorly understood, firms are less likely to transfer these through the contracting mode (Anderson and Gatignon, 1986). The positive relationship between transaction complexity and control has been confirmed by several empirical studies (Wilson, 1980; Gatignon and Anderson, 1988).

Hypothesis H7 The greater the transaction complexity, the greater the likelihood that firms will employ joint ventures.

Transaction Uncertainty

When two firms engage in business, there obtains a small-numbers condition which tends to enhance the possibility of opportunistic behaviour and costly haggling, since it is in the interest of each party to seek terms most favourable to them. Drawing on Williamson (1975), Teece (1981) argued that because contracts cannot be complete, uncertainty implies the existence of a large number of possible contingencies. For example, contractual breach may often be difficult to prove to the appointed third-party enforcer. In order to solve these problems and reduce transaction costs, Williamson (1975) advocated that opportunism and the small-numbers problem could be best dealt with in a hierarchy which permits interdependent units to adapt to unforeseen contingencies in a coordinated way, and in addition serves to 'absorb' uncertainty. Opportunism and the small-numbers problem can be curbed through organisational hierarchy by permitting additional incentive and control techniques to be brought to bear in a more selective manner. It has been discovered that US firms tended to invest in China through joint ventures rather than employ licensing because of China's past failure to join international patent and trademark agreements (Daniels *et al.*, 1985).

Hypothesis H8 The higher the transaction uncertainty, the more likely it is that firms will favour joint ventures.

Marketing Strategies

Standardised technology reduces transaction complexity and uncertainty in the process of technology transfer, which leads to lower transaction costs. When the transaction cost is low, an entry mode offering a lower degree of control is more likely to be employed by firms. When firms pursue a diversified marketing strategy, asset-specificity increases. As a result, a high control mode might be preferred to reduce transaction uncertainty.

Hypothesis H9 Firms employing a marketing mix with standardised elements are more likely to use licensing.

Servicing Policy

In the literature on entry-mode choice, a neglected issue has been whether or not a company's international market servicing base policy has an effect on the decision on entry-mode choice. Dunning (1988b) argued that a firm might choose not to become a MNC. Some firms, although they have all the sufficient conditions to produce abroad, might prefer to do so in their own country rather than to face all the additional risks and costs of operating abroad. Moreover, some might not be in a position to manage a manufacturing

Table 8.1 Summary of hypotheses: joint ventures versus licensing

Hypothesis		*Variables*	*Expected sign* of coefficient*
H1		Motives	+
H2		Country risk	–
H3		Psychic distance	
	H3a	Cultural distance	+
	H3b	Political and economic distance	–
H4		Firm's experience	+
H5		Firm size	+
H6		Type of technology	
	H6a	Tacit know-how	+
	H6b	Non-tacit know-how	–
H7		Transaction complexity	+
H8		Transaction uncertainty	+
H9		Standardisation	–
H10		Servicing policy	–

Note: *the movement from licensing to joint venture represents an increase in both resource commitment and in control
+ve coefficient indicates a likely move from licensing to joint venture, -ve coefficient the reverse

operation overseas due to the lack of expertise and personnel. There might be cases in which firms feel that it is adequate for them to service the international market through licensing because of limited market share. Thus it can be hypothesised that:

Hypothesis H10 The more that firms service international markets from a home base, the less likely it is that they will use joint ventures.

Table 8.1 presents a summary of all the above hypotheses, a brief description of the variables used, and the expected signs for each coefficient.

METHODOLOGY

The Sample

The sample for this research was drawn based on six steps suggested by Churchill (1991). The population for this study comprises EC firms doing business in China, as the theme of the research is to understand the entry-mode choice of EC firms into the Chinese market. However, it was very difficult to get hold of a detailed and accurate list of firms from which the actual sample could be drawn, as there was no published directory on EC firms doing business in China. Nevertheless, a comprehensive list containing more than one thousand firms was finally obtained by combining the lists given by the Commercial Consulate of EC member states' embassies in China, by the China Desk of the Department of Trade and Industry (UK), the European Federation of Management Development and by selecting from the Dictionary of Foreign, Hong Kong and Macao Resident Offices in China.

A simple random sampling method was used to obtain the sample. Three-hundred manufacturing firms from eight EC countries were chosen for contacts. There were no firms chosen from Greece, Ireland, Luxembourg and Portugal because they had either very few or no firms operating in China at the time. Only firms in the manufacturing sector were chosen because the service sector has a quite different set of factors affecting the decision on the choice of entry mode into a foreign market (Erramilli and Rao, 1990). To ensure that all respondents were upper-level managers, managing directors at the head office in the EC were selected as the receivers of the questionnaires. To guarantee the accuracy of the information, it was stressed in the covering letter that the questionnaire should be filled in by managers who were involved in entry-mode decisions on business in China. The data was collected in the early part of 1991.

The Instrument

A questionnaire was chosen as the best research instrument because it was the only method able to reach respondents effectively as they are scattered around the EC. It is an inexpensive method as personal interviews and telephone methods would have made research on this scale impossible. A pretest was conducted by sending questionnaires to several companies to check whether there were any problems such as ambiguity of statements or improper wording. Several questions were later revised as a result of the exercise. The questionnaire was written in English, and all respondents received this English version. The reason why no translation was made is that there is strong evidence that senior managers in EC MNCs can understand English without any difficulty, and the fear that translators may misinterpret the meanings of questions, posing problems later on during the data analysis.

Finally, a questionnaire of more than 200 items was sent to general managers at EC firms' headquarters in Europe, together with a covering letter. The letter was designed to contain most of the necessary elements suggested by Churchill (1991). It stressed the importance of the study to the general society, to the respondent firm and to the researcher. Anonymity and confidentiality were emphasised.

A total of 75 usable questionnaires were obtained with an overall response rate of 25 per cent, which is quite acceptable considering that eight countries have been covered. It is widely accepted and confirmed that the response rate is usually much lower in cross-border mail surveys than in domestic surveys (Jobber and Saunders, 1988). Of 75 firms, 21 were from the UK, 20 from Germany, 16 from Belgium, nine from France, six from Italy, two from the Netherlands and one from Denmark.

Operational Measures

A literature review and pre-study interviews with company executives and British government officials in charge of China business were instrumental in designing the operational measures for the study. Some of the items were measured through multiple choice. Most of the dimensions identified in the model are continuous variables measured by a 5-point Likert-type scale ranging from '1' (strongly disagree) to '5' (strongly agree). Each construct consists of more than five items, although two constructs were reduced to two items because of the initial low-construct alpha. The multi-items method has been suggested to yield a stronger hypothesis-testing and to reduce reliance on single-item measures of complex constructs (Nunnally, 1978; Anderson and Gatignon, 1986).

RESULTS

Measure Purification

In order to have reliable analysis of the data, measures should be purified. According to Churchill (1979), in the multi-item measurement, if all the items in a measure are drawn from the domain of a single construct, responses to these questions should be highly intercorrelated. Low inter-item correlations, in contrast, indicate that some items are not drawn from the appropriate domain, and are producing error and low reliability.

Cronbach coefficient alpha was used to carry out the task of purifying the measures. As suggested by Churchill, coefficient alpha should be the first measure one calculates to assess the quality of the instrument. Coefficient alpha was also regarded by Nunnally (1978) as the basic formula for determining the degree of reliability based on internal consistency. The statistical package SPSSPC was used to conduct this task, as it can provide the item-to-total correlations and the other necessary data which can help improve the measures. Nunnally pointed out that in the early stages of basic research, a reliability of 0.50 to 0.60 was sufficient. Because this research may be the first of its kind in respect of EC firms' entry-mode choice into the Chinese market, a coefficient alpha of 0.60 was chosen as the target for improving the measure if required.

Nine constructs out of twelve had finally obtained an alpha higher than 0.60 with three slightly lower than the target, but all higher than 0.50. The resulting constructs were confirmed by factor analysis. This indicates that the remaining items are relatively reliable for further analysis and hypothesis testing.

Findings

Although multiple regression can give predicted values, these cannot be interpreted as probabilities. Logistic regression models are particularly appropriate when (a) the dependent variable is binary, (b) independent variables are qualitative or quantitative, and (c) underlying assumptions of multivariate normality cannot be met.

For the binary dependent variable (licensing and joint venture), the probability of EC firms choosing joint venture is modelled as follows:

$$P(Joint\ venture = 1) = 1/\{1+e^{-y}\}$$

Where: $y=f$ (motives, firm's experience, firm size, cultural distance, economic distance, non-tacit know-how, tacit know-how, servicing policy, marketing strategies, country risk, transaction complexity and uncertainty)

In order to check for any problems of multicollinearity, a correlation analysis was conducted for the sample. No significant problems were detected except for one pair of variables: *tacit know-how* and *firm size*. A backward method was used to eliminate variables with the largest probability of F value for those with a value larger than 0.1. A full model was obtained in the first instance. Following that, all the variables that showed no significance were dropped at the later stages. Four shorter versions of the model resulted, in which each coefficient was significant (see Table 8.2).

For this binary model, licensing is coded as 0 and joint venture as 1. The results of the logistic regressions are reported in Table 8.2. After the collinearity problem was controlled for the pair (*tacit know-how* and *firm size*), it was revealed (Model 1 and Model 2) that both factors obtained a significant coefficient without the presence of the other. When these two variables were present in the same model (Model 4), only *tacit know-how* had a significant coefficient. All models have a relatively high classification rate, indicating that models obtained from the logistic regressions are robust.

Country risk has been found to have no significant effect on the choice between licensing and joint venture, and the same is found for *cultural distance*. Hypotheses 4 (Model 1 and 4) and 8 (Model 3) were rejected. However, all the other hypotheses have been confirmed and supported. Four models (Models 1, 2, 3 and the Full Model) all indicate that when *economic and political distance* is large, firms are likely to use licensing rather than committing higher resources (joint ventures) in China. Hypothesis 9 has also been confirmed here (Models 1, 2, and 3). Support is also found for the argument that *non-tacit know-how* is less likely to be transferred internally (Model 1). The *motive* variable has a significant and positive coefficient, indicating that as the motives to produce in China become stronger, the probability of using a high control mode increases.

The negative sign and significant coefficient of (home base) *servicing policy*

Table 8.2 Results of logistic regressions for the choice between licensing and joint ventures

Variable hypothesis	*Model 1*	*Model 2*	*Model 3*	*Model 4*	*Full model*
H3b	−1.698[a]	−2.936[c]	−2.108[b]	*	−3.021[b]
H7	1.336[a]	1.137[a]	*	1.305[a]	2.325[a]
H9	−1.581[a]	−1.158[a]	−1.173[b]	−.895	−1.327
H6b	*	−1.559[b]	*	*	−1.633
H1	*	1.156[a]	*	*	.837
H8	*	*	−0.879[a]	*	−.702
H10	−0.766	*	*	−.973[a]	−.457
H6a	1.299[a]	*	*	1.127[a]	.596
H5	*	0.720[a]	*	.641	.967
H4	−1.926[b]	*	*	−1.998[b]	−1.787
H2	*	*	*	*	.421
H3a	−1.603	*	*	−1.657	−1.026
Constant	18.976[b]	12.822[b]	16.100[c]	8.004	19.709[a]
Model statistics:					
X^2 (df)	22.071[c]	(7) 21.899	(6) 13.325	(3) 19.488	(7) 26.977[c](12)
-2 log likelihood	34.548	33.738	45.703	33.935	26.446
Goodness of fit	30.447	37.262	38.287	30.651	27.022
Overall classification	75.61%	82.93%	69.77%	79.49%	87.18%

Notes:
[a] denotes significance at $p<0.10$, $N=50$
[b] denotes significance at $p<0.05$, $N=50$
[c] denotes significance at $p<0.01$, $N=50$

show that firms employing this policy are less likely to use an entry mode involving high resource commitments. Not surprisingly, the results (Model 2) support the contention that larger firms are more likely to commit resources than smaller firms.

DISCUSSION

The results obtained provide support for most of the fundamental predictions of the existing theories. Significant findings have been obtained for the variables that reflect the level of motives to invest in the Chinese market. These indicate why joint ventures have been the preferred mode for EC firms investing in China.

The finding that licensing is preferred to joint ventures under the condition of high transaction uncertainty cannot be justified by the control criteria. They predict that joint ventures should be favoured over licensing when *transaction uncertainty* is high. However, the finding can be explained very well by resource commitment criteria. It is reasonable to argue that when transaction uncertainty is high, in order to reduce the risks involved firms prefer low resource commitment modes (licensing) to joint ventures.

The results on *transaction complexity*, another internalisation variable, seem to confirm the expectations of transaction cost and internalisation theories. They support the findings reported by Davidson and McFetridge (1985) among others, suggesting that the desire to control the risk involved in a complex transaction is a prime driving force in entry-mode choice.

The prediction of transaction cost theories that *tacit know-how* should be linked with internalisation and *non-tacit know-how* with externalisation was also confirmed. This is in line with the findings of Davies (1977), among others, that joint ventures are used to transfer a much wider range of know-how, including tacit know-how, than the contractual mode.

The non-significance of *cultural distance* for the choice between licensing and joint venture needs some careful explanation. Although it has been found that there were relationships between degree of control and cultural distance (Agarwal and Ramaswami, 1991; Kogut and Singh, 1988), several major differences exist between the earlier researches and this study. A plausible explanation is that the target market is different. In Agarwal and Ramaswami's case, their sample is that of United States-based firms entering into various target markets around the world. As for this study, the sample is EC firms entering the same target market, China. Therefore, whether it is a licensing or an investing firm, their perception of cultural distance between their home countries and China would probably not be as great as the case in Agarwal and Ramaswami's study. As a result, cultural distance here fails to show any effects on the choice of entry mode. Another possible interpretation is that because the output of both licensing and joint ventures of those firms are directed towards the home and other developed countries or neighbouring countries of China, the cultural distance tended to have much less effect on the choice between licensing and joint ventures.

Nevertheless, the effects of *political and economic distance* on the entry mode have revealed a quite different story. Firms which perceived that there was a great political and economic distance between China and their home countries were found to be reluctant to commit resources in China. Political and economic systems are the major base for social turmoil and uprising which can adversely affect the outcome of business operations. The interesting new finding from this research is that the cultural distance and political and economic distance should be treated differently and not as a single variable as in previous research, for instance, Hwang (1988).

It was surprising to find that *country risk* had no significant influence on the choice between licensing and joint ventures. The possible explanation here is that where entry took place several years before responding to this questionnaire, the respondents might well be expressing their experience of country risk in China after their firms had entered the market. Another possible explanation is that for both modes the operational location is in China; therefore, the country risk they encountered might be more or less the same.

The semi-standardised marketing mix variable lends great support to the hypothesis. Licensing is more suitable for *standardisation* than joint ventures. One explanation is that it would not be feasible to use a semi-standardisation marketing mix in a joint venture, as the local partner may object to certain policies and may propose its own marketing ideas. Licensing firms are in a better position to employ an independent marketing strategy.

Another variable (*servicing policy*) influencing entry-mode choice also offers substantial support for the hypothesis that the more that firms service international markets from their home base, the less likely are they to commit higher resources. Dunning (1988a) stressed that there should be a will to do so, otherwise, international production will not occur. Therefore, firms employing a home-based servicing policy are less likely to engage in foreign production. The probable outcome of this policy is licensing rather than joint ventures. The significance of this finding is that entry-mode choice is not only determined by the external environment and internal environment in respect of resource constraints, but also intentionally by the management who may quite simply not like the idea of investing in another country. This is one of the reasons why some firms have expanded across borders and become MNCs, and why others remain local and small. The result also supports the concept put forward by Buckley (1993) that the management play a significant role in the internalisation efforts of firms.

Our findings on *firm size* confirm the theoretical argument that larger firms seem to be more capable of absorbing the cost and risk involved, and to possess more advantages to offset the disadvantageous positions (Buckley and Casson, 1976). Larger firms may perceive the potential risks in the Chinese market to be lower than smaller firms. They are also in a better position to cope with any unforeseen uncertainty because they have access to natural resources, finance, information on favoured terms and, most importantly of all, stronger lobbying power.

A surprising and interesting finding of the study is that EC firms' multinational and China-specific *experience* are inversely related to the degree of resource commitments, suggesting the less experienced firms are more likely to enter China through joint ventures. A possible explanation may be that less experienced firms are more likely to feel vulnerable in doing business in China; therefore, by linking with local firms, they can reduce some risks and obtain the necessary local knowledge, such as distribution channels and access to the right decision makers. Joint ventures can reduce the political risk for these firms through having joint ownership with local firms (Vernon, 1983).

MANAGERIAL IMPLICATIONS AND RECOMMENDATIONS

The results have strong managerial implications for EC firms which have entered and want to expand in the Chinese market, as well as for those who are intending to do so in the near future. China will be a great potential market for those firms wanting to use China as a manufacturing base for re-export by taking advantage of the cheap labour and land costs, raw materials and government incentives. With a decade of development, the infrastructure has been greatly improved. For example, China's largest suspension bridge, the Nanpu bridge in Shanghai, opened to traffic on 19 November 1991.[5] It can be expected that these developments will continue as long as China's open-door policy is adhered to. There were very good signs of this from the latest 14th Chinese Communist Party Congress. A new term 'socialist market economy' has been used frequently in the Chinese media recently (*Beijing Review*, 1992). Therefore, FDI may become increasingly suitable for those firms interested in cheap labour and land, with the added attraction of improved infrastructures within the Chinese market.

The negative relationship between resource commitments and transaction uncertainty implies that the entry mode of higher resource commitments should become the more commonly chosen mode for the Chinese market as the transaction uncertainty falls. In mid-January 1992, the United States and China reached an agreement on intellectual property rights. In the Memorandum of Understanding, the Chinese government agreed to join two international copyright conventions within the next 18 months. It also agreed to take necessary steps over the next two years to enact new laws and regulations that will expand the scope of protection for foreign firms' intellectual property. Progress in both legislation and enforcement has been steady and further improvements are clearly in the offing. Therefore, higher resource commitment modes such as joint ventures are expected to be used more frequently, with further improvements on legislation on the protection of intellectual property rights.

In terms of transaction complexity, one can expect that when know-how transferred to China becomes more and more complicated, entry modes with a higher degree of control will be preferred by most EC firms. The implication is that EC firms which are transferring complicated know-how to China should use the entry modes offering high control, for example joint ventures, in order to reduce transaction costs. In order to attract foreign advanced technologies, China has committed itself to further expanding its foreign investment fields, and has emphasised energy sources, transportation, communications, agriculture, forestry, water conservancy projects, production of major raw materials and environmental protection (Niu, 1992). Therefore, it is reasonable to expect that EC firms will transfer more sophisticated technologies to China, and transactions will become more complex. It follows that firms would be advised to use entry modes of higher control.

The implications of the results on tacit and non-tacit know-how are not fully clear. However, EC firms should employ entry modes of high control when transferring tacit know-how. When management skills are involved in the transfer, an internalised investment mode such as joint ventures and wholly-owned subsidiaries would be suitable for such a transfer. Therefore, it can be expected that, increasingly, joint ventures and wholly-owned subsidiaries will be established in China by foreign investors when there is a strong need to transfer such tacit know-how (particularly when factors such as political risk become somewhat less prominent in EC firms' decisions to invest in China). Some recent data bear witness to such a trend. During the first nine months of 1992, of new foreign investment projects roughly 19 000 were joint ventures, while over 3400 were cooperative ventures and 5200 were solely foreign-funded (Qu, 1992).

With the deepening of China's economic reforms, the political and economic distance from the EC will be narrowed. Consequently, EC firms are expected to commit greater resources. Therefore, it can be expected that FDI will be more frequently used in the Chinese market.

The implication of the finding that semi-standardisation is closely linked with low control/resource commitments is a significant one for EC firms. Those EC firms with standardised products or other standardised elements in their marketing mix, should consider using low resource commitment modes as part of their entry strategy into the Chinese market. This may not only save a great deal of money, but also provide a quicker method of entering the market. Another implication here is that EC firms employing a global strategy should be quite careful in using joint ventures as an entry mode. Local partners might object to the plans of the foreign partner to treat the local venture as part of their global strategy, which might be contrary to the interests of the local partners.

Of course, any EC firms which are employing home-based servicing policy are expected to prefer entry modes such as licensing rather than joint ventures or wholly-owned subsidiaries. The latter require higher resource commitments, such as expatriates, to manage the local venture and regional offices to monitor, instruct and coordinate the branches' or subsidiaries' business operations. Therefore, any firms which do not have such resources, or who are not well prepared, should avoid using high resource commitment modes in entering the Chinese market.

The positive relationship between firm size and resource commitments implies that increasingly larger firms will enter China through high resource commitment modes. Fierce competition by large multinational firms in the Chinese market can be expected. Therefore, it is advisable for many larger EC firms who are already in the Chinese market to strengthen their competitive advantage by expanding through high resource commitment modes. Volkswagen (VW) produces cars both in Shanghai and in the north-eastern city of Changchun. It is also considering another sedan manufacturing joint venture in China because the country is thought important in Volkswagen's overall overseas strategy (Chang, 1992).

The negative relationship between EC firms' international experience and China-specific experience and resource commitments raises a very interesting question. The finding that firms with earlier business experience in China failed to commit higher resources than less experienced firms implies that a firm's experience might not help it to commit higher resources. The possible resolution of this question is that it may depend on what kind of experience the firms actually had. In 1949, the Communists took power from the Nationalists and expropriated and nationalised all foreign assets. Firms which had this kind of experience might well be cautious in re-entering the market. It is, therefore, logical to expect that as the number of firms with experience of success in the Chinese market grows, more EC firms will commit higher resources. The above-mentioned case of VW is proof of this.

On the whole, it is recommended that Western firms, especially EC firms, should take advantage of direct investment modes to enter, expand and prosper in the Chinese market. Many firms are already doing so. For example, in 1991 China became the second largest recipient of inflows of FDI among all the developing countries. There are signs that this trend will continue: contracted investment in China during the first half of 1992 was about US$15 billion, compared to US$12 billion in the whole of 1991 (UNCTAD, 1993). In the first nine months of 1993, the Beijing government approved 62 789 projects involving foreign participation, with a contracted value of more than US$83 billion (Nicoll, 1993).

CONCLUSIONS

This study has provided an in-depth account of the determinants of EC firms' entry-mode choice between licensing and joint ventures. As the first study of this kind, the findings are especially significant. It has been found that existing theories can be successfully applied to explain EC firms' entry into the Chinese market. Most of the hypotheses have been confirmed. Cost motives were found to have a strong positive relationship with the entry mode of high resource commitment. The findings have confirmed the common belief that foreign firms have been lured into China because of her cheaper labour. Most of the findings point to the conclusion that internalisation is the key factor which affected EC firms' decisions to enter China through joint ventures. Therefore, with the further improvements of the investment environment in China, the stronger the need for EC firms to internalise, the more they will use high control and resource commitment modes such as joint ventures and wholly-owned subsidiaries to enter, expand and develop in the Chinese market. Evidence has shown that more and more firms are now investing either through joint ventures or wholly-owned subsidiaries in China (Qu, 1992). The findings have other wider implications. For example, these findings will be of high referential value to EC firms who intend to do business in the East European countries which, to a certain extent, are similar to the Chinese market. In particular, both them are moving away from a central planning economy to a market economy.

Inevitably, there are some limitations to this study. Because of the restricted number of EC firms which have entered the Chinese market, longitudinal research, while preferable, was not possible and, consequently, this research was obliged to be cross-sectional in nature. Another major inherent limitation of the study is the total reliance on the respondents' memories and personal opinions. Although this technique has been used widely and has often proved accurate, there are still problems, such as those of inaccurate responses and omissions. It is true that managing directors are the appropriate source for information, but the decision on entry mode is usually made by a group of people. Furthermore, as the target market is a single country, some variables which would have been more powerful had lost their vigour. For example, the 'cultural distance' variable would have been more potent if the target market had not been a single country but several dozen across the world.

In future research, an improved but similar approach is needed for the Chinese market. This research did not include wholly-owned subsidiaries owing to the fact that there were very few wholly-owned subsidiaries of EC firms operating in China at the time of the research. Otherwise, more meaningful comparisons could have been made. Another inherent drawback is the research method employed. Ideally, both a questionnaire and several in-depth case studies are needed at the same time. A combined method would be useful in deciphering some seemingly surprising findings. The preferred research method is an industry-based, longitudinal research approach. As this research is cross-sectional and for a single point in time, some of the issues may have not been well represented as firms from different industries may perceive existing variables in a very different way. The longitudinal approach is especially important for understanding variables such as a firm's international experience and country-specific experience. Finally, future research should include other major Western players in the Chinese market. A meaningful comparison between foreign operations from different source countries may well be the most promising way to discover the applicability of existing theories. To further test the applicability of the theories, Western firms doing business in East European countries should be the next target for such a task.

Notes

1. It was reported in the overseas edition of *People's Daily*, Beijing, China, 1 October 1993, p. 1.
2. The figures have been compiled by the author from the *Almanac of China's Statistics*, published by China Statistics Publisher, Beijing, 1993.
3. Non-affiliate licensing, hereafter, will be referred to as licensing.
4. The figures were collected by the author from the *Almanac of China's Economy 1992*, published by Jingji Guanli Publishers 1992.
5. This information was reported in various issues of the *China–Britain Trade Review*, 1992.

9 International Joint Ventures in China from a Managerial Perspective: A Comparison between Different Sources of Investment

Haochun Dong, Peter J. Buckley and Hafiz Mirza

INTRODUCTION

Since its adoption of an 'open door' policy in 1978, the People's Republic of China (PRC) has attracted increasing attention in the global economy. Its record of attracting foreign direct investment (FDI) is particularly impressive. As of the end of September 1994, more than 210 000 foreign-funded ventures were approved with pledged investment of US$275 billion. The actual investment to date is around US$85 billion (*Financial Times*, 1994).

As far as the origin of the investment is concerned, Hong Kong and Macao together account for the largest source of FDI, followed by the US, Japan and European countries. Equity joint ventures (EJVs) follow the same pattern (*Financial Times*, 1994). It is believed that many investors from Hong Kong and Macao are overseas Chinese, although accurate information is not available. In addition, overseas Chinese investment has come from many other parts of the world, notably from Singapore and most recently from Taiwan. Clearly, overseas Chinese investors have become a very important force in China's path to modernisation (*Economist*, 1992a).

In their pursuit of joint-venture (JV) opportunities in the Chinese market, foreign investors including the overseas Chinese have encountered various challenges at every stage of the venture arrangement, from venture negotiation and creation to its implementation and operation. Many problems arise because of differences in cultural, economic and business practice. The rapid transition of the economic and political system, which in turn brings enormous risks and uncertainty, compounds the complexity of doing business in China. Within a joint venture both the foreign and local partners are on a learning curve.

Multinational companies (MNCs) have rushed to China for many reasons, and investment strategies may vary from one firm to another. What are their intentions? How do they value the resources brought by their partner to the venture? How are the ventures managed? How well have the ventures performed and how do these MNCs evaluate this performance compared to their local partners? This study attempts to investigate these questions and issucs.

LITERATURE REVIEW AND THEORETICAL BACKGROUND

An increase in joint-venture activity is a major trend in the international business environment, and JVs are now a popular means of foreign market entry for MNCs. There is a body of literature addressing the theoretical aspects of this type of FDI arrangement (Beamish and Banks, 1987; Buckley and Casson, 1976, 1988; Caves, 1982; Dunning, 1980; Hennart, 1988; Kogut, 1988; Rugman, 1981) and EJV characteristics (Beamish, 1988; Geringer and Hebert, 1989; Harrigan, 1985; Killing, 1983; Lyles, 1988; Schaan, 1985; Shan, 1991).

The economic theory of joint ventures as expressed by Buckley and Casson (1988) suggests that there are three segments in the decision to set up a JV:

1. JVs are preferred to arm's-length trade because of the net benefits of internalising a market in one or more intermediate goods and services flowing between the joint venture and the parties' other operations.
2. Indivisibilities may make it economic for each firm to own part of a joint venture rather than the whole of another facility.
3. Net disadvantages to full merger exist, arising from managerial diseconomies, legal obstacles or constraints related to imperfections in financial markets.

Alternative and supplementary explanations arise from strategic motivations and competitive behaviour (Harrigan, 1988) or from organisational knowledge and learning (Kogut, 1988), including bandwagon behaviour (Knickerbocker, 1973; Dimaggio and Powell, 1983).

As Parker (1983) points out, the analysis of joint ventures leads into areas of analysis which are 'messy' or relatively intractable with conventional tools. It is often necessary to involve concepts such as forbearance, trust, reciprocity, relationships and cooperation. Many of these concepts are linked to cultural differences and distance between partners. This chapter sheds light on the impact of these concepts, in particular by including Overseas Chinese as JV partners, thereby permitting a contrast to be drawn with European, North American and Japanese investors.

There are more motives for entering a joint venture than there are separate investment decisions. The major advantages of EJVs are: they improve a firm's strategic position in a competitive market-place because a local partner can provide it with established environment relations (Awadzi, 1987; Kogut, 1988; Porter and Fuller, 1986); they 'block competition' by turning potential competitors into allies (Bernstein, 1965; Contractor and Lorange, 1988; Hennart, 1988); they provide horizontal or vertical integration opportunities for parents (Harrigan, 1985; Williamson, 1975); they permit the sharing of a firm's stock of knowledge (Berg, Duncan and Friedman, 1982; Lyles, 1988; Roberts, 1980); they help overcome host-government regulations (Beamish, 1985, 1988; Harrigan, 1988; UNCTC, 1987); they reduce transaction costs (Beamish and Banks, 1985; Buckley and Casson, 1985; Hennart, 1989), and they reduce financial risk.

Despite the growing popularity of the JV, it is not without complications and these create distinct disadvantages if they are overlooked or ignored (Roulac, 1983). Many studies have indicated a high rate of mortality of JVs (Beamish, 1985; Curhan, Davidson and Suri, 1977; Franko, 1971; Harrigan 1986; Janger, 1980; Killing, 1983; Kogut, 1986). The main contributors to the problems include, the incompatibility of partners (Beamish, 1988; Geringer, 1988a, 1988b; Killing, 1983); an uneven level of commitment or incongruence of goals (Anderson, 1990; Berg, Duncan, and Friedman, 1982; Harrigan, 1985; Roulac, 1983); an inappropriate division of control between partners or an imbalance of benefits (Geringer, 1989, 1990; Killing, 1983; Schaan, 1985); and poor cooperation between partners (Awadzi, 1987; Beamish, 1988; Buckley and Casson, 1988).

Research on foreign direct investments in China, in particular those involving EJVs, has been distinguished by numerous reports in both academic publications and the business press. The main areas of attention are related to the attractiveness of the market and cheap resources (Ho and Huenemann, 1984; Punnett and Yu, 1990; Shaw and Woetzel, 1992; and Wang, 1986); JV strategies including ownership and partner selection (Beamish, 1988; Campbell, 1988, 1989; Casson and Zheng, 1992; UNCTC, 1988); JV management and operating issues such as control and cooperation (Boisot and Child, 1990; Davidson, 1987; Rondinelli, 1993; Shenkar, 1990; Woodward and Liu, 1993; Zamet and Bovarnick, 1986); cultural differences (Holton, 1990; Tung, 1986; Wall, 1990); and differences in business practice (Campbell, 1987; Daniels, Krug and Nigh, 1985; Grow, 1986; Keonderman, 1990; Lee and Lo, 1988; Pye, 1982; Weiss and Bloom, 1990). Some of the literature focusing on cross-cultural cooperation examines JVs in terms of particular ownership groups (Lane and Beamish, 1990; National Council, 1987; Von Glinow and Teagarden, 1988; Baird, Lyles, Ji and Wharton, 1990; Baird Lyles and Wharton, 1990; Grow, 1990). However, research on Japanese, European and, especially, Overseas Chinese investors as JV partners in China has been less frequent than analyses of North American JV partnerships.

A successful joint venture is often described as one with a stable and healthy interpartner relationship, rather than one which is simply profitable. The relationship is based on cooperation and a two-way communication which meets the needs of both partners over the long term. 'Success is a mutual condition, not "a one-sided one"' (Lane and Beamish, 1990). The joint-venture arrangement is a process of learning and involves continuously improving cooperation and a fair sharing of benefits. It is, therefore, important for academics to choose or construct an appropriate methodology to obtain accurate and unbiased data, so as to be able to draw a balanced picture and reach appropriate conclusions (Adler, Campbell and Laurent, 1989; Baird, Lyles and Wharton, 1990). This study emphasises these aspects and investigates JV characteristics from three different perspectives:

1. The country/regional perspective, discriminating between different sources of investment;
2. The managerial perspective of both foreign and local partners;
3. The strategic management perspective.

DATA COLLECTION AND METHODOLOGY

Data Collection

Because of the large number and geographical dispersion of JVs in China, it is very difficult, if not impossible, to select a sample covering all the major sectors and locations. This research focuses on JVs:

- In manufacturing industries;
- Formed during 1985–1987;
- With foreign participants from North America, West Europe, Japan and Overseas Chinese;
- Located in three major areas – the South (Guangdong and Fujian provinces), the East (Shanghai, Jiangsu and Zhejian provinces) and the North (Beijing and Tianjin), since these three areas have played a leading role in attracting FDI.

Primary data collection was conducted in 1991 and 1992 so that all the ventures in the sample had had at least three years of operation. To obtain a listing of such JVs, a number of secondary sources were used, including the *China Investment Guide*, the *Almanac of China's Foreign Economic Relations and Trade*, and various government reports and publications. Although there were overlaps between these sources, no two sources provided exactly the same listings. The exact size of the target population is, therefore, uncertain. From these sources, 328 firms were randomly selected from a list of 1312. Two specially designed questionnaires were sent to both foreign and local partners of each JV. After three rounds, including follow-ups, 114 JVs were included in the final sample. In addition to a mail survey, interviews were conducted with 36 JVs at a later stage and with 20 government officials to (a) confirm responses and (b) explore some issues in more detail.

The Operationalisation of Variables

Except for general profile variables such as the investment amount, foreign equity, JV duration and location, the variables of JV characteristics are divided into three broad groups corresponding to the establishment, management and performance of JVs. The first group includes motivations underlying JV formation and partner selection. Each partner was asked to rate the importance of all factors in their decision to invest in China and in selecting partners, on a 5-point Likert-type scale with 1 being 'not important at all' and 5 'crucially important'.

The second group was used to examine the control of the JV, exercised by both parents and JV management over a number of decision areas, and the perceptions of conflict arising in these areas. The same 5-point Likert-type scale was used to measure the control with 1 indicating 'local completely dominant', 3 'shared' and 5 'foreign completely dominant'. To measure the conflict, the respondent was asked to give his/her rate on the frequency of disagreement arising over each decision-making area with 1 indicating 'never' and 5 'very often'.

The third group of variables assessed the JV performance using multiple measures which were derived from Awadzi (1987); that is, in terms of:

- Profitability
- Growth
- Comparison with competitors
- Overall satisfaction.

The scores were coded on a 5-point scale with 1 indicating 'very disappointed' and 5 indicating 'very satisfactory'. Perceptual measures rather than financial measures were chosen because of the unavailability of objective financial information, the dispersion of business lines, and a wide spectrum of investment objectives. However, early studies (Beamish, 1988; Geringer and Hebert, 1991) show that there are significant positive correlations between objective financial and subjective measures; and a significant positive correlation between evaluations by JV general managers and parent companies of JV performance.

Data Analysis Techniques Employed

To find the differences and similarities of managerial perceptions on JV characteristics (that is, the three mentioned groups of variables) for each investment group, three types of comparisons were designed:

1. a comparison between overseas Chinese-invested JVs and the rest (North American, European and Japanese), referred in this paper as Group 1 and Group 2 respectively;
2. a comparison between the three sub-groups within Group 2, that is the North American, European and Japanese JVs; and
3. a comparison between foreign and local partners.

Analyses were conducted using SPSS/PC+, and non-parametric test procedures were chosen for all variables, including the ratio variables after their distribution was found to be far from normal. The Mann–Whitney procedure was used to test the difference between Groups 1 and 2, the Kruskal–Wallis one-way ANOVA between the three sub-groups within Group 2 and the Wilcoxon matched-pairs signed-ranks test for difference between foreign and local partners.

RESULTS AND DISCUSSION

Initial Observations of the Sample

The sample comprises 114 JVs, of which 77 belong to Group 2 (33 investors from North America, 20 from Europe and 24 from Japan), and the remaining 37 are Group 1 JVs. The sample shows a great variety in foreign investment, both in terms of absolute amounts and as a percentage of foreign equity (Table 9.1). Foreign investment ranges from US$45 thousand up to US$90 million with an average of about US$3 million, and foreign equity from 10 per cent to 80 per cent with an average of 43 per cent. American and European companies tend to have large and medium-sized investment, while Japanese and the Overseas Chinese have relatively small investment amounts ($p<0.05$, x^2-test). The JV contract duration ranges from 5 to 40 years with an average of 16 years. Over 60 per cent of the total are between 11 and 20 years. American companies appear to have joint-venture contracts of a longer duration, while the Overseas Chinese prefer a shorter one ($p<0.05$, x^2-test). There is a great geographical bias in the location of JVs. Overseas Chinese JVs are concentrated on the southern region, particularly Special Economic Zones (SEZs). US investors liked to locate investment in relatively developed regions such as the coastal areas, and Japanese MNCs preferred northern regions with which they are familiar. Table 9.1 also observes that Overseas Chinese-invested JVs are more export orientated than Group 2 JVs ($p<0.05$, x^2-test). In addition, MNCs in Group 2 are more likely to invest in technology-intensive industries, while the Overseas Chinese tend towards labour-intensive areas.

Table 9.1 Sample pattern summary

Investor group	*Foreign investment (US$10 000)*			*Row Total*
	<45	50–400	>400	
N. America	8	19	6	33 (29%)
Europe	2	14	4	20 (18%)
Japan	13	9	2	24 (21%)
Overseas Chinese	14	21	2	37 (33%)
Column Total	37 (33%)	63 (55%)	14 (12%)	114 (100%)
	Foreign equity (%)			
	10–49%	*50%*	*51–80%*	
N. America	13	16	4	33 (29%)
Europe	9	9	2	20 (18%)
Japan	14	9	1	24 (21%)
Overseas Chinese	25	7	5	37 (33%)
Column Total	61 (53%)	41 (36%)	12 (11%)	114 (100%)
	Duration of JV (year)			
	1–10	*11–20*	*21–40*	
N. America	8	18	6	32 (30%)
Europe	4	13	3	20 (18%)
Japan	5	15	4	24 (22%)
Overseas Chinese	8	24	2	34 (31%)
Column Total	25 (23%)	70 (64%)	15 (14%)	110 (100%)
	Location of JV			
	South	*East*	*North*	
N. America	9	12	12	33 (29%)
Europe	10	5	5	20 (18%)
Japan	5	7	12	24 (21%)
Overseas Chinese	31	3	3	37 (23%)
Column Total	55 (48%)	27 (24%)	32 (28%)	114 (100%)
	JV output for export (%)			
	0%	*1–40%*	*>40%*	
N. America	20	5	5	30 (28%)
Europe	10	2	7	19 (18%)
Japan	11	6	6	23 (22%)
Overseas Chinese	10	8	16	34 (32%)
Column Total	51 (48%)	21 (20%)	34 (32%)	106 (100%)

The Motivations Underlying JV Formation

As Table 9.2 shows, there is a great difference in motivations for entering China via a joint venture between the MNCs of Groups 1 and 2. The decision

Table 9.2 Comparison of foreign partners' motivations (Mann–Whitney test)

	Group 2			*Group 1: Overseas Chinese*			
Decision factors	*Mean*	*S.D.*	*Rank*	*Mean*	*S.D.*	*Rank*	*SIG*
Access to distribution	4.052	1.421	11	2.892	1.286	11	*
Access to raw matcrials	3.766	1.037	8	4.351	0.789	5	***
Avoid trade barrier	4.221	0.968	5	3.486	1.261	7	**
Build local image	4.519	0.660	4	4.297	0.702	6	*
Enter local market	4.870	0.338	1	4.595	0.498	4	***
Follow competitors	1.844	0.779	13	3.081	1.010	9	***
Geo-diversification	2.532	0.968	12	2.081	1.038	13	**
Low labour cost	4.558	1.019	3	4.692	1.646	3	
Low transportation cost	3.455	1.333	10	2.568	1.237	12	**
Make profit	4.766	0.456	2	4.811	0.397	2	
Minimum financial risk	3.026	0.887	7	3.297	0.878	8	*
Protect patents/tech	3.597	1.003	9	2.946	0.911	10	***
Use of incentives	4.078	0.885	6	4.838	0.442	1	***

Notes:
*** denotes $p<0.01$
** denotes $p<0.05$
* denotes $p<0.1$

to enter into a JV by MNCs in Group 2 is driven by such factors as the need to 'enter the Chinese market', 'generate profit', 'use of cheap labour', 'build local image', 'avoid trade barrier' and 'use of incentives'. Clearly, market-orientated motivations are paramount. In contrast, 'use of incentives', 'make profit', 'access to raw materials' rank high in the list of motives mentioned by the Overseas Chinese. This is because JVs with Overseas Chinese participation tend to invest in industries with low technology (Table 9.1), and therefore the local supply of raw materials is important. Although foreign investors in both groups appear to have the same level of desire to 'make profit', the Overseas Chinese investors' expectations of quick profit are higher when account is taken of their rating of other factors. Furthermore, Table 9.2 shows that it is competitive pressures, to a certain extent, which force investors in Group 1, especially those based in HK, to go to mainland China.

As far as the local partners' motivations are concerned (Table 9.3), clear differences also exist between the two groups. Local partners in JVs with North American, European and Japanese MNCs are more interested in their foreign partners bringing advanced technology, management skills and business expertise while being willing to sacrifice part of their desire to use the JV as a hard currency 'cash cow'. The significant difference in the rating of 'gain reputation' shows that local partners in Group 2 JVs believe that entering such an arrangement can greatly enhance their image and position/status in both the market-place and social context. With regard to earning hard currency, although foreign companies were expected by local partners

Table 9.3 Comparison of local partners' motivations (Mann–Whitney test)

	Group 2			*Group 1: Overseas Chinese*			*SIG*
Decision factors	*Mean*	*S.D.*	*Rank*	*Mean*	*S.D.*	*Rank*	
Access to financial resource	4.130	0.695	7	3.973	0.687	5	
Access to foreign market	4.221	0.955	6	4.297	0.702	4	
Earn hard currency	3.506	1.131	8	4.459	0.730	2	***
Follow competitor	3.445	0.732	9	3.604	0.682	8	
Gain reputation	4.273	0.737	5	2.946	0.702	9	***
Learn I B Skills	4.455	0.527	2	4.595	0.498	1	
Learn management skills	4.286	0.944	4	3.703	1.177	7	***
Tech transfer	4.584	0.656	1	3.730	0.769	6	***
Use of incentives	4.429	0.524	3	4.378	0.594	3	

Notes:
*** denotes $p<0.01$
** denotes $p<0.05$
* denotes $p<0.1$

to 'fulfil the obligation to export', many JVs in Group 2 are set up to produce import-substitution products. Many foreign companies found themselves in a better bargaining position in determining the percentage of output exported if they possessed alternative resources which were attractive to the local partners. These included the 'right' products, advanced manufacturing processes and management skills (but the value of the management skills was almost always underestimated by local Chinese companies). With regard to Overseas Chinese companies, however, other resources such as established channels to outside markets or assistance from technical personnel are more important to local partners.

Tests of differences in the motivations of both partners in JVs with North American, European and Japanese companies reveal some interesting results. For foreign partners, there are two factors which received significantly different ratings across the sub-groups. The Japanese regarded the need to 'protect patents and technology', perhaps unexpectedly, as being more important than did their American and European counterparts ($p<0.1$). They are more cautious of disclosure of their technology. This echoes other research (Conroy, 1986) which also shows that Japanese companies are reluctant to transfer technology through foreign direct investment, in contrast to European companies. Another significant result is that European investors scored the factor 'make profit' much lower than American and Japanese investors did ($p<0.1$). The interviews indicated that the Chinese market, or business environment in general, looks much more unfamiliar to them: in consequence they do not aim for high profits in the short term. American and Japanese

Table 9.4 Comparison of differences in selecting local partner (Mann–Whitney test)

	Group 2			*Group 1: Overseas Chinese*			*SIG*
Factors	*Mean*	*S.D.*	*Rank*	*Mean*	*S.D.*	*Rank*	
Environment relations	4.403	0.862	2	3.432	1.015	8	***
Estb'ed distribution channel	3.494	1.119	9	2.676	0.852	9	***
Financial resources	2.922	0.161	8	3.703	0.777	6	***
Good location	4.000	0.973	6	4.081	0.862	3	
Government relations	3.636	0.958	7	4.297	0.909	1	***
Local entity	4.468	0.864	1	3.676	1.029	7	***
Plant/facilities	4.377	0.539	3	4.108	0.699	2	*
Raw materials	4.104	0.804	5	3.946	0.941	4	
Strong market position	4.364	0.759	4	3.730	0.902	5	***
Well-known brands	3.571	0.870	10	2.568	0.765	10	***

Notes:
*** denotes $p<0.01$
** denotes $p<0.05$
* denotes $p<0.1$

firms, however, are more acquainted with the Chinese economy and culture, because of geographical closeness or other business associations.

As far as the local partners' motivations are concerned, it is very interesting to find that a significant emphasis was given by the local partners in the JVs with North American and European companies on their intention to 'learn management skills' ($p<0.05$). This indicates that the local partners have a stronger desire to learn from the 'West' than from the Japanese in this respect. The reason might be that they appreciate Western-style management, or perhaps they think that the Japanese management style is easier to learn because of similarities in cultural background. These views were expressed, to some extent, in the interviews with Chinese executives and government officials.

Partner Selection

Table 9.4 summarises foreign partners' ratings on ten factors in their decision to select a local partner. First, for foreign partners in Group 2 there are six factors receiving scores with means higher than 4, but there are three factors for those in Group 1. This indicates that what the local partner will bring to the JV is, in general, more important to Western and Japanese firms than it is for the Overseas Chinese. The local partner is indispensable, in

Table 9.5 Comparison of differences in selecting foreign partner (Mann–Whitney test)

	Group 2			*Group 1: Overseas Chinese*			*SIG*
Factors	*Mean*	*S.D.*	*Rank*	*Mean*	*S.D.*	*Rank*	
Assist of tech personnel	3.273	1.034	10	3.405	1.117	9	
Estb'ed distribution	4.078	0.791	6	3.946	0.705	5	
Financial resources	4.338	0.620	4	4.378	0.639	2	
Good market position	4.442	0.618	3	3.973	0.833	4	***
Licence/patents etc.	4.234	0.647	5	3.892	0.699	6	**
Management skills	4.122	1.128	7	3.541	1.145	8	***
R&D	3.826	0.984	9	3.378	0.953	10	**
Raw materials	3.792	0.908	8	3.622	0.794	7	
Technology/ equipment	4.468	0.528	2	4.432	0.603	1	
Well-known brand	4.584	0.496	1	4.297	0.661	3	**

Notes:
*** denotes $p<0.01$
** denotes $p<0.05$
* denotes $p<0.1$

particular, for many North American and European MNCs. Secondly, the ranking of the factors by the two groups are markedly different from each other. Two factors at the top of the list in Group 2 only rank seventh and eighth in Group 1. This reversal of positions supports the point mentioned above that the Overseas Chinese, having the same or similar cultural background as local firms, and possessing close social contacts in China, expect (need) less of local partners in building relationships. In a similar vein, Western and Japanese companies (because of their local market orientation) hope to share more of the local partners' established channels of distribution through JV arrangements, while overseas Chinese companies can do the marketing for export products themselves.

However, 'providing government relations' ranks seventh in Group 2, but surprisingly comes first in importance to Overseas Chinese firms. This implies that they are more aware of the crucial role of the government and bureaucratic involvement at many different levels in business. As Holton (1990) observes, the Chinese enterprise, in the sense of Western economies, is somewhat akin to a semi-autonomous unit of government since much of the critical decision-making is carried out in the upper reaches of the total system.

The local partners' rating of the factors in their decision to select a foreign partner is shown in Table 9.5. Firstly, the order of ranking of factors for both groups is roughly the same, but the level of importance appears different. There are five significant difference factors, namely, 'well-known brands', 'strong market position', 'R&D', 'patents and licences', and 'management skills'. They are all factors typically related to the Western 'sophistication' which attracts businesses from developing countries such as China. With respect to Group 1, local partners rely much more on resources such as outward channels of distribution and assistance from technical personnel to improve the quality of JV products and export.

As for partners' perceptions on partner selection between the three subgroups of Group 2 (that is, North American, European and Japanese JVs), there are three points worth making. First, no significant difference was identified between the JVs with North American and European participation for both local and foreign partners in their partner selections. Secondly, the considerably higher rating on 'government relations' given by Japanese investors ($p<0.01$) indicates that they are more similar to Overseas Chinese investors in understanding Chinese culture and, particularly, the current political environment in China, than are their American and European counterparts. Thirdly, Western rather than Japanese technology and management expertise ($p<0.05$) is more attractive to local Chinese partners.

Control Exercised by Foreign and Local Partners over Key Decision Areas

In this study, several questions were designed to analyse issues about the control of JVs and conflicts between the partners in a number of decision areas. The research has tried to address (i) whether differences relating to control exist between investment groups, and (ii) if there are, what relationship exists between these differences and conflicts. In order to do this, both partners in each JV were asked to give their views on control and conflicts over the range of decision areas.

Table 9.6 lists 15 decision areas in a JV and presents the foreign partners' views of the control exercised on different decision areas, with 1 being 'local completely dominant', 3 'shared' and 5 'foreign completely dominant'. First, as shown in Table 9.6, in both groups foreign partners have much more control over decision areas such as 'product planning' and 'quality control'; they have a bit more control over 'marketing'; while local partners have more control over 'production planning', 'wages and labour policy' and 'management recruitment'. On 'dividend policy', 'organisation', 'purchasing', 'budgeting', 'accounting' and 'export and import', the decisions are roughly shared between partners. Secondly, compared with investors in Group 2, the Overseas Chinese have relatively more control over 'pricing policy' ($p<0.1$), 'quality control' and 'export and import' ($p<0.05$) in JVs, leaving more control to their local partners over the decision areas of 'wages and labour policy' ($p<0.05$) and 'organisation' ($p<0.1$).

Table 9.6 Foreign partners' rates of control: comparison of the differences (Mann–Whitney test)

	Group 2			*Group 1: Overseas Chinese*			*SIG*
Decision area	*Mean*	*Mode*	*S.D.*	*Mean*	*Mode*	*S.D*	
Accounting	3.727	3	0.868	3.486	3	0.932	
Budgeting	3.325	4	1.019	3.324	3	1.056	
Capital expenditure	3.143	3	0.996	3.459	4	1.070	
Dividend policy	3.013	3	0.659	3.027	3	0.726	
Export and import	2.857	3	0.838	3.216	3	0.821	**
Loan funds	2.098	3	0.851	3.153	3	1.058	
Marketing	3.610	4	1.172	3.865	4	1.134	
Mgnt recruitment	2.403	2	0.847	2.703	2	0.740	*
Organisation	2.831	3	0.750	2.486	3	0.932	*
Pricing policy	3.338	3	0.982	3.703	4	1.127	*
Product planning	4.195	5	0.889	4.297	5	0.996	
Production planning	2.545	2	0.836	2.459	2	0.900	
Purchasing	3.208	2	1.092	3.108	3	1.100	
QC	4.182	5	0.884	4.514	5	0.768	**
Wage/labour policy	2.104	2	0.699	1.703	2	0.618	**

Notes:
*** denotes $p<0.01$
** denotes $p<0.05$
* denotes $p<0.1$

Table 9.7 Comparison of local and foreign partners' rates of control in Group 2 (N=77), (Wilcoxon matched-pairs signed-ranks test)

Decision areas	*–Rank*	*+Rank*	*Tie*	*SIG*
Accounting	13	24	40	**
Budgeting	25	27	25	
Capital expenditure	26	17	34	
Dividend policy	28	17	32	
Export and import	20	24	33	
Loan funds	29	26	22	
Marketing	42	20	15	***
Mgnt recruitment	28	11	38	**
Organisation	21	19	37	
Pricing policy	28	20	26	
Product planning	26	17	34	
Production planning	15	27	35	**
Purchasing	32	13	32	***
QC	24	25	18	
Wage/labour policy	16	16	45	

Notes:
*** denotes $p<0.01$
** denotes $p<0.05$
* denotes $p<0.1$

Table 9.8 Comparison of local and foreign partners' rates of control in Group 1 (N=37) (Wilcoxon matched-pairs signed-ranks test)

Decision areas	*–Rank*	*+Rank*	*Tie*	*SIG*
Accounting	7	14	16	**
Budgeting	11	12	14	
Capital expenditure	19	7	11	***
Dividend policy	11	12	14	
Export and import	14	8	15	*
Loan funds	16	8	13	*
Marketing	22	7	8	***
Mgnt recruitment	15	12	10	
Organisation	13	14	10	
Pricing policy	2	24	4	***
Product planning	14	7	16	
Production planning	12	12	13	
Purchasing	14	4	19	***
QC	17	10	10	*
Reporting	10	16	11	
Wage/labour policy	8	19	10	*

Notes:
*** denotes $p<0.01$
** denotes $p<0.05$
* denotes $p<0.1$

It is useful to know to what extent local partners agree with the foreign partners' views. Tables 9.7 and 9.8 highlight the comparison of local and foreign partners' perceptions on control for the two investment groups. Each table gives three columns of numbers entitled '−Ranks', '+Ranks and 'Tie'. These represent, respectively, the numbers of cases in which the local partner's score is lower, higher or equal to the foreign partner's score. In other words, in cases under '−Ranks' the local partners perceive that they have relatively *more* control over that decision area than the foreign partners' perception (although, only in the sense of a comparison of two scores rather than in absolute terms), while in cases under '+Ranks' the local partner perceives that the foreign counterpart has more control.

As indicated in Table 9.8, in JVs with Overseas Chinese, local partners agreed with their partners on the control exercised by each of them over the areas of 'product planning' (foreign dominant); 'production planning' and 'organisation' (local dominant); and 'dividend policy', 'export and import', 'reporting', 'management recruitment' and 'budgeting' (roughly shared) (see also Table 9.6). Over other decision areas, both sides had different perceptions. The local partners felt they exercised more control over the areas, of 'marketing', 'capital expenditure', 'quality control', 'export and import', 'purchasing' and 'loan fund' than was perceived by their foreign partners: while the opposite was the case over 'pricing policy', 'accounting' and 'wage and labour policy'. The reasons for these discrepancies of perceptions appear to be either (i) an unclear division of decision-making between partners over the areas, or (ii) inappropriate division of decision-making over these areas. Interviews revealed that when locals felt they were stronger than was conceded by their partners, this tended to reflect an inappropriate division of decision-power and responsibility: this indicated the discomfort of either partner over that decision area or could highlight where the seeds of potential disputes might lie. For instance, on 'accounting procedures' and 'pricing policy', many local parents, especially small and medium-size firms, have hardly any international business experience or channels to world markets and are not familiar with the accounting system used in JVs. As a result, they often cast a suspicious eye on activities relating to import and exports – such as the prices of products for export.

Compared with Group 1, local partners in JVs with Western and Japanese participation showed more consensus on decision-making areas (Table 9.7). Despite this, a divergence of perceptions occurred in several areas. In areas like 'purchasing', 'marketing' (perceived by foreign partners as 'shared with, but slightly foreign dominant'), 'production planning', and 'management recruitment' (perceived by foreign partners as 'shared with, but slightly local dominant'), local partners believed the decisions were entirely shared. However, on 'accounting' they strongly disagreed with their foreign partner's verdict for the same reasons as discussed above.

Conflicts between Partners over Key Decision Areas

Table 9.9 summarises foreign partners' rating on the frequency of disagreements arising in the given decision areas. First, both partners tend to be cooperative in decisions on 'capital expenditure', 'organisation', 'product planning', 'budgeting' and 'loan funds'. Disagreement arises most often in the areas of 'dividend policy' and 'quality control', which were frequently reported because of the exchange-control policies of the host government and the poor quality of products respectively. Secondly, disagreements also happen relatively frequently in the decisions over 'pricing policy', 'accounting' (particularly in Group 2 JVs). For 'accounting' and 'pricing policy', apart from the reasons discussed above, another underlying reason is that some of the investors in JVs with a high percentage of export sales are believed (at least by local partners) to be deliberately postponing the declaration of the JVs' profits in order to enjoy tax holidays. As for 'management recruitment', foreign partners find that a frequent change of top management on the local side seriously affects the JV's operation, both on a strategic and daily basis. This is particularly true for investors with a long-term strategy and commitment. For small firms, however, like many Overseas Chinese firms, the predominant objective is to generate profits. Therefore, they leave management recruitment decisions to local partners as long as

Table 9.9 Comparison of foreign partners' rates of conflict (Mann–Whitney test)

	Group 2			*Group 1: Overseas Chinese*			*SIG*
Decision area	*Mean*	*mode*	*S.D.*	*Mean*	*mode*	*S.D*	
Accounting	2.844	3	0.988	3.432	4	0.987	***
Budgeting	1.597	2	0.568	1.865	2	0.751	*
Capital expenditure	1.701	3	0.708	1.405	1	0.498	*
Dividend policy	3.545	4	0.680	3.541	3	0.898	
Export and import	2.662	2	0.681	2.541	2	0.558	
Loan funds	1.649	2	0.507	1.622	1	0.639	
Marketing	3.286	3	0.958	2.757	2	0.955	***
Mgnt recruitment	2.896	3	0.771	2.297	2	0.939	***
Organisation	1.494	1	0.503	1.568	2	0.502	
Pricing policy	2.883	3	0.917	3.216	4	0.821	*
Product planning	1.506	1	0.576	1.622	2	0.492	
Production planning	2.468	2	0.788	2.622	2	0.924	
Purchasing	2.701	3	0.778	2.757	3	0.863	
QC	3.649	4	0.807	4.108	4	0.616	***
Wage/labour policy	2.221	2	0.641	2.405	2	0.551	

Notes:
*** denotes $p<0.01$
** denotes $p<0.05$
* denotes $p<0.1$

this does not affect them too much. It is not unusual that JVs with Overseas Chinese participation select a local person as their representative. The representative focuses mainly on ensuring the quality of products and that delivery dates are met.

Moreover, frequent disagreements (a mode of three or more in Table 9.9) occur in four out of the five areas ('accounting', 'management recruitment', 'purchasing' and 'marketing') which received a significantly different control rating from the partners in Table 9.7 (see also the earlier discussion). The same relationship exists for Group 2 as well (see Tables 9.8 and 9.9). Thus, we can draw the empirical conclusion that in decision areas with significantly different perceptions of control by each partner, there is a higher probability of disputes and conflicts.

Looking at differences in the perception of disputes reveals some interesting points (Table 9.10). First of all, there are seven areas in which local partners' perceptions disagree with those of their foreign counterparts; and on six of these the local partners' rates (of conflict) are significantly lower ($p<0.001$), while on one (accounting) significantly higher than their foreign partner's ($p<0.05$). Local partners' extreme unhappiness with the current situation on accounting procedures has already been discussed. However, the reasons for the lower rating by local partners on the other five areas might be as follows:

1. They acknowledge the disputes or conflicts, but they do not want this to be known to others because of the idea of 'preserving a harmonious family' or 'saving face';
2. The Chinese tend to emphasise the positive side when a disagreement arises; and
3. They acknowledge the disputes, but believe decisions in some areas are simply beyond their control, such as foreign exchange control, which leads to disputes over dividend policy.

Table 9.10 Comparison of local and foreign partners' rates of conflict (N=114) (Wilcoxon matched-pairs signed-ranks test)

Decision area	*–Rank*	*+Rank*	*Tie*	*SIG*
Accounting	27	47	40	**
Budgeting	25	22	67	
Capital expenditure	30	26	58	
Dividend policy	96	0	18	***
Export and import	31	27	56	
Loan funds	25	26	63	
Marketing	36	45	33	
Mgnt recruitment	65	8	41	***
Organisation	23	20	71	
Pricing policy	52	10	52	***
Product planning	26	16	71	
Production planning	60	70	47	***
Purchasing	37	21	56	
QC	85	7	22	***
Wage/labour policy	78	4	32	***

Notes:
*** denotes $p<0.01$
** denotes $p<0.05$
* denotes $p<0.1$

Interviews with local partners and government officials reveal that the divergence of the partners' perceptions on conflict are often the results of the combined effects of these three factors.

The Performance of Joint Ventures

Performance is assessed on four measures: profitability, growth, comparison with competitors and overall satisfaction. Table 9.11 indicates the foreign and local partners' perceptions of JV performance. First, the foreign partners' level of satisfaction on the performance of JVs ranges between 'not too bad' to 'satisfactory'. Secondly, they are relatively more satisfied with profitability than other measures. This is particularly true for Overseas Chinese investors. Thirdly, foreign investors from Group 2 JVs rate growth

Table 9.11 Comparison of partners' perceptions of JV performance (Mann–Whitney test)

Criteria	*Foreign partner's perception*			*Local partner's perception*		
	Group 2 (mean)	*Group 1 (mean)*	*SIG*	*Group 2 (mean)*	*Group 1 (mean)*	*SIG*
Profitability	3.429	3.811	*	3.753	2.811	****
Growth	3.000	3.162		3.597	2.946	**
With competitors	3.182	3.432	*	3.818	3.703	
Overall perception	3.169	3.189		3.935	3.135	****

Notes:
*** denotes $p<0.01$
** denotes $p<0.05$
* denotes $p<0.1$

Table 9.12 Comparison of local and foreign partners' perceptions of JV performance (Wilcoxon matched-pairs signed-ranks test)

Criteria	*Group 2 (N=77)*				*Group 1 (N=37)*			
	–Rank	*+Rank*	*Ties*	*SIG*	*–Rank*	*+Rank*	*Ties*	*SIG*
Profitability	18	39	50	**	25	5	7	****
Growth	8	44	25	****	16	11	10	
With competitors	4	45	28	****	8	16	13	
Overall perception	9	56	12	****	13	14	10	

Notes:
**** denotes $p<0.001$
*** denotes $p<0.01$
** denotes $p<0.05$

significantly lower than Overseas Chinese investors because of their high expectations (also it is easier to grow 'outwards' than 'inwards' into the Chinese market). Fourthly, local partners in JVs with Western and Japanese MNCs have much higher levels of satisfaction of the performance JVs than their counterparts in JVs with Overseas Chinese partners. This is especially the case with regard to profitability and overall perception ($p<0.0001$). Finally, local partners with 'Group 2 JVs' are much more satisfied with the JV's performance than their partners on all measures ($p<0.01$, see Table 9.12); while in JVs with the Overseas Chinese, both partners are approximately at the same level of satisfaction on growth, comparison with competitors and overall perception. However, on profits, as might be expected from the earlier discussion, local partners believe that profits are not fairly distributed between the partners in line with their contribution. This reality of differences between the partners has been supported using the Wilcoxon matched-pairs signed-ranks test as shown in Table 9.12.

Analysis was also carried out to examine the relationship between JV performance and some key characteristics, such as investment source, amount, JV duration and foreign partner's equity share. Only the measure of overall perception was used to define the level of success of the JVs. The scores on overall satisfaction from both partners were first added together as a single measure with a range of one to ten: JVs with scores greater than seven were defined as 'successful', those with less than five as 'unsuccessful' and the rest as 'unknown'. This means that for successful JVs both partners have a rate no smaller than three, while for unsuccessful JVs there is no rate greater than three. For the remaining cases it may be that one partner is very happy, whereas the other is very dissatisfied, or both are neither satisfied nor dissatisfied. Although this manipulation looks arbitrary, it does not affect the analysis in this context. It appears that more American and European JVs are successful, while more Overseas Chinese ventures are unsuccessful. In terms of the scale of foreign investment and the JV's duration, it appears that more successful cases occur in investments of a large size and a longer contract duration. These three observations were tested for significance by the chi-square test, and Mann–Whitney test. The statistics do not show a significant relationship between performance and foreign equity.

CONCLUSIONS

The results of this study are consistent with earlier research findings on JVs and, in addition, bring to the fore some new findings. First of all, substantial differences have been found in JV characteristics between different sources of investment in China. Generally, investments from North American, Japanese and European companies are larger and have a longer venture duration. They are technologically more advanced and likely to invest in technology-intensive industries such as electronics, pharmaceuticals and automobiles. JVs with Western partners require a relatively highly-skilled work-force and usually purchase intermediate materials from the international market, in particular from the foreign parent company. These JVs produce more import-substitutes for the domestic market. In contrast, investments from the Overseas Chinese are generally smaller and with a shorter venture duration. The level of technology is not as high as their Western counterparts and so their investments tend to be in labour-intensive industries such as textiles and foods. They use more local resources, such as cheap labour and low-cost materials for offshore production. In terms of investment strategy, American and European investments are more market-orientated while Overseas Chinese investments are more profit-orientated. Western and Japanese MNCs enter into JVs in order to get familiar with the local environment and to build a strong position in order to establish a long-term competitive advantage. As the *Economist* (1992b) put it, if a MNC can position itself well in

China by the end of this century, it might achieve a great distance from its rivals in the next century. JV arrangements provide local Chinese partners with better opportunities to learn foreign management expertise, gain access to technology and earn hard currency. To achieve these goals, local partners in JVs with Western and Japanese MNCs value their partners' resources in areas such as the level of technology, patents and licences, R&D and management skills. In JVs with Overseas Chinese partners they count more upon resources such as outward channels of distribution, strong market position and quality-control techniques.

Secondly, the results of this study have not shown a relationship between JV performance and any particular type of control; that is, foreign dominant, local dominant or shared. Control can be exercised dominantly by either local or foreign partners over some areas, and shared between both partners in other areas. The pattern of control changes from case to case, but the results suggest that good cooperation between partners over key decision areas such as accounting, marketing, pricing policy and quality control is very important to the success of JVs. Previous research has found that it is important for each partner to have a clear understanding of what they contribute to the arrangement and what they can expect of the other partner, before entering the JV. This study has shown that a full awareness of the partner's needs is equally important. Each partner needs to identify the areas where potential disagreements of conflicts may arise, and remain aware of this through the whole life of the venture. As the sections on control and conflict show, those decision areas where partners do not have a clear understanding of the division of control are those most likely to cause frequent disagreements.

Thirdly, as far as location strategy is concerned, this study supports the theory and recent research finding (Buckley and Casson, 1985; Casson and Zheng, 1992) that companies with a high inclination to export tend to choose locations in coastal areas and particularly in SEZs where fiscal incentives for offshore production are more favourable. Firms with a long-term commitment to targeting the domestic market are more likely to select a fairly central location such as Beijing, Tianjin and Shanghai. Finally, local partners in JVs with Western and Japanese MNCs are relatively more satisfied with their JV's performance than those in JVs with Overseas Chinese partners. Interestingly, Western partners' level of satisfaction is much lower than that of their local counterparts.

The above results shed some light on current theoretical issues. While no clear relationship emerged between performance and formal control, it is clear that the achievement of mutual understanding and cooperation over key areas was crucial to JV success. This appears to be related to a clear definition of control between the partners, fully understood by both. The longer-term outlook of Western and Japanese JVs leads to a greater degree of satisfaction (for both foreign and local partners) than the short-term, profit-orientated outlook of Overseas Chinese partners. For foreign partners, this is partly due to the need for learning about China and its market: this learning is a key resource gain which substitutes for short-term profit. The Overseas Chinese 'cultural start' is, ironically, translated into rapid profit-taking with some loss of cooperation from the perspective of local owners and managers. As always, the complementary skills brought by the foreign partner exercise a huge influence on the venture's operations. Local partners value the learning, but differentiate between the technological learning derived from Western and Japanese MNCs and the production and distribution skills derived from Overseas Chinese partners. Further research would be valuable on these matters.

China is currently one of the most attractive locations for MNCs and will continue to draw further attention from academia and the business world alike. This research paves the way for further investigation, but research themes will undoubtedly evolve in tandem with the rapid development of the country's economy and the consequent changes in the nature of inward foreign direct investment.

10 The Impact of Strategic Choice on the Internationalisation of the Firm

Timothy Clark and Geoff Mallory

INTRODUCTION

Companies either seeking to expand into foreign markets or to alter their existing institutional arrangements have a choice between three forms of foreign market servicing: exporting, foreign licensing and foreign direct investment (FDI)[1] (Buckley 1991; Buckley and Casson 1976; Root 1987; Terpstra 1987). The 'stages theory of internationalisation' proposes that these options are chosen in a linear sequence in that firms initially export, then establish a sales subsidiary and only when they have built up knowledge and experience do they invest directly.

Andersen (1993) has distinguished between two ways of describing the sequential process by which firms internationalise:

- The 'Uppsala Internationalisation Model' which is associated with the seminal studies undertaken by Johanson and Wiedersheim-Paul (1975) and Johanson and Vahlne (1977);
- The 'Innovation-Related Internationalisation Models' as developed by Warren Bilkey and his colleagues (Bilkey and Tesar, 1977; Cavusgil, 1980; Czinkota, 1982).

This article focuses on the Uppsala Internationalisation Model, since a distinctive feature of this model is the stress on the development of different modes of marketing that are associated with an organisation's growing commitment to a foreign market. In contrast, the models derived from Bilkey's work are limited to the sequence of stages associated with export development.

The widespread popularity of the Uppsala Internationalisation Model is surprising since, as Reid (1984) indicates, it largely rests on a limited number of empirical studies: the initial research into the overseas expansion of four Swedish companies (Johanson and Wiedersheim-Paul, 1975), a case study of Pharmacia (cited in Johanson and Vahlne, 1977) and an Australian investigation which treated domestic expansion as analogous to export expansion (Wiedersheim-Paul, Olson and Welch, 1978). In addition, Luostarinen (1980) and Larimo (1985) have produced similar evidence for Finland (cited in Young, 1987, p. 33). However, a considerable amount of empirical research fails to support the stepwise development process identified by the Swedish researchers (see, for example, Young and Hood, 1976; Buckley, Newbould and Thurwell, 1979; Turnbull and Valla, 1986; Millington and Bayliss, 1990). Turnbull (1987) conducted a detailed critical review of the empirical evidence and concluded that, 'it does not support the proposition that the pattern of export organisational development follows an evolutionary path' (p. 36). Hedlund and Kverneland (1985) suggest such failings may result from the original Uppsala studies reflecting a particular period in the historical development of Swedish industry.

In addition to the lack of empirical support, there are a number of conceptual problems associated with the Uppsala Internationalisation Model. The first is definitional and relates to the level of analysis. It is not clear whether the theory relates to the company as a whole or the operational units which comprise the organisation, or both. In large multi-divisional/product firms, the organisational unit being observed can determine the extent and type of internationalisation observed. Operational units differ in their degree of export dependence, number of overseas markets served and institutional arrangements. For example, some multi-product firms may have distinct institutional arrangements for different product ranges. Overall, a company may have a high percentage of export sales, and whilst some product ranges may mirror this others may be more domestic in their focus. Hence, the degree and complexity of internationalisation depends on whether the empirical focus is at the group or operational level. With this in mind, the later discussion of research methods indicates the level of analysis in this study is the operational unit. This argument suggests multi-divisional/product firms may adopt several forms of foreign market servicing in a single country. Furthermore, the type of product (that is, whether it is a good or service) can influence the initial post-entry form of foreign market servicing by limiting the options available (Buckley, Pass and Prescott, 1991). For instance, Root (1987, p. 15) notes the export mode is not available to service companies. Hence, the proposition that increasing export dependency has similar institutional implications for all firms regardless of their product mix and/or market is doubtful.

Second, the institutional arrangements adopted are assumed to be a consequence of the stage in internationalisation obtained. For instance, exporting through agents is considered an initial stage of internationalisation, whilst FDI is viewed as the final stage. By contrast, Turnbull (1987), suggests that firms with considerable experience and well-developed international institutional arrangements continue to export extensively. The final stage, FDI, is achieved in a limited number of markets. This point is developed further in the discussion relating to our empirical results.

Finally, and related to the previous point, for every entrant, and each foreign market entered, the Uppsala Internationalisation Model predicts an identical sequential development. The internationalisation process is a step-by-step, country-by-country repetition of an identical sequence of stages. This arises since for most firms, in particular those without any international experience, decisions with regard to foreign market expansion are characterised by considerable uncertainty. This uncertainty stems from two sources:

1. The lack of detailed knowledge of a particular foreign market;
2. A lack of general knowledge of how to operate a particular mode of foreign market servicing in an unfamiliar setting.

Market-specific knowledge is gained mainly through the experience of operating in a particular foreign market, whereas knowledge of managing different modes of foreign market servicing can be transferred across countries and is therefore general. Both these types of knowledge are accumulated through a process of 'learning by doing'. For Johanson and Vahlne (1977), 'experiential knowledge is the critical kind of knowledge' (p. 28). The gradual acquisition of knowledge derived from direct experience of a foreign market underpins a firm's sequential move to FDI via agents and sales subsidiaries. This implies that the establishment of, and modifications to, institutional arrangements in each foreign market is due to the acquisition of market-specific knowledge. Briefly, the basic argument is that internationalisation is the consequence of overcoming a set of identical obstacles in each market entered, and that these present the same degree of difficulty on each occasion of entry. The most important of these are lack of knowledge and resources. Incremental participation in each market reduces these obstacles. Two basic assumptions underlie this argument. First, the degree of lack of knowledge is similar for each market entered. Second, the content and amount of information a firm is required to obtain is identical for each market. These pertain to all firms regardless of their international experience.

The literature relating to international strategy has tackled these two assumptions by arguing that it is the knowledge of operating internationally, rather than in specific markets, which is of greater importance (Agarwal and Ramaswami, 1992; Kim and Hwang, 1992). These writers make two important assumptions. First, the unit of analysis is the firm as a whole, not operating units in individual countries. Second, the emphasis is on the active management of the interdependencies between operating units. This shift in focus has a number of important implications. First, the strategic relationship between foreign operations has an impact on the entry-mode decision and subsequent modal shifts. Past experiences, resulting from entry into other markets, feed into current decisions relating to the form of foreign market servicing adopted in individual markets (Davidson, 1980). As a consequence, firms do not develop incrementally along an identical continuum in each market they enter. Second, interdependencies between foreign operations mean actions taken in one country have repercussions for units located elsewhere (Hamel and Prahalad, 1985; Watson, 1982). The portfolio of institutional arrangements which characterises a firm's foreign operations is continually assessed in terms of the situation within individual countries and the relationship between countries. Therefore, a shift in the mode of foreign market servicing within one country may be due to factors external to that country. This suggests that the location of activities comprising the marketing channel can be varied. However, varying the location of one activity has repercussions for activities in other national markets. Third, and related to the previous point, when entering a foreign market firms may have,

> motivations which go beyond the narrow calculus of choosing the most efficient entry mode; that is, they may have global strategic motivations. (Kim and Hwang, 1992, p.35)

These motivations range from establishing a competitive scanning post in an otherwise unprofitable market, to sacrificing the revenues of a subsidiary thereby limiting the cash flow of a global competitor and forestalling entry into the firm's domestic market. The interdependencies between foreign operations mean that the losses in one country are cross-subsidised by the profits generated in domestic or protected markets (Bartlett and Ghoshal, 1987).

Following the points enumerated above, this article places greater emphasis on firm-level rather than country-specific factors. We wish to suggest that it is the knowledge which comes from operating internationally in addition to the management of the relationship between foreign operations which determines the shifts between modes of foreign market servicing. In other words, firms are repositories of knowledge which assists them to learn about the nature of internationalisation and so pursue a range of options which are not conceivable within the narrow sequence of stages identified by the Uppsala Internationalisation Model. Therefore, progress from exporting to FDI is neither inevitable nor uni-directional, particularly if the decisions are taken within a company-wide and global, rather than country-by-country, perspective where the interdependencies between foreign operations are fully appreciated.

In pursuing this argument the chapter divides into three sections. The first suggests that the adoption of a strategic choice framework may free us from the view that there is a single path to internationalisation. The second outlines the sources of data which underpin the discussion in the final section. The final section empirically examines the framework developed in the first section.

STRATEGIC CHOICE FRAMEWORK

Given the problems with the Uppsala Internationalisation Model outlined above, there is an obvious need for a model with enough flexibility to take account of the full range of foreign market servicing options available to firms. The proposed model is based on the strategic choice framework (Child, 1972). He basically argues that contingency theorists, such a Lawrence and Lorsch (1967) and Woodward (1958), among others, attempted,

> to explain organisation at one remove by ignoring the essentially political process, whereby power-holders within organisations decide upon courses of strategic action. (p. 1)

Essentially, Child (1972) focuses the attention of organisational studies not only on the relationship between contextual factors and structural variables, but also 'the agency of choice by whoever have power to direct the organisation' (p. 1). He adopts the term 'dominant coalition' to refer to those power-holders who have considerable influence over decisions and subsequent changes that may occur. For instance, changes in organisational goals (that is, strategy) may modify size, technology and location. He concludes that the notion of strategic choice is critical to any theory of organisations. This leads to the view that managers in organisations are not passive actors restricted by the straight-jacket of numerous contingencies. Rather, they are able to determine many of their features, including the choice between market servicing options. One consequence of this argument is the proposition that there is no single route to foreign market servicing. Rather, there are a whole range of alternatives from which managers may choose. As outlined above, the selection of any particular option is a reflection of firm-level rather than market considerations. Figure 10.1 illustrates the range of options available to firms when initially entering a foreign market, and when subsequently altering their foreign market servicing arrangements in these countries.

Extending the model first proposed by Buckley, Pass and Prescott (1990), our analysis suggests fourteen possible options beyond minimal involvement. These can be divided into *between* and *within* mode shifts. The *between* mode shift refers to forward and backward movements between the three generic forms of market servicing: exporting, licensing and FDI (for example, exporting to licensing). The *within* mode adjustment concerns shifts within any one of the three generic forms of market servicing (for example, in export form, from agent to distributor). These can be simplified into four classes of moves, of which initial entry, move to FDI, and retrenchment are *between* mode shifts, and export adjustment is a *within* mode shift. Each is considered briefly below.

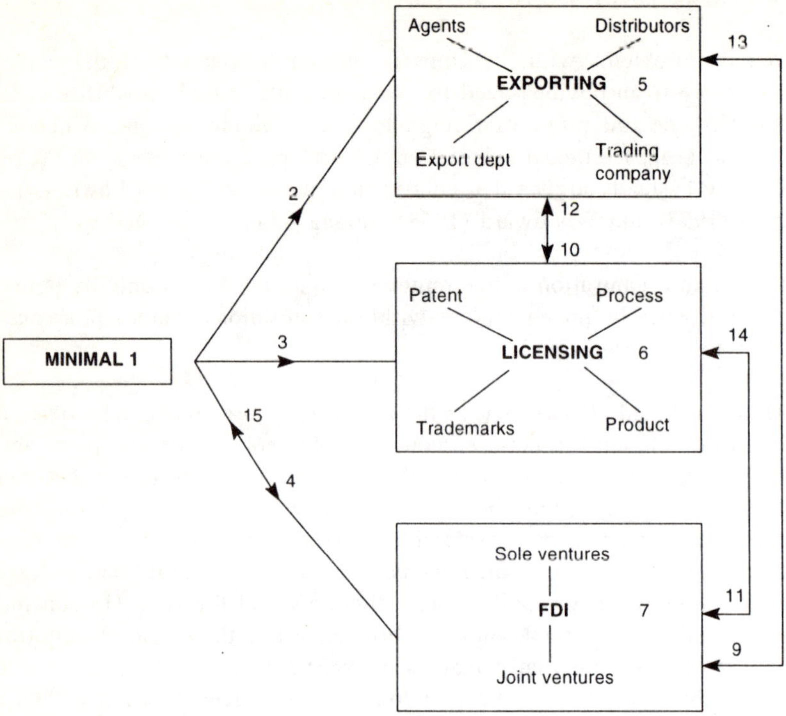

Figure 10.1 *Between* and *within* mode foreign market servicing shifts

Between Mode Shifts

(a) Initial Entry

This refers to the first significant attempt by a firm to penetrate a foreign market, and is similar to Cavusgil's (1980) 'experimental involvement stage' (pp. 276–7) where sporadic, intermittent and half-hearted exporting occurs in response to individual foreign orders. However, as Figure 10.1 shows, the first move is not confined to exporting; firms may initially engage in licensing and FDI, if they so choose. An experienced international firm may tend towards the latter.

(b) Move to FDI

This concerns the move towards the establishment of overseas production facilities. This can be likened to Cavusgil's 'committed involvement stage', where the firm has a long-run commitment to its international activities. The term 'global investment stage' (Young, Hamill, Wheeler and Davies, 1989, p. 33) is perhaps more precise since this recognises the fact that any one firm may have a broad spread of international institutional arrangements.

FDI is not the culmination of an internationalisation process, rather it is one alternative amongst several forms of market servicing.

(c) Retrenchment

This concerns the reduction of a firm's depth of involvement in a host country. A firm continues to be present in the market, whether it be via export, licensing or a sales and marketing subsidiary, but its previous resource commitment, as represented by its marketing mode, is reduced. This does not imply that the market becomes less significant for the firm; rather, its resource commitments within the individual market are reduced. Resources may be transferred to other markets. For instance, a firm may acquire a manufacturing facility in Country A which results in the closure of a plant in Country B. The product is then exported from Country A to B. The firm remains committed to Country B, but has transferred resources to Country A. Such moves may reflect the fact that firms are continually monitoring their mix of institutional arrangements. As the external and internal factors change, so do the relative advantages of their existing institutional arrangements.

Within Mode Shifts

These can be as significant as between mode shifts. Essentially, the firm retains its existing foreign market servicing mode, but adjusts the form this takes. This can be of two types. First, firms adjust their institutional arrangements within one mode. Examples include changing from a distributor to an agent, exporting directly to end users instead of using distributors as intermediaries, changing agents (that is, a change in export form), and changing licence or joint-venture partners (that is, a change in licensing and FDI form). Second, firms may add to their existing marketing modes thereby adopting a mixed marketing approach. Such shifts are *within* mode rather than *between* mode, since a firm complements the existing marketing structure(s) within an individual country. A number of classifications of mixed marketing approaches have been propounded (Young and Hood, 1976, p. 242; Turnbull and Valla, 1986, p. 33); the approach adopted in this study is identified in Table 10.3. (to be discussed more fully in the Results section). The various types of mixed marketing approaches are combinations of the modal shifts already noted.

A further important feature of Figure 10.1 is the recognition that modal shifts are not uni-directional; that is, from exporting through agents to production facilities. Following from the four classes of move presented above, it is clear that firms have a range of choices and that these options are multi-directional. Figure 10.1 illustrates the forward and reverse *between* and *within* mode shifts. This is a development to the existing analysis of foreign market servicing. It identifies a broader range of adjustments that firms make to their institutional arrangements. In contrast, previous analyses of the internationalisation process have in the main focused on forward *between* mode shifts. This may in part be due to small sample sizes. The original Uppsala studies (Johanson and Vahlne 1977; Johanson and Wiedersheim-Paul, 1975) considered the internationalisation of only four Swedish engineering firms (Atlas Copco, Facit, Sandvik and Volvo). The study conducted by Buckley, Pass and Prescott (1990), which originally distinguished *between* and *within* mode shifts, investigated 15 manufacturing firms across five industry groups – glass, industrial gases, pharmaceuticals, scientific instruments and consumer paint (glass and industrial gases were grouped together as 'national champions'), who made 25 entry-mode changes. Our sample is of 23 large manufacturing organisations. Between them they entered 687 foreign markets and made 203 market servicing mode changes.

RESEARCH METHODS

The empirical results presented in the next section of the chapter are founded upon the UK element of an international collaborative research project – the International Organisation Observatory (IOO). The IOO is a group of organisational researchers based in seven European business schools (Bocconi, Italy; ESADE, Spain; ESSEC, France; Saarlandes, Germany; Limburg, Holland; Open University, UK;[2] and Uppsala, Sweden). The group is developing a regular series of comparable Europe-wide surveys of a panel of large firms. The population from which the sample is taken was defined as the largest 1000 companies in each country as ranked by sales turnover, provided they manufactured in the country of study. Two levels within companies were distinguished: the holding and operating levels. Potential participants were approached at the level at which units operated (that is, manufactured rather than just held). Six industries were targeted: chemical, pharmaceutical, electronics, mechanical engineering, automobile production, and food and drink. The sample was stratified by industry to ensure cross-national comparability. The data were collected through structured interviews with normally five to six senior managers (for example, directorial heads of function). The structured interview schedule was designed in order to obtain reasonably complex information which is internationally comparable. A more detailed discussion of the comparative research methodology is contained in Mallory and Clark (1992).

That part of the interview schedule which relates to the data presented in this chapter sought to examine the emergence of each firm's international activities longitudinally. A detailed profile of how each firm developed its foreign market servicing arrangements for every market it had entered was constructed. Hence, data was obtained for those markets in which it currently operated as well as those from which it had subsequently withdrawn.

Table 10.1 Foreign market servicing options

Foreign market servicing options			*Number of moves*
1	Minimal		16
2	Minimal to export		387
3	Minimal to licence	Initial entry	78
4	Minimal to FDI		206
5	Change in export form		4
6	Change in licensing form	Within mode adjustment	9
7	Change in FDI form		21
8	Mixed marketing		36
9	Export to FDI		104
10	Export to licensing	Move to FDI	17
11	Licensing to FDI		7
12	Licensing to export		
13	FDI to export		3
14	FDI to licence	Retrenchment	2
15	FDI to minimal		

This information was supplemented by company histories, where they existed, and other documentation such as sales and marketing reports.

RESEARCH RESULTS

This section analyses the form of foreign market servicing adopted by our sample of 23 UK companies when entering a foreign market, and any subsequent modal shifts to these initial arrangements. The sample operated in a total of 687 markets and generated 203 modal shifts. The subsequent analysis is derived from Tables 10.1 to 10.3. A major feature of Table 10.1 is the stability of initial foreign market servicing entry modes. A third were subsequently adjusted. Of these, 34.5 per cent were within mode adjustments, 63 per cent involved a move to FDI and only 2.5 per cent were retrenchments.

Table 10.1 indicates that export is the most frequent method by which the sample entered a foreign market, accounting for 387 initial entry moves (56 per cent). Interestingly, 30 per cent of first moves were directly to FDI, missing out the intermediary steps suggested by the Uppsala Internationalisation Model. This direction was dominated by five firms in the sample who accounted for 83 per cent of such moves. Each of these firms was part of a larger group, suggesting considerable international experience existing within the group of which the unit of analysis was a part. The unit of analysis was therefore able to draw on the experience of the wider group when developing its international operations. Similarly, a number of participants in the study exported to units controlled by other divisions within the group.

Essentially, they entered foreign markets by 'piggybacking' on the international network which existed in other parts of the group.

The least frequent initial entry mode was the move from minimal to licensing. This is not surprising for two reasons. First, not all firms in the sample could engage in licensing agreements. The basic motivation for licensing depends upon a firm having an exclusive advantage which is identifiable and in some way transferable (saleable) (Buckley and Davies, 1981). Licensing is not possible, even for an identifiable advantage, if that advantage cannot be transferred between firms. If this condition is violated, it may be difficult to make the asset the subject of a licence agreement. Such a limitation resulted in only six firms in the sample engaged in licensing. Second, as Buckley and Prescott (1989) indicate, the use of licensing is limited to those markets which are difficult to penetrate by other modes of market servicing. Where barriers to import prevent export sales and government regulation makes direct investment difficult, licensing may be the only option available even if it is the 'third-best' alternative. Thus, licensing is limited to those companies which have a transferable advantage (for example a patent, a trademark or a separable process), and those markets where other modes of market servicing are restricted.

Despite the various criticisms levelled at the Uppsala Internationalisation Model earlier, some supporting evidence is provided by Table 10.1. The majority of moves within the sample were from minimal to export (387), and subsequently to FDI (104). Initially, comparing this route with that proposed by the Uppsala Internationalisation Model is problematic since this study takes a broader definition of FDI than that used by Johanson and Wiedersheim-Paul (1975). They view FDI as constituting wholly-owned production within a foreign market. We have used a wider definition to include any form of market servicing which involves direct investment in the host country. This leads to a distinction between direct investment in marketing operations (for example, sales subsidiaries) and direct investment in production operations (for example, wholly-owned and joint ventures). Such a definition permits greater sensitivity to the variety of shifts involving FDI. These are shown in Table 10.2. Of the 206 moves from minimal to FDI, 42 involved joint-venture agreements, 123 sales subsidiaries and 41 manufacturing facilities. Subsequently, 57 changes were made to the form of FDI. Table 10.2 shows that 17 of these shifts were from sales subsidiaries to manufacturing facilities, whilst in 36 instances firms adopted mixed modes of marketing in individual countries. Hence, in this sample the export–sales subsidiary–manufacturing route was not as frequent as the export–sales subsidiary–mixed mode route. This indicates that whilst the former route is an important path to internationalisation, it is only one amongst several options available to firms. Indeed, a detailed analysis of the data presented in Table 10.1 indicates that the 23 firms in the study adopted four routes to establishing a production facility. These are:

- Route 1 – Direct move to foreign production;
- Route 2 – Export to foreign production;
- Route 3 – Export to sales subsidiary to foreign production;
- Route 4 – Export to licence to foreign production.

The shortest and most direct path, Route 1, was the most frequent accounting for 53 per cent of cases. Route 2 was the second most common route accounting for 18 per cent of cases. Route 3 accounted for 14 per cent of cases, with Route 4 only occuring in 5 per cent of cases. These data support our earlier contention that the sequence of stages proposed by the Uppsala Internationalisation Model is too restrictive since it fails to take account of the full range of options available to firms.

Table 10.2 Types of foreign direct investment shifts

Basic moves[a]	*Type of move*	*Number of moves*	*Frequency (%)*
Minimal to FDI	1 to 3	42	
	1 to 4	123	56
	1 to 5	41	
Export to FDI	2 to 3	13	28
	2 to 4	76	
	2 to 5	15	
Changes to FDI form	3 to 4	1	
	3 to 5	1	
	4 to 3	1	6
	4 to 5	17	
	5 to 3	1	
	5 to 4		
Mixed approaches[b]		36	10
Total		367	100

Notes:
[a] 1 = minimal; 2 = export; 3 = joint venture; 4 = sales subsidiary; 5 = manufacturing facility
[b] combinations of more than one mode of foreign market servicing in an individual overseas market

However, when discussing the various routes to establishing a production facility, it should be noted that this is the third most frequent way of operating in a foreign market amongst the sample. A greater number of markets were serviced by export and sales subsidiaries. Hence, the internationalisation process as conceived by the Uppsala Internationalisation Model is completed by few firms in few markets. More commonly, firms limit their foreign market servicing activities to export and sales subsidiaries.

A total of 36 cases were identified in which companies combined two or more marketing modes in a single foreign market. Table 10.3 indicates the

Table 10.3 Types of mixed marketing approaches and their frequency

*Type of mixed approaches**	*Number of moves*	*Frequency (%)*
1 + 2	4	
1 + 3		11
1 + 4		
1 + 5		
2 + 3	10	
2 + 4	4	50
2 + 5	4	
3 + 4	5	
3 + 5	2	28
4 + 5	3	
2 + 3 + 4	1	11
3 + 4 + 5	3	
Total	36	100

Notes:
* 1 = exporting; 2 = licensing; 3 = joint venture; 4 = sales subsidiary; 5 = manufacturing facility
Source: Based on Turnbull and Valla (1980), Table 2.11, p. 33

various mixed marketing approaches adopted by companies in the sample. Whilst 12 combinations are noted, 9 were used by the sample. The most frequent of these combinations includes licensing with the other three forms of foreign market servicing (53 per cent of cases).

The second most frequent solution (28 per cent of cases) combines the use of joint ventures with sales and manufacturing subsidiaries. The next two most popular ways of combining market servicing modes in individual countries were mixing exporting and manufacturing (11 per cent), and fusing a sales subsidiary with a manufacturing facility (8 per cent). Four instances of markets being serviced by more than two modes are noted in Table 10.3. In one case, a licensing agreement was combined with a joint venture agreement and a manufacturing facility; in the other four cases a joint venture, sales subsidiary and manufacturing subsidiary were combined.

The conclusions to be drawn from the analysis of mixed marketing approaches are twofold: first, at some point firms in the sample found that a single mode of marketing their products was inappropriate; second, instead of changing from one mode to another (as suggested by the stages model of internationalisation), firms preferred to complement existing marketing structures with additional servicing modes. This finding does not support an incremental organisational stages theory.

As defined by Buckley (1983), retrenchment is a reduction of 'involvement' in the host country. The data in Table 10.1 indicates few firms in the sample reduced their depth of involvement in foreign markets. Hence, this type of move is uncommon but does occur. The sample includes five cases where a firm closed a foreign production facility and moved to another form of market servicing. In three instances, firms moved to export from a neighbouring country, and in two cases they adopted a licensing approach.

CONCLUSION

This chapter has presented empirical evidence of the foreign market servicing modes adopted by a sample of 23 UK-based firms within a strategic choice framework. In total, the sample entered 687 foreign markets and made 203 market servicing mode adjustments. The evidence presented does not support a single route to FDI as propounded in the Uppsala Internationalisation Model. Whilst firms have a choice between three generic forms of foreign market servicing, 11 *between* mode shifts and 4 *within* mode shifts were identified. Export was the most common method by which firms in the sample initially entered foreign markets. The move from minimal to FDI was the second most common form of initial entry. Of these 206 moves, 42 involved joint-venture agreements, 123 sales subsidiaries and 41 manufacturing facilities. Of the subsequent changes to the form of FDI, mixed modes of marketing approaches were more frequent than moves to sales subsidiaries. Hence, in this sample the export–sales subsidiary–manufacturing route was not as frequent as the export–sales subsidiary–mixed mode route. This indicates that whilst the former route is an important path to internationalisation, it is one option amongst several available to firms. However, overall foreign production was the third most frequent foreign market servicing mode adopted by the sample of companies. It was more common for markets to be serviced via export and sales subsidiaries. Hence, the internationalisation process as enumerated in Uppsala Internationalisation Model is completed by few firms in a small number of markets.

The results clearly demonstrate that whilst firms may expand on a country-by-country basis, they do not apply the same foreign market servicing strategy to each market. Rather, new forms of foreign market servicing are pursued within the context of interdependencies between existing foreign operations. Firms continually monitor their overseas operations both as separate entities, but also as interrelated structures. Just as licensing is the only option if firms wish to enter a particular foreign market, the sequential approach suggested by the Uppsala Internationalisation Model is appropriate for some firms in some markets. In other markets the firm may use its accumulated experience from operating internationally, or that of the group of which it is a part, to jump the intermediate steps and adopt a direct route to FDI. As a consequence, generalised models of the internationalisation process which seek to impose a common framework, and in so doing limit the choices available to managers, should be discarded. Rather, the internationalisation process is best understood, and therefore analysed, at the firm level. It is then that the variety of options available to managers will become clear.

Notes

1. We use a wider definition of FDI to include any form of market servicing which involves direct investment in the host country. This leads to a distinction between direct investment in sales operations, and direct investment in production facilities. Such investments may be either wholly owned or joint ventures. This distinction permits greater sensitivity to the variety of shifts involving FDI.
2. The UK 100 research team consists of the present authors, with the addition of Professor D.S. Pugh.

11 Global Procurement: A Strategy for Improving International Business Competitiveness

Shan Rajagopal and Kenneth N. Bernard[1]

INTRODUCTION AND OBJECTIVES

The 1980s and early 1990s have seen a progressive reduction in trade barriers around the world, culminating in several agreements, notably those setting up the North American Free Trade Area, the European Economic Area, and that which brought to a close the 'Uruguay Round' of GATT negotations. Whilst the precise nature and extent of the benefits arising from those agreements will probably remain matters for debate for several years to come, there seems little doubt that they mark further steps along the road to a general easing of constraints upon the internationalisation of trade. The consequences are therefore likely to affect not only the ability of suppliers to open new markets for goods and services, but equally will have similar impacts for purchasers. The changes will not be limited to 'external' transaction environments, but will also bear upon environments previously considered to be 'internal' or domestic. Freedom of competition means not simply that marketers are released from restraints imposed by tariff or non-tariff discrimination, but also that customers have a greater ability to source on a truly competitive basis – without being confined to local or domestic suppliers. Thus, companies who have previously been accustomed to secure conditions in local, protected environments will now find themselves faced with increased competition from 'outside', as competitors seek new sources of revenue, business and supplies.

Procurement motives are varied: whilst they may overtly focus on cost reductions or the acquisition of secure supply sources, other issues such as innovation, enhancement of service, quality advantage, acquisition of 'new' technologies and time-to-market compression are all identifiable as driving forces. Risk minimisation, coupled with the ever-present need to offer customers increased levels of benefit, and pressures to offer shareholders an attractive investment prospect, combine to increase the attention given to the identification of the most advantageous sources of supply of goods and services at all levels. These pressures bear not only upon large diversified organisations, but also upon smaller businesses which are faced with the need to compete for customers and suppliers in more open and widespread trading environments.

The authors' objective is to suggest a framework for the application of an approach to global procurement which could be adopted managerially, to deal with competitive threats and pressures in both customer and supplier markets. Whilst there are essential relationships between marketing and procurement environments there are also crucial differences as noted, for example, by Rajagopal and Bernard (1993a). It should be noted that the conceptualisation of procurement activities and the development of a critical body of literature lag behind the established practices of many leading companies, and, further, that companies themselves are far from having adopted a consensus approach to procurement as a strategic force or profit centre.

The models which are offered are tested against specific case material; against a body of data accumulated as part of ongoing research in the area, and against the main strands of existing literature in the areas of both procurement and international business.

GLOBAL PROCUREMENT: AN INTRINSIC PART OF GLOBAL STRATEGY

Global competition has become a central issue for many multinational companies. The emergence of European, Japanese and Third World multinationals has created a new competitive environment, calling for globalisation of corporate strategy (Kotler *et al.*, 1985; Levitt, 1983; Ohmae, 1985; Porter, 1986). Numerous advantages are increasingly recognized in creating and integrating various business operations across the national boundaries (Kogut, 1985; Porter, 1986; Prahaled and Doz, 1987). This has resulted in an increasing number of multinational firms engaged in sourcing of components and products on a global scale. Indeed, cross-national marketing transactions encompass both the buying (that is, sourcing) and selling (that is, market selection) aspects of the exchange process. Although marketing institutions are examined primarily in their roles as sellers rather than as buyers, the buying side of the exchange process should not be ignored (Kotler and Levy, 1973).

To maintain competitive advantage, multinational firms need to look beyond their national boundaries for sourcing of components and/or finished products. The options open to those firms range from establishing a buyer/seller relationship across national boundaries, to entering into a joint-venture agreement with an existing foreign company, to investing directly in overseas production facilities. In developing viable sourcing strategies on a global scale, firms must consider not only manufacturing costs, the cost of various resources and exchange rate fluctuations, but also the availability of infrastructure including transportation, communications and energy, industrial and cultural environments, the ease of working with foreign host governments and so on (Hefler, 1981; Caddick and Dale, 1986). Hickman and Hickman (1992) identified political stability, a well-developed infrastructure and a well-educated, urban work-force as attributes of low-risk procurement success.

The complex nature of sourcing strategy on a global scale spawns many barriers to its successful execution. Monczka and Giunipero (1984) report that logistics/inventory/distance, nationalism, and lack of working knowledge about foreign business practices, among others, are major problems identified by both US and foreign multinationals who are engaged extensively in international sourcing. They further argue that sourcing development programmes should be arranged within organizations to foster development of a positive attitude regarding international purchases. Thus, the implementation of such a sourcing strategy calls for a well-integrated and efficient global corporate system and outlook (Fayerweather, 1981; Porter, 1986).

LINKING MODELS OF INTERNATIONALISATION TO GLOBAL SOURCING

Within this broad context, numerous models have been postulated to demonstrate and explain the various steps in the development of internationalisation strategies, and the factors which would or could influence companies in their choice of a market entry mode or operational programme (summarised in, for example, Rugman *et al.*, 1988; Keegan, 1989; Young *et al.*, 1989). During the 1980s, a great deal of rather sterile academic debate centred on the extent to which the existence of various identifiable categories of international business activity predicated the existence of a sequential hierarchy of stages of development through which operations progressed. The generally accepted conclusion at the present time is that the 'stages' concept is somewhat irrelevant but that, in any case, the central issue is not that of progression or otherwise, but rather that taxonomies of strategy and practice *can be identified* – one corollary of which is that implications for the nature and scale of investments required can be deduced.

The development of global sourcing strategies, vertical dis-integration and Just in Time programmes have been undertaken to avoid excessive inventories and to contain the costs of obsolescence and improve customer service. Businesses that have instituted these arrangements are highly dependent on reliable supplies available at short time intervals. Market research has revealed that global sourcing is expected to grow, and also that those businesses with plans to continue outsourcing their supply needs will consolidate the number of suppliers to provide better control over the supply lines and thereby minimize risk (World Bank Report, 1991).

As a consequence, quick response to orders and timely delivery have become decisive criteria for success in international trading. All this is putting great pressure on plant flexibility and the maintenance of high quality levels. A track record of consistent reliability has become prerequisite for improving industrial productivity. In short, throughout the world – whether in industrial or developing countries – business conditions are changing in two fundamental and closely related ways.

Rajagopal and Bernard (1993a) have postulated a model of the internationalisation process showing four basic scenarios (Figure 11.1). This model has formed the background to the programme of field research on which the remainder of this discussion is based. There might perhaps be a perception that the postulation of this '4-stage' model discussed above carries with it an implicit necessity for sequential progression from one classification to another. Whilst there is clearly no formal stipulation that 'progress' should be step-wise, it might well be considered that, in practice, 'skipping' stages might be impracticable, given that each scenario has its own requirements in terms of relationships, levels of information flow and basic skills. Conversely, whilst it is clearly not essential that purchasers should actively seek to 'progress', it is likely that for many companies the need to change and to become more proactive will be forced upon them by competitive pressures, quite apart from simple progression along a 'learning curve'.

THE FRAMEWORKS FOR THE DEVELOPMENT OF GLOBAL SOURCING STRATEGY

One of the basic 'laws' of growth of any organisation is that as growth occurs, the internal structure of the organisation changes. In particular, the functional roles of its component parts tend to become more specialised and the links between the parts become more complex. As the size, organisational complexity and geographical spread of MNCs have increased, so the internal interrelationships between their geographically separated parts have become a highly significant element in the global economy (Dicken, 1992). The precise manner in which the MNCs organise and distribute their production or value-added chains, arises from their strategic orientation which is influenced by history as well as geographical origins. Internationally competitive strategies can be regarded as falling along a spectrum ranging from global integration at one end to national responsiveness at the other. Although there has certainly been a trend towards the adoption of globally integrated strategies by an increasing number of MNCs, they must remain responsive to national and local differentiation. Both global and local perspectives need to be combined.

	Inhibiting characteristics	External stimuli	Resource committment	Integrative execution
EXTERNAL AND INTERNAL DETERMINANTS	• attitudinal barriers • lack of international purchasing skills • lack of understanding foreign markets and its opportunities • lack of knowledge on foreign business customs • lack of foreign supplier qualifications methods	• supply disruption • changing exchange rate • declining domestic supply base • emergence of foreign competitor INTERNAL STIMULI • managerial aspirations • pressure to reduce cost • stringent quality • shorter product development cycle	• availability of resources • willingness to commit resources • experience based expectations • top management support	• develop an integrative worldwide • sourcing strategy • worldwide information integration
	↓	↓	↓	↓
CRITICAL ACTIVITY	• purchase solely from local supply market • at time obtain foreign produced goods, but purchased through domestic sources	• preliminary evaluation on international sourcing • international sourcing as and when needed • international information needs increase	• global perspective of potential source market • establish IPO's, FBO, TC • provide training and education • establish support with foreign based suppliers	• long term committment to global sourcing • expand base of knowledge about global sourcing
STAGES IN PROCESS	Domestic purchasing	Experimental involvement	Active involvement	Commitment involvement
	REACTIVE / DEFENSIVE		PROACTIVE / AGGRESSIVE	

Figure 11.1 A model of incremental internationalisation in the purchasing process

Source: Rajagopal, S. and Bernard, K.N. (1993) 'Globalisation of the Procurement Process', *Marketing Intelligence and Planning,* vol. 11, no. 7, pp. 44–56

The generic choice of worldwide sourcing strategies depends on the competitive advantage to be gained from global supply markets; the standardisation of purchase which may be achieved by centralising activities in a few countries to maximise economies of scale; and the volume of overseas buying versus the stage of involvement in the international purchasing process. If the perceived advantages of overseas sourcing are plotted in matrix form against the degree of proactivity and level of internationalisation in the procurement process, four generic strategies emerge (Figure 11.2).

	Level of involvement **Internationalisation of purchasing process** **(Reactive)** *Low*	**(Proactive)** *High*
Low **Perceived advantages of global supply market, standardisation**	(A) Local sourcing strategy	(C) Offensive sourcing strategy
High **of purchase and volume of overseas buying**	(B) Defensive sourcing strategy	(D) Worldwide sourcing strategy

Figure 11.2 A matrix of generic choices for global procurement strategies

Source: Rajagopal, S. and Bernard, K. N. (1993) 'Globalisation of the Procurement Process', *Marketing Intelligence and Planning*, vol. 11, no. 7, pp. 44–56.

Porter (1986) proposed four general types of international competitive strategy which the MNC might pursue, in terms of their organisational (coordination) and geographical (configuration) dimensions:

- An export-based strategy;
- A multi-domestic strategy;
- A basic global strategy;
- A complex global strategy.

Further, Porter observes that, 'There is no such thing as one global strategy. There are many different kinds . . . depending on a firm's choices about configuration and coordination throughout the value chain'. Using his argument and to promote more analytical appraisal, the authors propose a set of four international sourcing strategies which a multinational might develop.

Figure 11.3 shows these four generic international strategies expressed in a sourcing context, in terms of their organisational (coordination) and

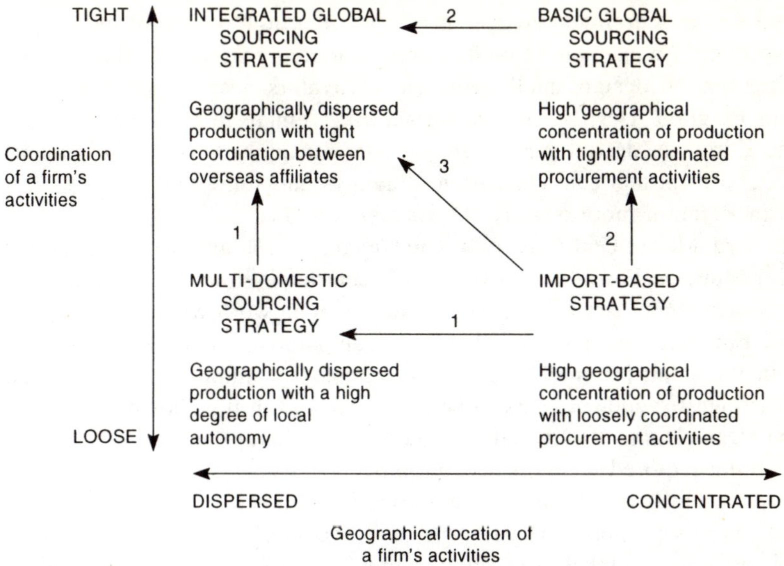

Figure 11.3 A typology of global sourcing strategies

Source: Rajagopal, S. and Bernard, K.N. (1993) 'Globalisation of the Procurement Process', *Marketing Intelligence and Planning*, vol. 11, no. 7, pp. 44–56; adapted from Porter, M.E. (ed.) (1986) *Competition in Global Industries* (Boston: Harvard Business School Press)

geographical (configuration) dimensions. The three sets of numbered arrows suggest possible strategic development paths, but it should not be assumed that only one path is inevitable. Each strategic quadrant involves different degrees of geographical concentration or dispersal of value activities. Two of the alternatives – the import-based strategy and the basic global sourcing strategy – involve a high degree of geographical concentration of production activities.

An interesting example of basic global sourcing strategy can be seen in Companhia Vale du Rio Doce (CVRD) in Brazil, which maintains complex relations with other firms both within the country and in its main external market in the processing of iron ore. CVRD, together with Kawasaki (Japan) and private enterprises in the USA, bought a steel-processing plant in California which was expanded to include a conglomerate in Mexico, and which imports mineral ore from Brazil for processing into steel plates which are then supplied to the California plant. Since this plant is the key provider of steel products to several car and equipment manufacturers on the West Coast, most of whom have adopted just-in-time production arrangements, the supply lines for ore and steel plates have to be well coordinated to ensure timely and reliable deliveries (World Bank Report, 1991).

The other two alternatives – the multi-domestic sourcing strategy and integrated global sourcing strategy – may involve a high degree of geographical dispersion. An example of multi-domestic sourcing strategy is the decision of Caterpillar to design small hydraulic excavators near its manufacturing plant in Belgium. Design control and auditing remain in the United States, but the European design group can react to changing market requirements on the Continent and can adapt basic drawings and source to plant requirements in Belgium more quickly (Davis *et al.*, 1974).

The Ford Motor Company is a good example for an integrated global sourcing strategy. Ford's strategy involves centralising the development of a car or a component wherever Ford has the greatest worldwide expertise. As Ford of Europe is recognised as having a comparative advantage over other firms in the small-car market, it has developed a common suspension and undercarriage for compact cars to be built and sold in the United States and Europe (Daniels and Radebaugh, 1989). Ford of Europe is also responsible for sourcing required component materials.

Based on the literature and the empirical evidence summarised later, the present authors propose that the process of deciding whether to, and who should, develop a global sourcing strategy can progress by understanding three fundamental dimensions: Figure 11.4 provides a general framework for the development of a global sourcing strategy. Within each of the three dimensions, crucial strategic questions can be considered to help devise a focused, tailored worldwide sourcing strategy unique to the organisation.

Step One: The Analytical and Motivational Dimension

This step enables the firm to assess the worldwide business situation, and especially the market factors influencing the need to 'go overseas': for example, supply disruptions, declining domestic supply base and access to worldwide technology. Environmental factors (for example changes in government and international regulations), foreign exchange fluctuations and general economic conditions need to be appraised carefully. Conjointly, firms need to review internal factors, particularly top management vision, corporate objectives and global strategy. The human factor, including individual managers' skills, knowledge and aspirations can be considered as a motivator for being involved in the international arena. Other firm-specific factors like cost, quality, product development and delivery requirements must also be considered. Thus, the starting point for global strategy development is an accurate assessment of the present and prospective extent of global opportunity, which will be determined by the presence and intensity of the following underlying forces and trends:

- Increasing homogenisation of customer needs and behaviour, and likewise the development of a supply base in these markets;
- Competitors that think and behave globally;

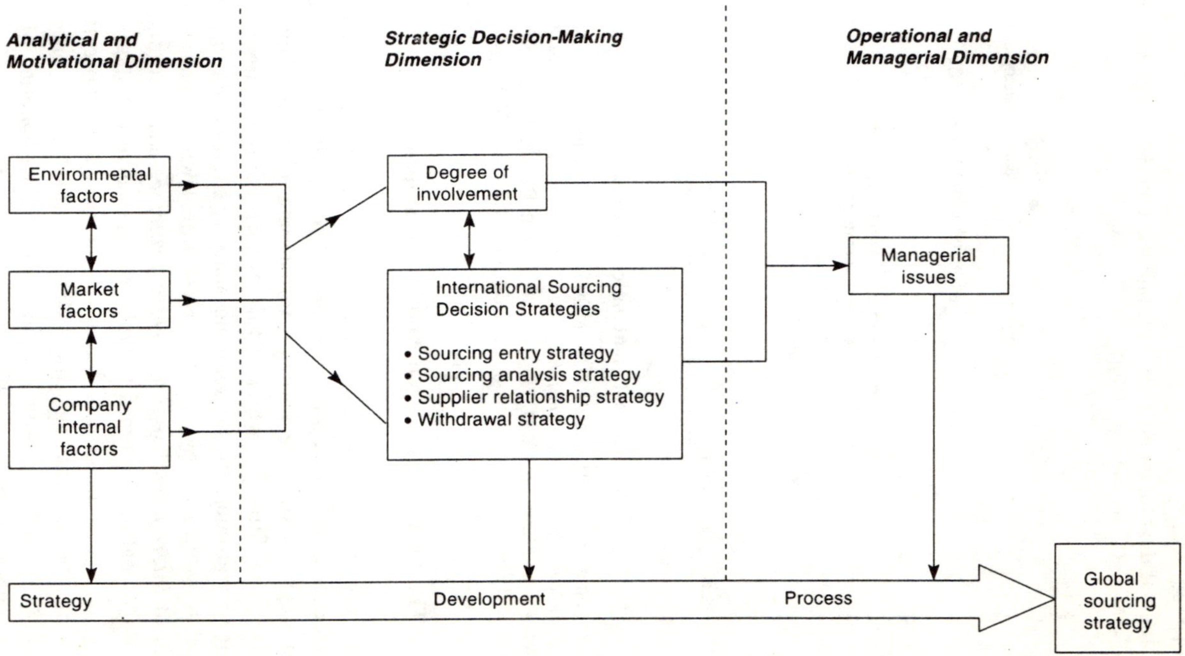

Figure 11.4 A framework for developing a global sourcing strategy

- Opportunities for substantial economies of scale or scope in key value-creating activities;
- Supportive macroeconomic environments that encourage and even demand a global presence;
- Technological developments that facilitate the coordination of wide-spread networks of activities (Day, 1990).

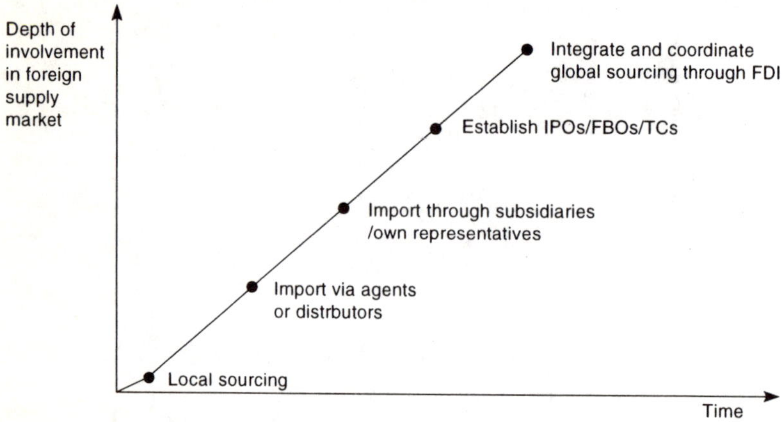

Figure 11.5 Modes of international sourcing entry strategies

Source: Rajagopal, S. and Bernard, K.N. (1993) 'Globalisation of the Procurement Process', *Marketing Intelligence and Planning*, vol. 11, no. 7, pp. 44–56; adapted from Figure 4.2 in Rugman, A.M., Lecraw, D.J. and Booth, L.D. (1988) *International Business Firm and Environment,* 3rd edn. Fig. 4.2 (New York: McGraw-Hill)

Step Two: The Strategic Decision-Making Dimension

A business contemplating sourcing from global markets has numerous strategic choices to make. Three of these choices are fundamental to any competitive strategy. Firstly, the strategic thrust determines the 'International Sourcing Decision Strategy' which in turn entails: the international sourcing entry strategy; the international sourcing analysis strategy; the international supplier relationship strategy; and the international withdrawal strategy.

Analysis of *international sourcing entry strategies* has been discussed in detail by Rajagopal and Bernard (1993b) who perceive the stages of internationalisation in procurement to be closely analogous to those familiar in the context of international marketing. Market entry criteria as proposed by Terpstra (1987), *inter alia*, give rise to various classifications of strategy. The present authors propose that Rugman *et al.*'s (1988) market entry model can be adapted with equal validity to illustrate the procurement options, and is capable of accommodating organisational objectives, structure and information availability, using Depth of Involvement as a key variable (Figure 11.5).

International companies must determine the sourcing entry alternatives if they expect to maintain a global perspective of their supply market. A company may want to import directly or indirectly, or engage in some mode of direct investment which views global sourcing as a strategic component of corporate strategy. These decisions on foreign sourcing entry mode tend to be of medium- to long-term importance, leaving little room for change once a commitment has been made. Therefore, it is important to treat these decisions with the utmost care. Not only is the financial welfare of the company at stake, but also the end market advantages to be gained depend on these decisions. In many respects the choice of entry mode represents a classic strategic trade-off evaluation between 'costs' and managerial 'control'.

Importation

Whether this be indirectly through agents or distributors, or directly through corporate subsidiaries/representatives – it is an option favoured by many companies in that it is usually perceived to minimise costs and maximise freedom of subsequent manoeuvre.

Arm's-length relationships may however lead to problems of product quality and delivery punctuality where dependence on intermediaries arises, and firms face a potential risk of inefficiencies in the conduct of their operations. On the other hand, use of corporate affiliates can assist in enhancing control, and is generally more likely to be favoured when there is a need for increased levels of information. Monczka and Giunipero (1983) identified four particular benefits from the use of affiliates:

- Knowledge of local suppliers;
- Physical proximity to sources;
- Knowledge of local business practices;
- Easier communications especially where language differences exist.

Establishment of International Procurement Offices

This has evolved as a logical response to deficiencies which have been detected in the levels of support available from distributors or affiliates. Qua and Thian (1991) stated that many original equipment manufacturers (OEM) have established IPOs in Asia due to Asia's tremendous manufacturing capacities and creditable capabilities. These IPOs buy parts, components and manufacturing and product development services for their plants worldwide. An interesting example is Singapore: since the 1970s, Singapore has attracted IPOs, and over the past ten years the number of IPOs and their roles have increased substantially. The number of IPOs operating or based in Singapore increased from 12 in 1985, to 75 in 1990 to over 100 in 1993. American and a few European companies were the first to set up IPOs in Singapore, followed by Japanese companies in the mid-80s. Towards the late-80s, Taiwanese and even Thai companies began to set up their IPOs in Singapore (Singapore Trade Development Board Report, 1991, authors' research).

Global Sourcing through Direct Investment
This provides an opportunity to maximise control over the procurement function, but demands worldwide integration of activities and a coordinate management system. Whilst maximising buying leverage, this approach is still compatible with the use of IPOs and with the concept of comparative advantage in designing, building and sourcing items. Firms can also go for joint production or co-production involving the sharing of manufacturing facilities to achieve economies of scale and production cost efficiencies. Requiring the supplier to invest in physical assets represents a form of transaction relationship. In addition, finding a partner with production efficiencies or combining production to achieve the economies of scale can provide a solution to maintaining costs at a competitive level. However, corporations need to be careful in selecting partners and generally limit their numbers because of the amount of management time and attention they require. Typically such agreements will feature:

- Increased sole sourcing between companies;
- Deeper technological interchanges involving process technology in addition to parts or products;
- Joint development of emerging technology;
- Commitments intended to last decades.

The shift from independence to interdependence stems from the growing understanding that, 'you are not buying parts, but you are buying capacity'. Joint product development is a form of technical tie-up combining R&D, production and occasionally some marketing (Yeoh and Cavusgil, 1990). This is the approach frequently taken by the Japanese in setting up a local captive supplier: they supply equipment, materials and technology and sometimes assist the local suppliers in acquiring finance as well as being a potential source of marketing support.

Finally, joint ventures and foreign subsidiaries represent a direct investment mode which views global sourcing as a strategic component of corporate strategy, which is based on the accumulation of common procurement requirements across worldwide business units to achieve superior performance for the corporation as a whole (Electronics Purchasing, 1989).

The modes of international sourcing entry strategy can best be represented as a continuum of domestic versus global sourcing orientation, where at one end the strategy focuses on local sourcing with little or no involvement with foreign suppliers. At the other end, integrated, coordinated relationships developed through joint ventures and direct investments are characterised by increasing complexity and a stronger focus on competitiveness. The organisational choice for most firms must involve a thorough evaluation of all the options which lie between these two extreme positions. Some firms may find that a choice to source locally or globally may optimise the ability of their purchasing department to contribute. However, the vast majority of companies will end up with a hybrid organisational choice positioned between these two extremes. Such a hybrid approach must be customised by each company, and this organisational choice should offer a reasonable trade-off by maximising perceived organisational strengths with avoidance of perceived weaknesses.

In respect of sourcing entry strategies the research shows that the majority favour direct and/or indirect import. An *international sourcing analysis strategy* is necessary for firms to consider the resource impact of deploying potential entry strategies. Again, from the study, cost and risk are considered significant in analysis of international sources.

Thirdly, an *international supplier relationship strategy* is fundamental to a firm considering long-term perspectives of global sourcing: the research identified only a minority of respondents who consider a formal policy for developing relationships with international suppliers. Out of these, contractual agreements, partnership agreements and licensing are popular modes of establishing and regulating relationships with foreign vendors.

Finally, it is important for a firm to have a contingency *withdrawal strategy*. Factors like failure to meet international purchasing objectives, international sanctions, political instability and changes in government regulations can influence the supply markets. For example, MSA (Britain), which manufactures high technology safety apparatus for the oil and coal industry, bought platinum from South Africa. When international sanctions against South Africa were imposed, MSA had difficulty in sourcing elsewhere due to short lead times: MSA had not been proactive and they almost stopped their production. It is critical for firms to consider their withdrawal strategy and to have an alternative supply source always ready.

The second strategic ingredient is the 'Degree of Involvement'. This involvement identifies the firm's stage in international development and the top management commitment to involvement in the international market place. A firm can have total commitment to global strategy, be active or only be involved experimentally.

The above elements have been identified as major stages in the internationalisation of the procurement process, which interrelate with the organisational objectives, structure, network and channel of information integration (Rajagopal and Bernard, 1993b).

Step Three: The Operational and Managerial Dimension

To implement a global sourcing strategy, a firm not only requires a tight central direction and harmonisation of the selection of sources, but also the managerial resources to carry out the strategy. These include having the right personnel with appropriate skills backed up by necessary training and development programmes, and having adequate channels for collection of information to control and coordinate worldwide sourcing activities. For firms to implement a global sourcing strategy successfully, they need to achieve congruency at two levels – managerial coordination and organisational structure; – collectively they facilitate international sourcing.

EMPIRICAL EVIDENCE

This section is devoted to a discussion of research investigations undertaken by the authors in several different, but complementary, circumstances. The aim of the programme was to identify and evaluate the relationships between the procurement internationalisation process, the concerns and motivations of the purchasers and the evolution of global sourcing strategies.

The studies had three principal dimensions:

- A large-scale survey to provide a longitudinal perspective of the habits, practices and perceptions across a range of industrial organisations,
- A series of in-depth case studies of specific organisations in the UK;
- A number of in-depth interviews with multinational organisations operating International Procurement Organisations (IPOs) in several different environments, in SE Asia as well as in Europe.

The large-scale survey replicated important aspects of previous research using a stratified random sample survey to produce longitudinality of perspective whilst employing large samples to provide breadth of cover – and hopefully of understanding of international sourcing perceptions and practices across industries and across classifications of size and country of ownership. For this survey a postal questionnaire was employed, circulated to a sample of 350 companies identified from Jordan's List of British Manufacturers. A total of 76 usable responses was received – a response rate of 21.7 per cent. The first section of the survey sought descriptive data regarding the firm, its motivations and its international procurement activities. The second section focused on the identification of relationships between the age of the company, the type of ownership of the firm and the motivational factors involved in determining international procurement activities.

The case studies were derived from in-depth interviews with a convenience sample of companies physically located in the UK, supplemented by two in-depth discussions with IPOs of multinationals – one domiciled in the EU, the other in the USA, but both based in Singapore.

The survey data uncovered factors affecting international procurement strategy formulation from a broad spectrum of industries and from a range of companies. The evidence thus derived has been used in the preparation of the normative model discussed above (Figure 11.4). However, the data were sufficiently rich to permit the illustration of several other points of interest – and potential significance – in both managerial and academic contexts. As noted above, the survey covered companies domiciled in several geographical regions. Although it is not surprising that, in a UK based survey, the largest single representation of companies should originate from the UK, it is noteworthy that:

1. UK companies did *not* form the majority of the companies in the sample, despite the random basis of selection;
2. There was a sufficiently large representation of companies domiciled elsewhere to permit formulation of some qualitative distinctions between companies, based on their domicile.

Table 11.1 presents comparative listings of motivational factors, broken down by country of domicile. These comparisons might be subject to modification if larger samples were to be used, especially for non-UK companies, but, despite that, the responses received show very marked divergences by country/region. Whilst, perhaps, these outcomes might not in themselves be surprising, and indeed confirm much conventional wisdom, the facts that:

1. They emerge from data expressly collected for the specific purpose;
2. They are based on quantitative, objective research;
3. The polarisations between the geographic segments are so clear;

may be taken, collectively, both to validate the findings themselves and to permit their interpretation in a generalised respect, as well as their use as indicators for managerial strategic planning.

From Table 11.1, it is clear that European, American and Japanese companies' motivations to enter and remain involved in the international purchasing arena have radically different foundations, but conversely that there is a very strong element of agreement as to the major problems to be faced in practice. The data show up basic differences in strategic approach to business:

- European companies emerge as being primarily concerned with competitiveness, with particular emphasis on prices/costs – perhaps driven by habits of responsiveness, rather than innovativeness, and perhaps indicative of their having been 'forced' into 'follower' positions by external constraints such as funding and investment limitations and short-term reporting necessities.
- American companies enter the international procurement arena primarily when driven to do so by inabilities to source domestically, although it should be remembered that their domestic market is extremely large and there has been a long tradition of 'buying American' wherever possible, especially when faced with Japanese competition.

Table 11.1 Principal expectations regarding motivations for internationalisation by country of domicile

<table>
<tr><th rowspan="2">Factors</th><th colspan="4">Corporate nationality/domicile</th></tr>
<tr><th>Britain</th><th>Europe</th><th>USA</th><th>Japan</th></tr>
<tr><td>Importance of factors leading to international purchasing</td><td colspan="2">On time delivery
Lower prices</td><td>Non-availability of local suppliers
Supplier willingness to help in problem solving</td><td>Better quality</td></tr>
<tr><td>Motivation to commence international purchasing</td><td colspan="2">Seek strategic advantage
Competitors already sourcing abroad</td><td>Non-availability of local supplies</td><td>Immediate performance improvement</td></tr>
<tr><td>Motivation to continue with international purchasing</td><td colspan="2">Lower prices
Gain competitive advantage
On time delivery</td><td></td><td>Better quality
Establishment of long-term relationships</td></tr>
<tr><td>Perceived serious problems in international purchasing</td><td>Company integrity
Foreign exchange risks</td><td>Quality assurance
Foreign exchange risks</td><td>Foreign exchange risks</td><td>Foreign exchange risks
Transportation delays
Political instability</td></tr>
<tr><td>Perceived benefits derived from international purchasing</td><td>Increased sourcing options
Lower prices</td><td>Lower prices
Increased competitiveness</td><td>Access to worldwide technologies
Better quality</td><td>Better quality
Lower prices</td></tr>
</table>

Source: Rajagopal, S. and Bernard, K. N. (1994) 'Global Procurement: Motivations and Strategy', *Market Intelligence and Planning*, vol. 12, no. 4, pp. 4–17

- Japanese businesses are fundamentally motivated by quality considerations and perceive quality/performance enhancement to be the key to achievement of price advantage and overall competitiveness.

To illustrate the varieties of approaches possible to yield gains from strategic sourcing, the strategies of the respondent companies have been profiled by country of domicile, plotting the dimensions of global sourcing strategy development (from Figure 11.4) against the four levels of commitment outlined in Figure 11.1 (see Figure 11.6). The sharpness of this comparison for the *analytical and motivational dimension* indicates the influence of the country of origin's perception in developing international purchasing strategy. Both British and European-based companies tend to be at the initial stages of procurement internationalisation, while Japanese and American-based firms show greater commitment and involvement in the motivation and analysis of the global supply market.

These findings are consistent with the perception that European/American organisations tend to be driven by short-term considerations, whereas Japanese companies base their strategic plans on longer-term objectives geared to gaining both competitive advantage and profitability from providing better products with lower levels of wastage. This is entirely consistent with the marketing philosophy and the notion of a 'win–win' strategy based on strict principles of cost containment (Bernard and Rajagopal, 1992; and Rajagopal and Bernard, 1993c).

In respect of perceived problems in international sourcing, respondents from all geographic areas highlighted foreign exchange risks, but it is noteworthy that Japanese companies also raised issues of delays in transit and of threats caused by political instabilities. This confirms and amplifies the observation that key de-motivators from persistence with international business activities are strongly associated with uncertainties and also with the threats or actualities of external intervention or regulation (Young *et al.*, 1989). The findings also suggest that such perceived risks are second only to matters of quantifiable costs as matters of management concern.

With the strategic *decision making dimension*, the Americans appear to have the greatest committed involvement in respect of entry sourcing and analysis strategy. With respect to the development of international supplier relationships, British-based firms appeared relatively uninvolved and largely to be in the early stages of procurement internationalisation. The *operational and managerial dimension*, however, indicated that all firms tend to be either experimentally or actively involved in international sourcing activity. It is important to note that, in terms of personnel capabilities and training and development in international purchasing, the American-based firms showed the greatest commitment and involvement.

This comparative profile provides an overview of the behavioural aspects of companies when developing international sourcing strategies, and provides

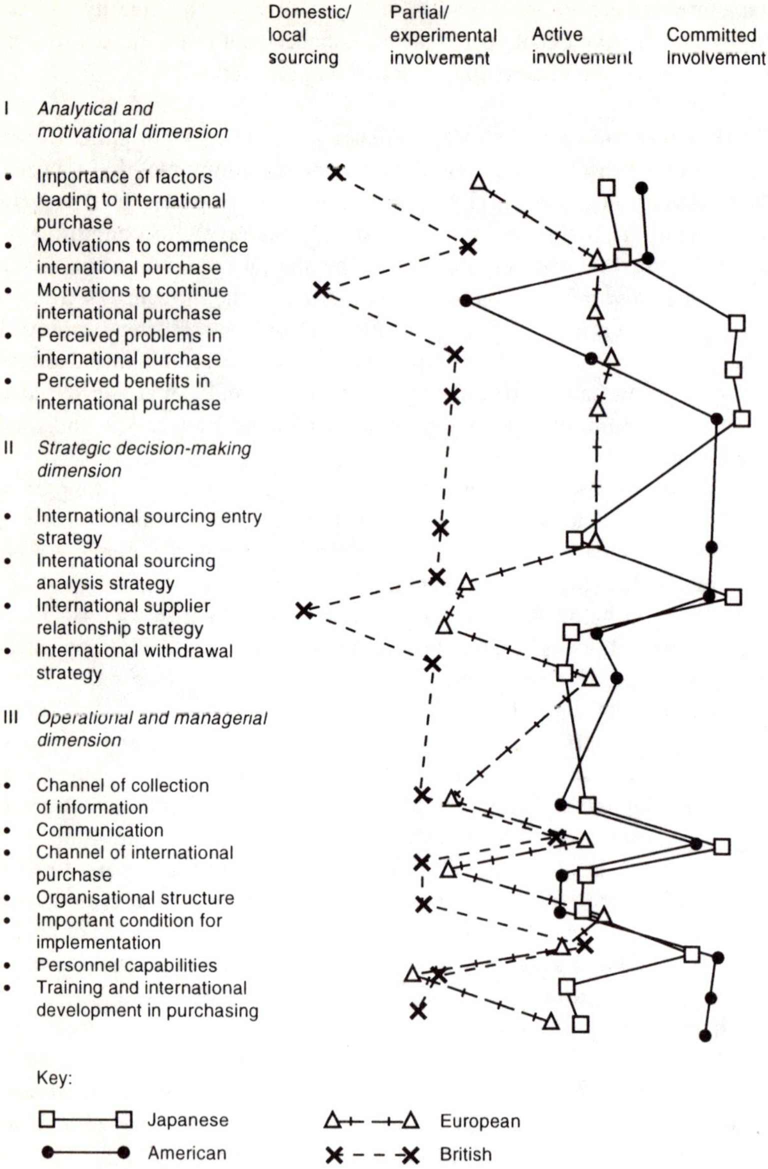

Figure 11.6 Profiling globalisation of procurement process by country of domicile

a useful insight into firms from different countries of origin. Firms can assess their own procurement internationalisation position and this in turn can assist them to develop an international sourcing strategy. Nevertheless, whilst a pessimist can always find a host of good reasons for doing nothing, the clear conclusion drawn from this sample of respondents is that the benefits derivable and the risks of being left behind through non-participation in international purchasing programmes are sufficient to outweigh the operational risks involved in participation. It also appears likely that amongst the companies surveyed, the existence of strategic plans and objectives and the establishment of performance monitoring systems provide a basis for constructive management of the purchasing function, even though only just over half of the companies identify purchasing strategy as a matter of top management concern.

CONCLUSION

The internationalisation of the entire business environment is no longer just a hypothetical possibility, but in many industries has already become established fact. Marketers have been faced with that scenario in commodity and basic raw materials markets for many years, and increasingly this is extending to manufactured goods. Whilst it remains arguable whether global products will come to dominate the marketing environment, or whether global marketing will become the norm, it does appear that global procurement will have a major role to play in the competitive strategies of increasing numbers of companies, whether or not the resultant product is traded worldwide or more locally.

To achieve such an objective requirement, a broad view of the coordination of supply sources and production facilities is necessary in order to optimise deliverability of desired outputs to customers, wherever they may be. That has organisational implications for the supply side of the firm; for internal relationship management between supply-side and marketing functions; and for the fabric, focus, centre of gravity and strategic management of the firm as a whole.

Success in competitive procurement on a global scale has the potential to enhance the product offering and thus lead to competitive marketing success – leading to virtuous circle gains in competitive advantage, enhanced attractiveness to suppliers and bargaining leverage – and so back to further strategic procurement advantages. It is clear that some companies have already identified the possibilities – others will need progressively to reappraise their philosophies or become procurement 'followers', with consequent impact on their strategies for marketing, on their competitive standing and indeed on their ability to survive and develop in the longer term.

Note

1. The authors gratefully acknowledge receipt of financial support from the Carnegie Trust for the Universities of Scotland and from the Department of Marketing of the University of Strathclyde for the research upon which this paper is based.

Bibliography

Abell, M. (1990) *The International Franchise Option* (London: Waterlow).

Adams, J. and M. Mendelsohn (1986) 'Recent Developments in Franchising', *Journal of Business Law*, 206–19.

Adler, N.J., N. Campbell and A. Laurent (1989) 'In Search of Appropriate Methodology: From Outside the People's Republic of China Looking In', *Journal of International Business Studies*, 20(1), 61–74.

Adler, N.J. and M. Jelinek (1986) 'Is Organisational Culture "Culture Bound"?', *Human Resource Management*, 25, 73–90.

Agarwal, S. and S.N. Ramaswami (1991) 'Ownership Structures of US Joint Ventures in the 1980s', *The International Trade Journal*, 6(1), 127–49.

Agarwal, S. and S.N. Ramaswami (1992) 'Choice of Foreign Market Entry Mode: Impact of Ownership, Location and Internalisation Factors', *Journal of International Business Studies*, 23(1), 1–27.

Aharoni, Y. and J.P. Sticht (1990a) 'Ownership, Networks and Coalitions', paper presented at the conference 'Competition and Coalitions: The Globalisation of Professional Services', Duke University.

Aharoni, Y. and J.P. Sticht (1990b) 'Globalisation of Services, With Special Reference to Professional Business Services – A Survey of Major Issues and Research', paper presented at the Annual Conference of the Academy of International Business.

Allaire, Y. and M.E. Firsirotu (1984) 'Theories of Organisational Culture', *Organisation Studies*, 5(3), 193–226.

Anderson, E. (1985) 'The Salesperson as Outside Agent or Employee: A Transaction Cost Analysis', *Marketing Science*, 4(3), 234–54.

Anderson, E. (1990) 'Two Firms, One Frontier: On Assessing Joint Venture Performance', *Sloan Management Review*, 19, Winter.

Anderson, E. and H. Gatignon (1986) 'Modes of Foreign Entry: A Transaction Cost Analysis and Propositions', *Journal of International Business Studies*, 17(3), 1–26.

Anderson, E. and H. Gatignon (1987) 'International Market Entry and Expansion via Independent or Integrated Channels of Distribution', *Journal of Marketing*, 51 (January), 71–82.

Anderson, K. and R. Blackhurst (1993) 'Introduction and Summary', in K. Anderson and R. Blackhurst (eds), *Regional Integration and the Global Trading System* (Hemel Hempstead: Harvester-Wheatsheaf), 1–15.

Anderson, O. (1993) 'On the Internationalisation Process of Firms: A Critical Analysis', *Journal of International Business Studies*, 24(2), 209–31.

Argyris, R. and D. Schon (1978) *Organisational Learning: A Theory of Action Perspective* (Reading, Mass.: Addison-Wesley).

Awadzi, W.K. (1987) 'Determinants of Joint Venture Performance: A Study of International Joint Ventures in the United States', Ph.D. dissertation, Louisiana State University.

Aydin, N. and M. Kacker (1990) 'International Outlook of US-based Franchisors', *International Marketing Review*, 7(2), 43–53.

Baillie, I.C. (1987) 'Franchising in the International Regime of Intellectual Property', *Journal of International Franchising and Distribution Law*, 2, December, 67–73.

Baird, I.S., M.A. Lyles and R. Wharton (1990) 'Attitude Differences between American and Chinese Managers Regarding JV Management', *Management International Review*, 30, Special Issue.

Baird, I.S., M.A. Lyles, S. Ji and R. Wharton (1990) 'Joint Venture Success: A Sino-US Perspective', *International Studies of Management and Organisation*, 20(1/2).

Balasubramanyam, V.N. and D. Greenaway (1993) 'Regional Integration Agreements and Foreign Direct Investment', in K. Anderson and R. Blackhurst (eds) *Regional Integration and the Global Trading System* (Hemel Hempstead: Harvester–Wheatsheaf), 147–66.

Bamberger, I. (1986) 'Values and Strategic Behaviour', *Management International Review*, 36(4), 57–69.

Bandura, A. (1977) *Social Learning Theory* (Englewood Cliffs, N.J.: Prentice-Hall).

Barley, S.R. (1983) 'Semiotics and the Study of Occupational and Organisational Cultures', *Administrative Science Quarterly*, 28(4), 393–413.

Bartlett, C. and S. Ghoshal (1987) 'Managing across Borders: New Strategic Requirements', *Sloan Management Review*, Summer.

Bartlett, C.A. and S. Ghoshal (1987) 'Managing Across Borders: New Organisational Responses', *Sloan Management Review*, 29, 43–53.

Bartunek, J.M. (1984) 'Changing Interpretive Schemes and Organisational Restructuring: The Example of a Religious Order', *Administrative Science Quarterly*, 29(3), 355–72.

Beamish, P. (1985) 'The Characteristics of Joint Ventures in Developed and Developing Countries', *Columbia Journal of World Business*, 20(3).

Beamish, P. (1988) *Multinational Joint Ventures in Developing Countries* (London & New York: Routledge).

Beamish, P. and J. Banks (1987) 'Equity Joint Ventures and the Theory of the Multinational Enterprise', *Journal of International Business Studies*, 18(2), 1–16.

Beijing Review (1992) 'Socialist Market Economy – A New Term in Reform' (Beijing), 4.

Bennis, W. (1985) *Taking Charge* (New York: Harper & Row).

Berg, S., F. Duncan and P. Friedman (1982) *Joint Venture Strategies and Corporate Innovation* (Cambridge: Oelgeschlager, Gunn & Hain).

Berger, P. and T. Luckmann (1967) *The Social Construction of Reality* (Harmondsworth: Penguin).

Bernard, K.N. and S. Rajagopal (1992) 'Integrated Marketing and Procurement: A Conceptual Approach for Profitability', *Proceedings of the 21st Annual Conference of the European Marketing Academy*, Aarhus, 1229–32.

Bernstein, L. (1965) 'Joint Ventures in the Light of Recent Antitrust Development: Anticompetitive Joint Venture, *Antitrust Bulletin*, 10.

Bhagwati, J. (1990) 'Multilateralism at Risk: the GATT is Dead, Long Live GATT', *The World Economy*, 13, 149–69.

Bilkey, W.J. and G. Tesar (1977) 'The Export Behaviour of Smaller-Sized Wisconsin Manufacturing Firms', *Journal of International Business Studies*, 8(1), 93–8.

Bishop, M. (1990) 'European or National? the EEC's New Merger Regulation', in J. Fairburn and J. Kay (eds), *Continental Mergers are Different, Strategy and Policy for 1992*, Centre for Business Strategy Report (London: London Business School).

Bleeke, J. and D. Ernst (1993) *Collaborating to Compete: Using Strategic Alliances and Acquisitions in the Global Marketplace* (New York: John Wiley & Sons).

Boddewyn, J.J., M.B. Halbrich and A.C. Perry (1986) 'Service Multinationals: Conceptualisation, Measurement and Theory', *Journal of International Business Studies*, 17(3), 41–57.

Boisot, M. and J. Child (1990) *The Management of Equity Joint Ventures in China* (Beijing: China–EC Management Institute).

Boje, D.M., D.B. Fedor and K.M. Rowland (1982) 'Myth-making: A Qualitative Step in OD Interventions', *Journal of Applied Behavioural Science*, 18, 17–28.

Bradley, F. (1991) *International Marketing Strategy* (Englewood Cliffs, N.J.: Prentice-Hall).

Brittan, Sir L. (1990) 'The Law and Policy of Merger Control in the EEC', *European Law Review*, 15, October, 351–7.

Brooke, M.Z. (1986) *International Management: A Review of Strategies and Operations* (London: Hutchinson).

Brown, R. (1978) 'Bureaucracy as Praxis: Toward a Phenomenology for Formal Organisations', *Administrative Science Quarterly*, 23, 365–82.

Buckley, P.J. (1983) 'New Forms of International Industrial Co-operation: A Survey of the Literature and Special Reference to North–South Technology Transfer', *Aussenwirtschaft*, 38, 195–222.

Buckley, P.J. (1990) 'Problems and Developments in the Core Theory of International Business', *Journal of International Business Studies*, 21(4), 657–65.

Buckley, P.J. (1991) 'Alliances, Technology and Markets: A Cautionary Tale', in P.J. Buckley (ed.), *International Business* (London: Macmillan).

Buckley, P.J. (1993) 'The Role of Management in Internalisation Theory', *Management International Review*, 33(3), 197–207.

Buckley, P.J. and M.C. Casson (1976) *The Future of Multinational Enterprise* (London: Macmillan).

Buckley, P.J. and M.C. Casson (1981) 'The Optimal Timing of a Foreign Direct Investment', *Economic Journal*, 91, 75–87, reprinted as Chapter 5 in P.J. Buckley and M.C. Casson (1985) *The Economic Theory of the Multinational Enterprise* (London: Macmillan).

Buckley, P.J. and M.C. Casson (1985) *The Economic Theory of the Multinational Enterprise* (London: Macmillan).

Buckley, P.J. and M.C. Casson (1988) 'The Theory of Co-operation in International Business', in F.J. Contractor and P. Lorange (eds) *Cooperative Strategies in International Business* (Lexington, Mass.: Lexington Books).

Buckley, P.J. and M.C. Casson (1992) 'Economics as an Imperialist Social Science', *University of Reading Discussion Papers in Economics*, no. 260.

Buckley, P.J. and H. Davies (1981) 'Foreign Licensing in Overseas Operations: Theories and Evidence from the UK', in R.G. Hawkins and B.J. Prasad (eds), *Research in International Business and Finance* (Greenwich, Conn.: JAI Press), 75–89.

Buckley, P.J. and P.N. Ghauri (eds) (1993) *The Internationalisation of the Firm: A Reader* (London: Academic Press).

Buckley, P.J. and A.M. Mathew (1979) 'The Motivation for Recent First Time Direct Investments in Australia by UK Firms', *Management International Review*, 19(1), 57–69.

Buckley, P.J., G.D. Newbould and J.C. Thurwell (1979) *Foreign Direct Investment by Smaller UK Firms: The Success and Failure of First-time Investors* (London: Macmillan).

Buckley, P.J., C.L. Pass and K. Prescott (1990) 'The Implementation of an International Market Servicing Strategy in UK Manufacturing Firms', *British Journal of Management*, 1, 127–36.

Buckley, P.J., C.L. Pass and K. Prescott (1991) 'Foreign Market Servicing Strategies in UK Retail Financial Firms in Europe', paper presented to an Economic and Social Research Council (ESRC) Conference, Chatham House, 21 June.

Buckley, P.J., C. Pass and K. Prescott (1992) *Servicing International Markets: Competitive Strategies of UK Firms* (Oxford: Blackwell).

Buckley, P.J. and K. Prescott (1989) 'The Structure of British Industry's Sales in Foreign Markets', *Managerial and Decision Economics*, 10, 189–208.

Burton, F.N. and A.R. Cross (1994) 'The International Franchise Entry Mode: An Analysis', in M. Yamin, F.N. Burton and A.R. Cross (eds) *The Changing European Environment*, Proceedings of the 21st Annual Conference of the UK Academy of International Business, UMIST, 209–27.

Caddick, J.R. and B.G. Dale (1986) 'Sourcing from Less Developed Countries: A Case Study', *Journal of Purchasing and Materials Management*, Fall, 17–23.

Campbell, N. (1987) 'Experiences of Western Companies in China', *Euro–Asia Business Review*, July.

Campbell, N. (1988) 'The Pattern of Equity Joint Venture in China', *Management Research News*, 11(4/5).

Campbell, N. (1989) *A Strategic Guide to Equity Joint Ventures in China* (Oxford: Pergamon Press).

Campbell, Nigel and P. Adlington (1988) *China Business Strategies: Survey of Foreign Business Activity in the People's Republic of China* (Oxford: Pergamon).

Casson, M.C. (1979) *Alternatives to Multinational Enterprises* (London: Macmillan).

Casson, M.C. (1990) *Enterprise and Competitiveness: A Systems View of International Business* (Oxford: Clarendon Press).

Casson, M.C. (1992a) 'Cultural Factors in Innovation: An Economic Analysis', *University of Reading Discussion Papers in Economics*, no. 259.

Casson, M.C. (1992b) *The Economics of Business Culture: Game Theory, Transaction Costs and Economic Performance* (Oxford: Clarendon Press).

Casson, M.C. (1982) *The Entrepreneur: An Economic Theory* (Oxford: Martin Robertson).

Casson, M.C. (1988) 'Economic Man', in J. Creedy (ed.) *Fundamental Concepts in Economics* (Oxford: Blackwell).

Casson, M.C. and F. Chukujama (1991) 'Countertrade: Theory and Evidence', in P.J. Buckley and J. Clegg (eds) *Multinational Enterprises in Less Developed Countries* (London: Macmillan).

Casson, M.C. and J. Zheng (1992) 'Western Joint Ventures in China', in M.C. Casson (ed.) *International Business and Global Integration* (London: Macmillan).

Caves, R.E. (1982) *Multinational Enterprise and Economic Analysis*, Cambridge Surveys of Economic Literature (Cambridge: Cambridge University Press).

Caves, R.E. and S.K. Mehra (1986) 'Entry of Foreign Multinationals into US Manufacturing Industries', in M.E. Porter (ed.), *Competition in Global Industries* (Boston: Mass: Harvard Business School Press), 449–81.

Caves, R.E. and W.F. Murphy (1976) 'Franchising: Firms, Markets and Intangible Assets', *Southern Economic Journal*, 42, 572–85.

Cavusgil, S.T. (1980) 'On the Internationalisation Process of Firms', *European Research*, 8, November, 273–81.

Cecchini, P. (with M. Catinat and A. Jacquemin) (1988) *The European Challenge 1992: The Benefits of a Single Market* (Aldershot, Hants: Wildwood House).

Chang, W. (1992) 'VW May Launch New Auto Project', *Shanghai Focus, China Daily*, 8–14 November, 3.

Charles, R. (1989) 'Canada–United States Free Trade Agreement: A Canadian's Personal Perspective', *National Westminster Bank Quarterly Review*, May, 17–26.

Child, J. (1972) 'Organisational Structure, Environment and Performance: The Role of Strategic Choice', *Sociology*, 6, 1–22.

Child, J. and A. Kieser (1979) 'Organisational and Managerial Roles in British and German Companies: an Examination of the Culture-Free-Thesis', in C.J. Lammers and D.J. Hickson (eds), *Organisations Alike and Unlike* (London: Routledge & Kegan Paul), 251–71.

China International Economic Consultants Inc. (1984/85, 86, 87) *The China Investment Guide* (London: Longman).

Churchill, G.A. (1979) 'A Paradigm for Developing Better Measures of Marketing Constructs', *Journal of Marketing Research*, 16, February, 64–73.

Churchill, G.A. (1991) *Marketing Research: Mythological Foundations*, 5th edn (London: Dryden Press).

Coase (1937) 'The Nature of the Firm', *Economica*, 4(4), 386–405.

Colchester, N. and D. Buchan (1990) *Europe Relaunched: Truths and Illusions on the Way to 1992* (London: Economist Books).

Cole, R.E. (1973) 'Functional Alternatives and Economic Development: An Empirical Example of Permanent Employment in Japan', *American Sociological Review*, 38, 424–38.

Commission of the European Communities (1966) *Problem of Concentration in the Common Market*, Study No. 3.

Commission of the European Communities (1985) *Completing the Internal Market*, White Paper from the Commission to the European Council (Brussels: Office for Official Publications of the European Communities).

Commission of the European Communities (1992) *XXIst Report on Competition Policy* (Brussels: Office for Official Publications of the European Communities).

Commission of the European Communities (1993) *Review of the Application of Council Regulation (EEC)* No 4064/89 of 21 December 1989 on the Control of Concentrations between Undertakings (mimeo).

Conroy, R. (1986) 'China's Technology Import Policy', *Euro–Asia Business Review*, 3(3), July.

Contractor, F.J. (1985) *Licensing in International Strategy: A Guide for Planning and Negotiations* (Westport, Conn.: Quorum Books).

Contractor, F.J. (1990) 'Contractual and Cooperative Forms of International Business: Towards a Unified Theory of Modal Choice', *Management International Review*, 30(1) 31–54.

Contractor, F.J. and P. Lorange (1988) 'Why Should Firms Cooperate: The Strategy and Economic Basis for Cooperative Ventures', in F.J. Contractor and P. Lorange (eds) *Cooperative Strategies in International Business* (Lexington, Mass.: Lexington Books).

Council Regulation (EC) (1989) No 4064/89 of 21 December 1989 on the Control of Concentrations between Undertakings, *Official Journal*, L 395/1.

Cowhey, P.F. and J.D. Aronson (1993) *Managing the World Economy: The Consequence of Corporate Alliances* (New York: Council on Foreign Relations Press).

Curhan, J.P., W.H. Davidson and R. Suri (1977) *Tracing the Multinationals* (Cambridge, Mass.: Ballinger).

Cutler, T., C. Haslam, J. Williams and K. Williams (1992) *1992 The Struggle for Europe. A Critical Evaluation of the European Community* (Oxford: Berg).

Cyert, R.M. and J.G. March (1963) *Behavioural Theory of the Firm* (Englewood Cliffs, N.J.: Prentice-Hall).

Czinkota, M.R. (1982) *Export Development Strategies: US Promotion Policies* (New York: Praeger).

Czinkota, M.R. and I.A. Ronkainen (1988) *International Marketing* (Hinsdale, Ill.: Dryden Press).

Daniels, J.D., J. Krug and D. Nigh (1985) 'US Joint Ventures in China: Motivation and Management of Political Risk', *California Management Review*, 27(4), Summer, 46–58.

Daniels, J.D. and L.H. Radebaugh (1989) 'Ford in Europe – The Early Years' in *International Business: Environments and Operations* (Reading, Mass.: Addison-Wesley), 215–6.

Davidson, W.H. (1980) 'The Location of Foreign Direct Investment Activity: Country Characteristics and Experience Effects', *Journal of International Business Studies*, 11(2), 9–22.

Davidson, W.H. (1987) 'Creating and Managing Joint Ventures in China', *California Management Review*, 29(4).

Davidson, W.H. and D.G. McFetridge (1985) 'Key Characteristics in the Choice of International Technology Transfer Mode', *Journal of International Business Studies*, 16(2), 5–21.

Davies, H. (1977) 'Technology Transfer Through Commercial Transactions', *Journal of Industrial Economics*, 26(2), 161–75.

Davis, E. (1990) 'Synergies and Motivations for Cross Border Merger', in J.A. Fairburn and J. Kay (eds), *Continental Mergers are Different; Strategy and Policy for 1992*, Centre for Business Strategy Research Report (London: London Business School), 47–63.

Davis, H.L., G.D. Eppen and L-G. Mattson (1974) 'Critical Factors in World-wide Purchasing', *Harvard Business Review*, November–December.

Davis, S.M. (1984) *Managing Corporate Culture* (Cambridge, Mass.: Ballinger).

Day, G. (1990) *Market-Driven Strategy* (New York: The Free Press).

De Bettignies, H.C. (1973) 'Japanese Organisational Behaviour: A Psychological Approach', in G. Graves (ed.) *Management Research: A Cross Cultural Perspective* (San Francisco: Jossey Bass).

Deal, T.E. and A.A. Kennedy (1982) *Corporate Cultures* (Reading, Mass.: Addison-Wesley).

Department of Trade and Industry (1988) *Mergers Policy* (London: HMSO).

Dicken, P. (1992) *Global Shift: The Internationalisation of Economic Activity*, 2nd ed. (London: Paul Chapman).

Dimaggio, J. and W. Powell (1983) 'The Iron Cage Revisited: Institutional Isomorphism and Collective Rationality in Organisational Fields', *American Sociological Review,* 48.

Doise, W. and D. Mackie (1981) 'On the Social of Cognition', in J.P. Forgas (ed.) *Social Cognition: Perspectives in Everyday Understanding* (London: Academic Press), 51–83.

Donnellon, A. (1986) 'Language and Communication in Organisations', in D.A. Gioia and H.P. Sims Jr (eds) *The Thinking Organisation: Dynamics of Organisational Social Cognition* (San Francisco: Jossey Bass), 136–64.

Duhaime, I.M. and C.R. Schwenk (1985) 'Conjectures on Cognitive Simplification in Acquisition and Divestment Decision Making', *Academy of Management Review*, 10(2), 287–96.

Dunning, J.H. (1973) 'The Determinants of International Production', *Oxford Economic Papers,* 25(3), November, 289–336.

Dunning, J.H. (1979) 'Explaining Changing Patterns of International Production: In Defence of the Eclectic Theory', *Oxford Bulletin of Economics and Statistics*, Special Issue: The Multi-National Corporation, 41(4), November, 255–67.

Dunning, J.H. (1980) 'Toward an Eclectic Theory of International Production: Some Empirical Tests', *Journal of International Business Studies*, 80(1), 9–31.

Dunning, J.H. (1981) *International Production and the Multinational Enterprise* (London: George Allen & Unwin).

Dunning, J.H. (1988a) 'The Eclectic Paradigm of International Production: A Restatement and Some Possible Extensions', *Journal of International Business Studies*, 19(1), 1–31.

Dunning, J.H. (1988b) *Explaining International Production* (London: Unwin Hyman).

Dunning, J.H. (1989) *Transnational Corporations and the Growth of Services: Some Conceptual and Theoretical Issues*, UNCTC Current Studies, Series A, No. 9 (New York: United Nations).

Dunning, J.H. and R.D. Pearce (1981) *The World's Largest Industrial Companies* (London: Gower Press).

Dunning, J.H. and R.D. Pearce (1985) *The World's Largest Industrial Enterprises 1962–83* (Aldershot: Gower).

Durkheim, E. (1938), *The Rules of Sociological Method* (New York: Free Press).

Dutton, J.E., L. Fahey and V.K. Narayanan (1983) 'Towards Understanding Strategic Issues Diagnosis', *Strategic Management Journal*, 4, 307–23.

Economist (1992a) 'The Overseas Chinese: A Driving Force', 18 July.

Economist (1992b) 'Invest in China', 14 December.

Edvardsson, B., L. Edvinsson and H. Nyström (1992) *Internationalisering i tjänsteföretag*, Studentlitteratur, Lund.

Edvardsson, B. and E. Gummesson (1988) *Management i tjänstesamhället* (Stockholm, Sweden: Liber).

Eiser, R.J. (1986), *Social Psychology* (Cambridge: Cambridge University Press).

El-Agraa, A.M. (1988) 'The Theory of Integration', in A.M. El-Agraa (ed.) *International Economic Integration* (London: Macmillan).

Electronics Purchasing (1989) 'Global Sourcing Grows More Complex', F. Gardner (ed.), 16 February.

Eroglu, S. (1992) 'The Internationalisation Process of Franchise Systems: A Conceptual Model', *International Marketing Review*, 9(5), 19–30.

Erramilli, M.K. (1990) 'Entry Mode Choice in Service Industries', *International Marketing Review*, 7(5), 50–62.

Erramilli, M.K. (1991) 'The Experience Factor in Foreign Market Entry Behaviour of Service Firms', *Journal of International Business Studies*, 22(3), 479–501.

Erramilli, M.K. and C.P. Rao (1990) 'Choice of Foreign Market Entry Modes by Service Firms: Role of Market Knowledge', *Management International Review*, 30(2), 135–50.

Etzioni, A. (1988) *The Moral Dimension: Towards a New Economics* (New York: Free Press).

Euromonitor (1987) *Franchising in the European Economy: Trends and Forecasts 1980–1990* (London: Euromonitor).

Evans, P. and J. Walsh (1994) *The EIU Guide to the New Gatt* (London: The Economist Intelligence Unit).

Evered, R. (1983) 'The Language of Organisations', in L.R. Pondy, P. Frost, G. Morgan and T. Dandridge (eds) *Organisational Symbolism* (Greenwich, Conn.: JAI Press), 125–43.

Falbe, C.M. and T.C. Dandridge (1992) 'Franchising as Strategic Partnership: Issues of Co-operation and Conflict in a Global Market', *International Small Business Journal*, 10(3), 40–52.

Fayerweather, J.C (1981) 'Four Winning Strategies for the International Corporation', *Journal of Business Strategy*, Fall.

Felstead, A. (1993) *The Corporate Paradox: Power and Control in the Business Franchise* (London: Routledge).

Ferdows, K. *et al.* (1985) 'Evolving Manufacturing Strategies in Europe, Japan and North America', *INSEAD Working Research Paper* 85:07.

Financial Times (1994) Financial Times Survey: China, 7 November.

Fishwick, F. (1989) 'Definition of Monopoly Power in the Antitrust Policies of the UK and EC', *Antitrust Bulletin*, 34(3), 451–88.

Fiske, S.T. and S.E. Taylor (1984), *Social Cognition* (New York: Random House).

Fombrun, C. and E. Zajac (1987) 'Structural and Perceptual Influences on Intraindustry Stratification', *Academy of Management Journal*, 30(1), 33–50.

Forgas, J.P. (1981b) 'What is Social about Social Cognition', in J.P. Forgas (ed.) *Social Cognition: Perspectives in Everyday Understanding* (London: Academic Press), 1–26.

Forgas, J.P. (1981a) 'Epilogue: Everyday Understanding and Social Cognition', in J.P. Forgas (ed.) *Social Cognition: Perspectives in Everyday Understanding* (London: Academic Press), 259–72.

Form, W. (1979) 'Comparative Industrial Sociology and the Convergence Hypotheses', *Annual Review of Sociology*, 5, 1–25.

Franko, L. (1971) *Joint Venture Survival in Multinational Corporations* (New York: Praeger).

Gagliardi, P. (1986) 'The Creation and Change of Organisational Culture: A Conceptual Framework', *Organisation Studies*, 7(2), 117–34.

Galbraith, J. (1973) *Designing Complex Organisations* (Reading Mass.: Addison-Wesley).

Gatignon, H. and E. Anderson (1988) 'Multinational Corporation's Degree of Control over Foreign Subsidiaries: An Empirical Test of A Transaction Cost Explanation', *Journal of Law, Economics and Organisation*, 4(2), 305–36.

Geertz, C. (1975) *The Interpretation of Cultures* (New York: Basic Books).

George, K. and A.P. Jacquemin (1990) 'Competition Policy in the European Community', in W.S. Comanor *et al.* (eds) *Competition Policy in Europe and North America: Economic Issues and Institutions* (Switzerland: Harwood Academic Publishers).

Geringer, J. (1988a) *Joint Venture Partner Selection: Strategy for Developed Countries* (Westport, Conn.: Quorum Books).

Geringer, J. (1988b) 'Selection of Partners for International Joint Ventures', *Business Quarterly*, Summer.

Geringer, J. and L. Hebert (1989) 'Control and Performance of International Joint Ventures', *Journal of International Business Studies,* 20(2), 235–54.

Geringer, J. and L. Hebert (1991) 'Measuring Performance of International Joint Ventures', *Journal of International Business Studies*, 22(2), 249–63.

Geroski, P. (1989) 'The Choice between Diversity and Scale', in *1992 Myths and Realities* (London: London Business School).

Goll, I. and C. Zeitz (1991) 'Conceptualising and Measuring Corporate Ideology', *Organisation Studies*, 12(2), 191–207.

Gordon, G.G. (1985) 'The Relationship of Corporate Culture to Industry Sector and Corporate Performance', in R.H. Kilman, M.J. Saxon, R. Serpa, and associates, *Gaining Control of the Corporate Culture* (San Francisco: Jossey Bass), 103–25.

Götberg, G. (1989) 'Franchising in International Marketing', Chapter 8 in *Marketing at the Gothenburg School of Economics*, Proceedings from a Symposium for Professor Bo Wickström, BAS (Gothenburg: University of Gothenburg).

Graves, D. (1973) 'The Impact of Culture upon Managerial Attitudes, Beliefs and Behaviour in England and France', in G. Graves (ed.) *Management Research: A Cross Cultural Perspective* (San Francisco: Jossey Bass), 282–304.

Green, R.T. and W.H. Cunningham (1975) 'The Determinants of US Foreign Investments: An Empirical Examination', *Management International Review*, 15(2–3) February, 113–20.

Greenaway, D. (1990) 'Trade Related Investment Measures: Political Economy Aspects and Issues for GATT', *The World Economy*, 13(3), September, 367–85.

Greenaway, D. and C. Milner (1990) 'South–South Trade: Theory, Evidence and Policy', *World Bank Research Observer*, 5, 47–68.

Grow, R.F. (1986) 'Japanese and American Firms in China: Lessons of a New Market', *Columbia Journal of World Business*, Spring.

Guth, W. and R. Tagiuri (1965) 'Personal Values and Corporate Strategy', *Harvard Business Review*, 43(5), 123–32.

Hackett, D.W. (1976) 'The International Expansion of US Franchise Systems: Status and Strategies', *Journal of International Business Studies*, 7(1), 65–76.

Haire, M., E.E. Ghiselli and L.W. Porter (1966) *Managerial Thinking: An International Study* (New York: John Wiley).

Hakansson, H. (ed.) (1982) *International Marketing and Purchasing of Industrial Goods: An Interaction Approach* (Chichester: Wiley).

Hambrick, B. (1981) 'Environmental Strategy and Power within Top Management Teams', *Administrative Science Quarterly*, 26, 253–75.

Hambrick, D. and P. Mason (1984) 'Upper Echelons: The Organisation as a Reflection of Its Top Managers', *Academy of Management Review*, 9(2), 193–206.

Hamel, G. and C.K. Prahalad (1985) 'Do You Really Have a Global Strategy?' *Harvard Business Review*, 63 (July–August), 139–48.

Hamill, J. (1992) 'Cross border Mergers, Acquisitions and Alliances in Europe', in S. Young and J. Hamill (eds), *Europe and the Multinationals: Issues and Responses for the 1990s* (Aldershot: Edward Elgar), 137–58.

Hampton, C. (1993) 'Cross Border Manoeuvres', *Financial Times*, 23 February.

Harr, R. (1981) 'Rituals, Rhetoric and Social Cognition', in J.P. Forgas (ed.) *Social Cognition: Perspectives in Everyday Understanding* (London: Academic Press), 211–24.

Harrigan, K.R. (1983) 'A Framework for Looking at Vertical Integration', *Journal of Business Strategy*, 3, 30–7.

Harrigan, K.R. (1985) *Strategies for Joint Ventures* (Lexington, Mass.: Lexington Books).

Harrigan, K.R. (1986) *Managing for Joint Venture Success* (Lexington, Mass.: Lexington Books).

Harrigan, K.R. (1988) 'Joint Ventures and Competitive Strategy', *Strategic Management Journal*, 9.

Harrigan, K.R. (1988) 'Joint Ventures: A Mechanism for Creating Strategic Change', in A. Pettigrew (ed.) *The Management of Strategic Change* (Oxford: Basil Blackwell) p. 370.

Hawk, B.E. and H.L. Huser (1993) 'A Bright Line Shareholding Test to End the Nightmare Under the EEC Merger Regulation', *Common Market Law Review*, 30(6), 1155–83.

Hedlund, G. and Å Kverneland (1985) 'Are Strategies for Foreign Markets Changing? The Case of Swedish Investment in Japan', *International Studies of Management and Organisation*, 15(2), 41–59.

Hefler, D.F. (1981) 'Global Sourcing: Offshore Investment Strategy for the 1980s', *Journal of Business Strategy*, Summer, 7–12.

Hennart, J.F. (1982) *A Theory of Multinational Enterprise* (Michigan: University of Michigan Press).

Hennart, J.F. (1986) 'What is Internalisation?', *Weltwirtschaftliches Archiv*, 122, 791–804.

Hennart, J. (1988) 'A Transaction Cost Theory of Equity Joint Ventures', *Strategic Management Journal*, 9(4).

Hennart, J.F. (1989) 'Can the "New Forms of Investment" Substitute for the "Old Forms": A Transactions Costs Perspective', *Journal Of International Business Studies*, 20(2), 211–34.

Herzberg, F., B. Mansner and B.B. Snyderman (1959) *The Motivation to Work* (New York: John Wiley).

Hickman, J. and S.C. Hickman (1992) *Global Procurement* (Homewood, Illinois: Business One – Irwin).

Hickson, D.J., C.R. Hinings, C.J. McMillan and J.P. Schwitter (1974) 'The Culture-free Context of Organisation Structure: A Tri-National Comparison', *Sociology*, 8, 59–80.

Hickson, D.J., C.J. McMillan, K. Asumi and D. Howard (1979) 'Grounds for

Comparative Organisation Theory: Quicksand or Hard Core?', in C.J. Lammers and D.J. Hickson (eds), *Organisations Alike and Unlike* (London: Routledge & Kegan Paul), 25–41.

Hill, C.W.L., P. Hwang and W.C. Kim (1990) 'An Eclectic Theory of the Choice of International Entry Mode', *Strategic Management Journal*, 11(2), 117–28.

Hirch, P. and J. Andrews (1983) 'Ambushes, Shootouts, and Knights of the Roundtable: The Language of Corporate Takeovers', in L.R. Pondy, P. Frost, G. Morgan and T. Dandridge (eds) *Organisational Symbolism* (Greenwich, Conn.: JAI Press), 145–55.

Hirsch, P.M. (1975) 'Organisational Analysis and Industrial Sociology: An Instance of Cultural Lag', *American Sociologist*, 10, 3–12.

Hirsch, S. and A. Meshulach (1991) 'Towards a Unified Theory of Internationalisation', paper presented at the 17th Annual Conference of the European International Business Association (EIBA), Copenhagen, 15–17 December.

Ho, P.S. and R.W. Huenemann (1984) 'China's Open Door Policy: The Quest for Foreign Technology and Capital', working paper: University of British Columbia.

Hofer, C.W. and D.E Schendel (1978) *Strategy Formulation: Analytical Concepts* (St Paul, Minn.: West Publishing).

Hoffman, R.C. and J.F. Preble (1991) 'Franchising: Selecting a Strategy for Rapid Growth', *Long Range Planning*, 24(4), 74–85.

Hofstede, G. (1980) *Culture's Consequences* (Beverly Hills, Calif.: Sage).

Hofstede, G. (1983) 'The Cultural Relativity of Organisational Practices and Theories', *Journal of International Business Studies*, 14(2), 75–90.

Hofstede, G. *et al.* (1990) 'Measuring Organisational Culture: A Qualitative and Quantitative Study across Twenty Cases', *Administrative Science Quarterly*, 35, 286–316.

Hogarth, R.M. and S. Makridakis (1981) 'Forecasting and Planning: An Appraisal', *Management Science*, 27, 115–38.

Hogg, M. and D. Abrams (1988) *Social Identifications* (London: Routledge).

Holton, R. (1990) 'The Myth of the Chinese Enterprise', in N. Campbell (ed.) *Advances in Chinese Industrial Studies*, Vol. 1, Part B (Greenwich, Conn.: JAI Press).

Holzman, F.D. (1985) 'Comecon: a "Trade-Destroying" Customs Union?' *Journal of Comparative Economics*, 9, 410–23.

Hood, N. and S. Young (1979) *The Economics of Multinational Enterprise* (New York: Longman).

Huff, A.S. (1983) 'A Rhetorical Examination of Strategic Change', in L.R. Pondy, P. Frost, G. Morgan and T. Dandridge (eds) *Organisational Symbolism* (Greenwich, Conn.: JAI Press), 167–83.

Huff, A.S. (1982) 'Industry Influences on Strategy Reformulation', *Strategic Management Journal*, 3, 119–31.

Hughes, K. (1992) 'Competition and the Single European Market', *Policy Studies*, 13(3), Autumn.

Hwang, P.J-H. (1988) 'Multinationals' Strategic Choice of Institutional Mode: A Decision Model For Market Entry', unpublished Ph.D. thesis, Michigan State University.

Hymer, S. (1960) *The International Operations of National Firms: A Study of Direct Foreign Investment*, Ph.D. thesis, MIT (Cambridge, MA: The MIT Press) (published1976).

Jacquemin, A.P. (1990) 'Mergers and European Policy', in P.H. Admiraal (ed.), *Mergers and Competition Policy in the European Community* (Oxford: Basil Blackwell), 3–38.

Jacquemin, A.P., P. Buigues and F. Ilzkovitz (1989) 'Horizontal Mergers and

Competition Policy in the European Community', *European Economy*, 40, May, 11–95.

Janger, A. (1980) *Organisation of International Joint Ventures* (New York: Conference Board).

Jenny, F. (1993) 'EEC Merger Control: Economies as an Antitrust Defence or an Antitrust Attack', in B. Hawk (ed.) *International Antitrust Law and Policy*, Annual Proceedings of the Fordham Corporate Law Institute, Irvington on Hudson (New York: Transnational Juris Publications).

Jobber, D. and J. Saunders (1988) 'An Experimental Investigation into Cross-National Mail Survey Response Rates', *Journal of International Business Studies*, 19(3), 483–9.

Johanson, J. and L-G. Mattsson(1986) 'International Marketing and Internationalisation Processes – A Network Approach', in S. Paliwoda and P.W. Turnbull (eds) *Research in International Marketing* (London: Croom Helm).

Johanson, J. and L-G. Mattsson (1988) 'Internationalisation in Industrial Systems – A Network Approach', in N. Hood and J-E. Vahlne (eds), *Strategies In Global Competition* (New York: Croom Helm), 287–314.

Johanson, J. and D.D. Sharma (1987) 'Technical Consultancy in Internationalisation', *International Marketing Review*, Winter.

Johanson, J. and J-E. Vahlne (1977) 'The Internationalisation Process of the Firm – a Model of Knowledge Development and Increasing Foreign Market Commitment', *Journal of International Business Studies*, 8(1), 23–32.

Johanson, J. and J-E. Vahlne (1990) 'The Mechanism of Internationalisation', *International Marketing Review*, 4.

Johanson, J. and J-E. Vahlne (1992), 'Management of Foreign Market Entry', *Scandinavian International Business Review*, 1(3), 9–27.

Johanson, J. and F. Wiedersheim-Paul (1975) 'The Internationalisation of the Firm – Four Swedish Case Studies', *Journal of Management Studies*, 12(3), 305–22.

Johnson, G. (1987) *Strategic Change and the Management Process* (Oxford: Blackwell).

Jones, G.R. (1983) 'Transaction Costs, Property Rights and Organisational Culture: An Exchange Perspective', *Administrative Science Quarterly*, 28, 454–67.

Julius, D. (1990) *Global Companies and Public Policy: The Growing Challenge of Foreign Direct Investment*, Chatham House Papers (London: Pinter).

Kagono, T. *et al.* (1985) *Strategic vs. Evolutionary Management* (Amsterdam: North-Holland).

Kanter, M.R. (1989) 'Becoming PALS: Pooling, Allying and Linking across Companies', *Academy of Management Executive*, 3(3), August.

Kaynak, E. (ed.) (1988) 'Global Franchising: European and North American Perspectives', Chapter 4 in *Transnational Retailing* (Berlin: de Gruyter).

Keegan, W.J. (1989) *Global Marketing Management*, 4th edn (Englewood Cliffs, N.J.: Prentice-Hall).

Kemp, Lynette (1987) *Investing in China: Where, How and Why?*, Special Report No. 1071 (London: The Economist Intelligence Unit).

Keonderman, P.P. (1990) 'Doing Business in China', *Business Quarterly*, Spring.

Killing, P. (1983) *Strategies for Joint Venture Success* (New York: Praeger).

Kim, W.C. and P. Hwang (1992) 'Global Strategy and Multinationals' Entry Mode Choice', *Journal of International Business Studies*, 23(1), 29–53.

Kindleberger, C.P. (1969) *American Business Abroad* (New Haven: Yale University Press).

Kirkbride, P.S. and S.T.Y. Tang (1990) 'Negotiation: Lessons from Behind the Bamboo Curtain', *Journal of General Management*, 17(1), 1–13.

Kirkpatrick, C. (1994) 'Regionalisation, Regionalism and East Asian Economic Cooperation', *The World Economy*, 17(2), 191–202.

Kitching, J. (1974) 'Winning and Losing with European Acquisitions', *Harvard Business Review*, March–April, 84.

Kluckhohn, C. (1954) 'Culture and Behaviour', in G. Lindzey, (ed.) *Handbook of Social Psychology* (Reading, Mass.: Addison-Wesley), 921–76.

Kluckhohn, F.R. and F.L. Strodtbeck (1961) *Variations in Value Orientations* (Evanston, Ill.: Row, Peterson).

Knickerbocker, F.T. (1973) *Oligopolistic Reaction and the Multinational Enterprise* (Boston: Harvard University Press).

Kobrin, S.J. (1976) 'The Environmental Determinants of Foreign Direct Manufacturing Investment: An Ex Post Empirical Analysis', *Journal of International Business Studies*, 7(2), 29–42.

Kogut, B. (1985) 'Designing Global Strategies: Comparative and Competitive Value-Added Chains', *Sloan Management Review*, 26, Summer, 15–28.

Kogut, B. (1986) 'Cooperative and Competitive Influences on Joint Venture Stability under Competing Risks of Acquisition and Dissolution', working paper: University of Pennsylvania, December.

Kogut, B. (1988) 'Joint Venture: Theoretical and Empirical Perspectives', *Strategic Management Journal*, 9(4), 319–32.

Kogut, B. and H. Singh (1988) 'The Effect of National Culture on the Choice of Entry Mode', *Journal of International Business Studies*, 19(3), 411–32.

Konigsburg, A.S. (1987) 'A Compendium of Franchising Terms', *Journal of International Franchising and Distribution Law*, 2, December, 58–67.

Konigsburg, A.S. (1990) 'The Use of Joint Ventures in International Franchising', *Journal of International Franchising and Distribution Law*, 5(1) 2–9.

Korah, V. and P. Lasok (1988) 'Philip Morris and its Aftermath – Merger Control', *Common Market Law Review*, 25(2), 333–68.

Kotler, P., L. Falhey and S. Jatusripitak (1985) *The New Competition* (Englewood Cliffs, N.J.: Prentice-Hall).

Kotler, P. and S.J. Levy (1973) 'Buying is Marketing Too', *Journal of Marketing*, January, 54–9.

Kotter, J. and J. Heskett (1992) *Corporate Culture and Performance* (New York: The Free Press).

Krauss, R.M. (1980) 'Cognition and Communication', paper presented at the Society for Experimental Social Psychology Meeting, Stanford University.

Lane, W.H. and P. Beamish (1990) 'Cross-cultural Cooperative Behaviour in Joint Ventures in LDCs', *Management International Review*, 30, Special Issue.

Langeheine, B. (1991) 'Substantive Review under the EEC Merger Regulation', in B. Hawk (ed.), *International Mergers and Joint Ventures* (New York: Transnational Juris Publications), 481–502.

Larimo, J. (1985) 'The Foreign Direct Manufacturing Investment Behaviour of Finnish Firms', paper presented at the 11th Annual Conference of the European International Business Association (EIBA), Glasgow, December.

Laurent, A. (1983) 'The Cultural Diversity of Western Conceptions of Management', *International Studies of Man and Organisation*, 13, 75–96.

Lawrence, P.R. and J.W. Lorsch (1967) *Organisation and Environment* (Boston, Mass.: Harvard Graduate School of Business Administration).

Lee, K-H. and T.W-C. Lo (1988) 'American Businesspeople's Perceptions of Marketing and Negotiating in the People's Republic of China', *International Marketing Review*, Summer.

Levitt, B. and J. March (1988) 'Organisational Learning', *Annual Review of Sociology*, 14, 319–40.

Levitt, T. (1983) *The Marketing Imagination* (New York: The Free Press).

Li, J. and S. Guisinger (1992) 'The Globalisation of Service Multinationals in the Triad Regions: Japan, Western Europe and North America', *Journal of International Business Studies*, 23(4), 675–96.

Likert, R. (1967) *The Human Organisation* (New York: McGraw-Hill).

Lo, W-C.T. (1989) 'New Developments in China Trade: Industrial Co-operation with the West', unpublished Ph.D. thesis, City University Business School, London.

Lodge, G.C. and E.F. Vogel (eds) (1987) *Ideology and National Competitiveness: An Analysis of Nine Countries* (Boston: Harvard Business School Press).

Lorsch, J.W. (1986) 'Managing Culture: The Invisible Barrier to Strategic Change', *California Management Review*, 28(2), 95–109.

Löwendahl, B. (1992) 'Global Strategies for Professional Business Service Firms', unpublished Doctoral Dissertation, University of Pennsylvania.

Luostarinen, R. (1978) *Internationalisation Process of the Firm – Different Research Approaches*, FIBO Working Paper, Helsinki.

Luostarinen, R. (1980) *Internationalisation of the Firm* (Helsinki: Helsinki School of Economics).

Lyles, M. (1988) 'Learning Among Joint Venture-Sophisticated Firms', in F.J. Contractor and P. Lorange (eds) *Cooperative Strategies in International Business* (Lexington, Mass.: Lexington Books).

Mallory, G.R. and T.A.R. Clark (1992) 'Cross-Cultural Organisational Research: A Methodological Minefield', paper presented to the International Organisation Development Association, 7th Annual World Conference, University of Coventry.

Maister, D.H. (1982) 'Balancing the Professional Service Firm', *Sloan Management Review*, Fall.

Markides, C.C. and D. Oyon (1991) 'Are the European Markets for Corporate Control Competitive? An (Indirect) Empirical Test', in H. Vestergard (ed.), *An Enlarged Europe in the Global Community. Proceedings of the 17th Annual EIBA Conference* (Copenhagen: Copenhagen Business School), 1055–82.

Maslow, A.H. (1954) *Motivation and Personality* (New York: Harper & Row).

Maurice, M. (1979) 'For a Study of the Societal Effect: Universality and Specificity in Organisation Research', in C.J. Lammers and D.J. Hickson (eds), *Organisations Alike and Unlike* (London: Routledge & Kegan Paul), 42–60.

McCosker, C.F. (1992) *Motivations and Methods of Australian Firms Franchising Internationally*, research report prepared for the Department of Business, Industry and Regional Development, University of Southern Queensland, August.

McGregor, D. (1960) *The Human Side of Enterprise* (New York: McGraw-Hill).

Mendelsohn, M. (1992) *The Guide to Franchising*, 5th edn (Oxford: Pergamon).

Meyer, J. and B. Rowan (1977) 'Institutionalised Organisations: Formal Structure as Myth and Ceremony', *American Journal of Sociology*, 83(2), 340–63.

Millar, C.C.J.M. (1989) *International Advertising: How do Culture and Globalisation Affect Management Decision Making?* (London: City University).

Millington, A.I. and B.T. Bayliss (1990) 'The Process of Internationalisation: UK Companies in the EC', *Management International Review*, 30(2), 151–61.

Mirus, R. (1980) 'Note on the Choice between Licensing and Direct Foreign Investment', *Journal of International Business Studies*, 11(1), 86–91.

Mitroff, I.I. and R.H. Kilmann (1976) 'On Organisational Stories: An Approach to the Design and Analysis of Organisations through Myths and Stories', in R.H. Kilmann, L.R. Pondy and D.P. Slevin (eds), *The Management of Organisations Design, 1* (New York: Elsevier/North-Holland), 189–207.

MOFERT (1987) *Almanac of China's Foreign Economic Relations and Trade* (Beijing: China Prospect Publishing House).

Monczka, R.M. and L. Giunipero (1983) 'International Purchasing: Characteristics and Implementation', *Journal of Purchasing and Materials Management*, Fall, 2–9.

Morgan, E.J. (1994) 'Supranational Competition Policy? Merger Control in the "Single" European Market and Beyond', in M. Yamin, F. Burton and A.R. Cross (eds), *The Changing European Environment*, Proceedings of the 21st Annual Conference of the UK Chapter of the Academy of International Business (AIB), UMIST, March, 35–52.

Moscovici, S. (1981) 'On Social Representations', in J.P. Forgas (ed.) *Social Cognition: Perspectives in Everyday Understanding* (London: Academic Press), 181–209.

Moscovici, S. (1984) 'The Phenomenon of Social Representations', in R.M. Farr (ed.) *Social Representations* (Cambridge: Cambridge University Press).

National Council for US–China Trade (1987) *US Joint Ventures in China: A Progress Report* (Washington, D.C.: US Department of Commerce), March.

Neisser, U. (1967) *Cognitive Psychology* (New York: Appleton-Century-Crofts).

Neumann, M. (1990) 'Industrial Policy and Competition Policy', in K. Cowling and H. Tomann (eds), *Industrial Policy after 1992 An Anglo German Perspective* (London: Anglo German Foundation), 222–33.

Neven, D., R. Nuttall and P. Seabright (1993) *Merger In Daylight: The Economics and Politics of European Merger Control* (London: Centre for Economic Policy Research).

Nicolaidis, C. (1992a) 'Cultural Determinants of Corporate Excellence in an Integrated World Economy: The Impact of National Cultures on Economic Performance', in M.C. Casson (ed.) *International Business and Global Integration* (London: Macmillan).

Nicolaidis, C. (1992b) 'Ethnic Entrepreneurs: The Persistence of National Culture on Expatriate Enterprises', paper presented at the Annual World Conference of the Academy of International Business (AIB), Brussels, November.

Nicoll, A. (1993) 'Big Surge of Interest', *Financial Times Survey*, 18 November, p. vi.

Niu, G. (1992) 'Opening up China's Markets with High Technology', *Beijing Review*, 35(13), 4–5.

Noel, A. (1988) 'The Interpretation of Strategies: A Study of the Impact of CEOs on the Corporation', *INSEAD Working Paper*, No. 88/14.

Normann, R. (1992) *Service Management – ledning och strategi i tjänsteproduktionen* (Stockholm: Almqvist and Wiksell Förlag AB).

Normann, R. and R. Ramírez (1993) 'From Value Chain to Value Constellation: Designing Interactive Strategy', *Harvard Business Review*, July–August.

Norton, S.W. (1988) 'An Empirical Look at Franchising as an Organizational Form', *Journal of Business*, 61(2), 197–218.

Nunnally, J. (1978) *Psychometric Theory* (New York: McGraw-Hill).

Ohmae, K. (1985) *Triad Power* (New York: The Free Press).

Oman, C. (1984) *New Forms of International Investment* (Paris: OECD Publications).

Organisation for Economic Cooperation and Development (OECD) (1987) *International Technology Licensing: Survey Results* (Paris: OECD Publications).

Ouchi, W.G. (1980) 'Markets, Bureaucracies and Clans', *Administrative Science Quarterly*, 25, 129–41.

Ouchi, W.G. (1981) *Theory Z: How American Business Can Meet the Japanese Challenge* (Reading, Mass.: Addison-Wesley).

Overbury, C. (1992) 'Politics or Policy? The Demystification of EC Merger Control', Address to the Fordham Law Institute, October (mimeo).

Parker, A. (1993) '"Messy" Research, Methodological Predispositions and Theory

Development in International Joint Ventures', *Academy of Management Review*, 18(2).

Parsons, T. and E. Shils (1951) 'Values, Motives and Systems of Action', in T. Parsons and E. Shils (eds) *Toward a General Theory of Action* (Cambridge: Harvard University Press).

Pascale, R.T. and A.G. Athos (1981) *The Arts of Japanese Management* (New York: Simon & Schuster).

Payne, R. (1990) 'The Concepts of Culture and Climate', *Manchester Business School Working Paper*, No. 202.

Pennings, J.M. and C.G. Gresov (1986) 'Technoeconomic and Structural Correlates of Organisational Culture: An Integrative Framework', *Organisation Studies*, 7(4), 317–34.

Perkins, J.S. (1987) 'How Licensing, Franchising Differ', *Les Nouvelles*, 22(4), 15.

Peters, T.J. and R.H. Waterman (1982) *In Search of Excellence* (New York: Harper & Row).

Pettigrew, A.M. (1979) 'On Studying Organisational Cultures', *Administrative Science Quarterly*, 24, 570–81.

Pfeffer, J. (1981) 'Management as Symbolic Action: The Creation and Maintenance of Organisational Paradigms', in L.L. Cummings and B.M. Staw (eds) *Research in Organisational Behaviour, 3* (Greenwich, Conn.: JAI Press), 1–52.

Pondy, L.R. (1983) 'The Role of Metaphors and Myths in Organisation and in the Facilitation of Change', in L.R. Pondy, P. Frost, G. Morgan, and T. Dandridge (eds) *Organisational Symbolism* (Greenwich, Conn.: JAI Press), 157–66.

Porac, J.F. *et al.* (1987) 'Knowing the Competition: The Mental Modes of Retailing Strategists', in G. Johnson (ed.) *Business Strategy and Retailing* (New York: John Wiley), 59–79.

Porter, M.E. (1980) *Competitive Strategy* (New York: Free Press).

Porter, M.E. (1985) 'The Value Chain and Competitive Advantage', in M.E. Porter, *Competitive Advantage* (New York: Free Press), 33–61.

Porter, M.E. (1986) 'Competition in Global Industries: A Conceptual Framework', in M.E. Porter (ed.), *Competition in Global Industries* (Boston: Harvard Business Press), 15–60.

Porter, M.E. (1990) *The Competitive Advantages of Nations* (London: Macmillan).

Porter, M.E. and M.B. Fuller (1986) 'Coalitions and Global Strategy' in M.E. Porter (ed.) *Competition in Global Industries* (Boston: Harvard Business School Press), 315–43.

Powell, W. and P. DiMaggio (eds) (1991) *The New Institutionalism in Organisational Analysis* (Chicago: The University of Chicago Press).

Prahalad, C.K. and R.A. Bettis (1986) 'The Dominant Logic: a New Linkage between Diversity and Performance', *Strategic Management Journal*, 7(6), 485–501.

Prahalad, C.K. and Y.C. Doz (1987) *The Multinational Mission* (New York: The Free Press).

Punnett, B.J. and P. Yu (1990) 'Attitudes toward Doing Business with the PRC: A Comparison of Canadian and US Companies', *International Studies of Management and Organisation*, 20(1/2).

Pye, L.W. (1982) *Chinese Commercial Negotiating Style* (Cambridge, Mass.: Oelgeschlager, Gunn & Hain).

Qing, S. (1993) *China 1993* (Beijing: Xin-Xing).

Qu, Y. (1992) 'Overseas Capital Inflow Surges on', *China Daily*, p. 1.

Qua, C.F. and T.C. Thian (1991) 'Procurement from Asia: Emerging Sources in S.E. Asia', *Proceeding of the 76th International Purchasing Conference*, (Tempe, Arizona: National Association of Purchasing Management), 219–22.

Rajagopal, S. and K.N. Bernard (1993a) 'Globalisation of the Procurement Process' *Marketing Intelligence and Planning*, 11(7) pp. 44–56 based on *Proceedings of the 20th Annual Conference of the UK Academy of International Business*, April 1993, University of Glamorgan, 399–425.

Rajagopal, S. and K.N. Bernard (1993b) 'Strategic Procurement in the Airline Industry: An Examination of the Impact of Purchasing Effectiveness on Market Competitiveness', *Proceedings of the 22nd Annual Conference of the European Marketing Academy*, Barcelona, 1301–22.

Rajagopal, S. and K.N. Bernard (1993c) 'Cost Containment Strategies: Challenges for Strategic Procurement in the 1990s', *International Journal of Purchasing and Materials Management*, 29(1), 17–24.

Reid, S. (1981) 'The Decision Maker and Export Entry and Expansion', *Journal of International Business Studies*, 12(2), 101–12.

Reid, S. (1983a) 'Firm Internationalisation, Transaction Costs and Strategic Management', *International Marketing Review*, 2, Winter, 44–56.

Reid, S. (1983b) 'Export Research in a Crisis', in M. Czinkota (ed.), *Export Promotion: The Public and Private Sector Interaction* (New York: Praeger).

Reid, S. (1984) 'Market Expansion and Firm Internationalisation', in E. Kaynak (ed.), *International Marketing Management* (New York: Praeger).

Roberts, E. (1980) 'New Ventures for Corporate Growth', *Harvard Business Review*, July–August.

Robock, S. (1971) 'Political Risk: Identification and Assessment', *Columbia Journal of World Business*, July–August, 6–20.

Rogers, E.M. (1962) *History of Economic Analysis* (New York: The Free Press).

Root, F.R. (1987) *Entry Strategies for International Markets* (Lexington, Mass.: Lexington Books/D.C. Heath & Co).

Rosch, E. (1978) 'Principles of Categorisation', in E. Posch and B. Lloyd (eds), *Cognition and Categorisation* (Hillsdale, N.J.: Erlbaum), 27–48.

Rosch, E. *et al.* (1976) 'Basic Objects in Natural Categories', *Cognitive Psychology*, 8, 382–439.

Rose, M. (1985) 'Universalism, Culturalism and the Aix Group: Promises and Problems of a Societal Approach to Economic Institutions', *European Sociological Review*, 1, 65–83.

Roulac, S.E. (1983) 'Structuring the Joint Venture', *Mergers and Acquisitions*, Spring.

Rubin, P.H. (1978) 'The Theory of the Firm and the Structure of the Franchise Contract', *Journal of Law and Economics*, 21, 223–33.

Rugman, A.M. (1981) *Inside the Multinationals* (London: Croom Helm).

Rugman, A.M. (1985) 'Internalisation is Still a General Theory of FDI', *Weltwirtschaftliches Archiv*, 121, 564–69.

Rugman, A.M. (1986) 'New theories of Multinational Enterprises: An Assessment of Internalisation Theory', *Bulletin of Economic Research*, 38(2), 101–18.

Rugman, A.M., D.J. Lecraw and L.D. Booth (1988) *International Business: Firm and Environment*, 3rd edn (New York: McGraw-Hill).

Sanghavi, N. (1990) *Retail Franchising in the 1990's* (London: Longman).

Sapienza, A.M. (1986) 'Believing is Seeing: How Culture Influences the Decisions Top Managers Make', in R. Kilmann *et al.* (eds), *Gaining Control of the Corporate Culture* (San Francisco: Jossey Bass), 66–83.

Sawyer, M. (1992) 'Reflections on the Nature and Role of Industrial Policy', *Metroeconomica*, 43(1–2), 51–73.

Schaan, J. (1985) 'Managing the Parent Control in Joint Ventures', paper presented at the Fifth Annual Conference of the Strategic Management Society, Barcelona, Spain.

Schein, E.H. (1983) 'The Role of the Founder in Creating Organisational Culture', *Organisational Dynamics*, Summer, 13–28.

Schein, E.H. (1984) 'Coming to a New Awareness of Organisational Culture', *Sloan Management Review*, Winter, 3–16.

Scherer, F.M. and D. Ross (1990) *Industrial Market Structure and Economic Performance* (Boston: Houghton Mifflin).

Schroath, F.W., M.Y. Hu and H. Chen (1993) 'Country-of-Origin Effects of Foreign Investments', *Journal of International Business Studies*, 24(2), 277–90.

Schwartz, H. and S.M. Davis (1981) 'Matching Corporate Culture and Business Strategy', *Organisational Dynamics*, Summer, 30–48.

Schwenk, C.R. (1988) 'The Cognitive Perspective on Strategic Decision Making', *Journal of Management Studies*, 25(1), 41–55.

Scott, R. and R. Meyer (1991) 'The Organisation of Societal Sectors: Propositions and Early Evidence', in W. Powell and P. DiMaggio (eds), *The New Institutionalism in Organisational Analysis* (Chicago: University of Chicago Press).

Selznick, P. (1957) *Leadership in Administration: A Sociological Interpretation* (New York: Harper & Row).

Sethia, N. and M. Glinow (1986) 'Arriving at Four Cultures by Managing the Reward System', in R. Kilmann *et al.* (eds), *Gaining Control of the Corporate Culture* (San Francisco: Jossey Bass), 400–20.

Shan, Weijin (1991) 'Environmental Risks and Joint Venture Sharing Arrangements', *Journal of International Business Studies*, 22(4), 555–78.

Shenkar, O. (1990) 'International Joint Ventures' Problems in China: Risks and Remedies', *Long Range Planning*, 23(3), 89–90.

Shrivastava, P. (1985) 'Integrating Strategy Formulation with Organisational Culture', *Journal of Business Strategy*, 5(3), 103–11.

Siehl, C. (1985) 'After the Founder, An Opportunity to Manage Culture', in P. Frost *et al.* (eds), *Organisational Culture* (London: Sage), 125–40.

Simon, H.A. (1957) *Models of Man* (New York: John Wiley).

Simon, H.A. (1976) *Administrative Behaviour* (New York: Free Press).

Singapore Trade Development Report (1991).

Smirich, L. (1983) 'Organisations as Shared Meanings', in L.R. Pondy, P. Frost, G. Morgan and T. Dandridge (eds), *Organisational Symbolism* (Greenwich, Conn.: JAI Press), 55–65.

Smirich, L. and C.I. Stubbart (1985) 'Strategic Management in an Enacted World', *Academy of Management Review*, 10(4), 724–36.

Smith, P.B. (1984) 'The Effectiveness of Japanese Styles of Management: A Review and Critique', *Journal of Occupational Psychology*, 57, 121–36.

Spender, J. (1989) *Industry Recipes* (Oxford: Basil Blackwell).

Srinivasan, T.N., J. Whalley and I. Wooton (1993) 'Measuring the Effects of Regionalism on Trade and Welfare', in K. Anderson and R. Blackhurst (eds), *Regional Integration and the Global Trading System* (Hemel Hempstead: Harvester-Wheatsheaf), 52–79.

Stewart, S. and C.F. Keown. (1989) 'Talking with the Dragon: Negotiating in the People's Republic of China', *Columbia Journal of World Business*, 24, Fall, 68–72.

Stonich, P.J. (1982) *Implementing Strategy: Making Strategy Happen* (Cambridge, Mass.: Ballinger).

Strange, R. (1993) *Japanese Manufacturing Investment in Europe: Its Impact on the UK Economy* (London: Routledge).

Stubbart, C.I. (1989) 'Managerial Cognition: A Missing Link in Strategic Management Research', *Journal of Management Studies*, 26(4), 325–47.

Sturdivant, F. *et al.* (1985) 'Manager's Conservatism and Corporate Performance', *Strategic Management Journal*, 6, 17–38.

Sullivan, D. and A. Bauerschmidt (1990) 'Incremental Internationalisation: A Test of Johanson and Vahlne's Thesis', *Management International Review*, 30(1), 19–30.

Swann, D. (1992) *The Economics of the Common Market*, 7th edn (Harmondsworth: Penguin).

Tajfel, H. and J.P. Forgas (1981) 'Social Categorisation: Cognitions, Values and Groups', in J.P. Forgas (ed.), *Social Cognition: Perspectives in Everyday Understanding* (London: Academic Press), 113–40.

Tayeb, M.H. (1988) *Organisations and National Culture: A Comparative Analysis* (London: Sage).

Teece, D.J. (1986) 'Transaction Cost Economics and the Multinational Enterprise: An Assessment', *Journal of Economic Behaviour and Organisation*, 7.

Teece, D.J. (1981) 'The Multinational Enterprise: Market Failure and Market Power Considerations', *Sloan Management Review*, 22(3), 3–17.

Teece, D.J. (1986) 'Transaction Cost Economics and the Multinational Enterprise', *Journal of Economic Behaviour and Organisation*, 7, 21–45.

Terpstra, V. (1987) *International Marketing*, 4th edn (New York: Dryden Press).

Terpstra, V. and C.M. Yu (1988) 'Determinants of Foreign Investment of US Advertising Agencies', *Journal of International Business Studies*, 19(1), 33–46.

Thompson, R.S. and M. Wright (1988) *Internal Organisation, Efficiency and Profit* (Oxford: Philip Allan).

Tookey, D. (1969) 'International Business and Political Geography', *British Journal of Marketing*, 3, 136–51.

Triandis, H.C. (1972) 'The Analysis of Subjective Culture', in H.C. Triandis and associates, *The Analysis of Subjective Culture* (New York: John Wiley), 299–335.

Tung, Rosalie L. (1982) *U.S.-China Trade Negotiations* (New York: Pergamon).

Turnbull, P.W. (1987) 'A Challenge to the Stages Theory of the Internationalisation Process', in P.J. Rosson and S.D. Reid (eds), *Managing Export Entry and Expansion* (New York: Praeger).

Turnbull, P.W. and J-P. Valla (1986) *Strategies for International Industrial Marketing* (London: Croom Helm).

Vahlne, J-E. and K. Nordstrom (1988) 'Choice of Marketing Channel in a Strategic Perspective', in N. Hood and J-E. Vahlne (eds), *Strategies in Global Competition* (London: Croom Helm).

Vernon, R. (1966) 'International Investment and International Trade in the Product Life Cycle', *Quarterly Journal of Economics*, 80(2), 190–207.

Venit, J. (1991) 'The Evaluation of Concentrations under Regulation 4064/89: The Nature of the Beast', in B. Hawk (ed.) *International Mergers and Joint Ventures*, Fordham Corporate Law Institute (New York: Transnational Juris).

United Nations Centre on Transnational Corporations (UNCTC) (1987) *Arrangements between Joint Venture Partners in Developing Countries*, UNCTC Advisory Studies Series B, No. 2 (New York: United Nations Centre on Transnational Corporations).

United Nations Centre on Transnational Corporations (UNCTC) (1988) *Foreign Direct Investment in the People's Republic of China*, report of the Round-Table organised by the UNCTC in cooperation with the MOFERT of the Peoples' Republic of China, Beijing, 25/26, 1987 (New York: United Nations).

United Nations Centre on Transnational Corporations (UNCTC) (1991) *World Investment Report 1991: The Triad in Foreign Direct Investment* (New York: United Nations).

United Nations Centre on Transnational Corporations (1992) (UNCTC) *World Investment Directory 1992, Volume I, Asia and the Pacific* (New York: United Nations).

United Nations Conference on Trade and Development (UNCTAD) (1993) *World Investment Report 1993: Transnational Corporations and Integrated International Production*, Programme on Transnational Corporations (New York: United Nations).

United Nations Department of Economic and Social Development (1992) *World Investment Report 1992: Transnational Corporations as Engines of Growth* (New York: United Nations).

United Nations Department of Economic and Social Development (1993) *World Investment Directory 1992, Volume III, Developed Countries* (New York: United Nations).

Usunier, J.C. (1993) *International Marketing, A Cultural Approach* (London: Prentice-Hall).

Utton, M. (1993) 'Market Concentration and Merger Policy', in M.C. Casson and J. Creedy (eds), *Industrial Concentration and Economic Inequality: Essays in Honour of Peter Hart* (Aldershot: Edward Elgar).

Vernon, R. (1983) 'Organisational and Institutional Responses to International Risk', in R.J. Herring, (ed.), *Managing International Risk* (Cambridge: Cambridge University Press), 191–216.

Von Glinow, M. and M.B. Teagarden (1988) 'The Transfer of Human Resource Management Technology in Sino–US Cooperative Ventures: Problems and Solutions', *Human Resource Management*, 27(2).

Walker, G. and D. Weber (1984) 'A Transactions Cost Approach to Make-or-Buy Decisions', *Administrative Science Quarterly*, 29(3), 373–91.

Wall, J.A. Jr (1990) 'Managers in the People's Republic of China', *Academy of Management Executive*, 4(2).

Walter, I. (1988) *Global Competition in Financial Services* (Cambridge, Mass.: Ballinger).

Wang, N.T. (1986) 'United States and China: Business beyond Trade – an Overview', *Columbia Journal of World Business*, Spring.

Watson, C.M. (1982) 'Counter-Competition Abroad to Protect Home Markets', *Harvard Business Review*, 60, January–February, 40–2.

Weber, M. (1947) *The Theory of Social and Economic Organisation, being Part I of Wirtschaft und Gesellschaft*; trans. A. R. Henderson and T. Parsons, rev. and ed. T. Parsons (London: William Hodge).

Weick, K.E. and M.G. Bougon (1986) 'Organisations as Cognitive Maps', in D.A. Giogia and H.P. Sims, Jr (eds), *The Thinking Organisation: Dynamics of Organisational Social Cognition* (San Francisco: Jossey Bass), 102–35.

Weick, K.E. (1979) *The Social Psychology of Organising* (Reading, Mass.: Addison-Wesley).

Weiss, J.W. and S. Bloom (1990) 'Managing in China: Expatriate Experiences and Training Recommendations', *Business Horizons*, 33(3).

Welch, L.S. (1989) 'Diffusion of Franchise System Use in International Operations', *International Marketing Review*, 6(5) 7–19.

Welch, L.S. and F. Wiedersheim-Paul (1980) 'Initial Exports – a Marketing Failure?' *Journal of Management Studies*, 17, October, 333–44.

Welford, R. and K. Prescott (1996) *European Business: An Issue Based Approach* (London: Pitman).

Whipp, R., R. Rosenfeld and A. Pettigrew (1989) 'Culture and Competitiveness: Evidence from Two Mature UK Industries', *Journal of Management Studies*, 26(6), 561–85.

Whitley, R. (1989) 'Enterprise Structures in their Societal Contexts: The Comparative Analysis of Forms of Business Organisations', *Manchester Business School Working Paper, no. 175*.

Whitley, R. (1991) 'The Social Construction of Business Systems in East Asia', *Organisation Studies*, 12(1), 1–28.

Wiedersheim-Paul, F., H.E. Olson and L.S. Welch (1978) 'Pre-Export Activity: The First Steps in Internationalisation', *Journal of International Business Studies*, 9(1), 47–58.

Wilkins, A. and J. Martin (1980) 'Organisational Legends', *Graduate School of Business Working Paper* (Stanford: Stanford University).

Wilkins, A.L. (1983) 'The Culture Audit: A Tool for Understanding Organisations', *Organisational Dynamics*, Autumn, 24–38.

Williamson, J. and C. Milner (1991) *The World Economy: A Textbook in International Economics* (Hemel Hempstead: Harvester-Wheatsheaf).

Williamson, O.E. (1975) *Markets and Hierarchies: Analysis and Antitrust Implications: A Study in the Economics of Internal Organisation* (New York: Free Press).

Williamson, O.E. (1979) 'Transaction-Cost Economics: The Governance of Contractual Relations', *Journal of Law and Economics*, 22(2), 233–61.

Williamson, O.E. (1981) 'The Modern Corporations: Origins, Evolution, Attributes', *Journal of Economic Literature*, 19, December, 1537–68.

Williamson, O.E. (1985) *The Economic Institutions of Capitalism* (New York: Free Press).

Wilson, B. (1980) 'The Propensity of Multinational Companies to Expand Through Acquisitions', *Journal of International Business Studies*, 12(1), 59–65.

Wind, Y., S.P. Douglas and H.V. Perlmutter (1973) 'Guidelines for Developing International Marketing Strategies', *Journal of Marketing*, 37, 14–23.

Winters, L.A. (1993) 'Expanding EC Membership and Association Accords: Recent Experience and Future Prospects', in K. Anderson and R. Blackhurst (eds), *Regional Integration and the Global Trading System* (Hemel Hempstead: Harvester-Wheatsheaf), 104–25.

Wolf, M. (1993) 'US Follows the EC towards Discrimination', *Financial Times*, 23 August, p. 4.

Woodward, D.G. and B.C.F. Liu (1993) 'Investing in China: Guidelines for Success', *Long Range Planning*, 26(2).

Woodward, J. (1958) *Management and Technology* (London: HMSO).

Yeoh, P.L. and S.T. Cavusgil (199) 'Global Sourcing Entry Strategies: A Contingency Approach Based on Transaction Cost Analysis', *Proceedings of the Summer American Marketing Association Conference*, pp. 350–4.

Young, S. (1987) 'Business Strategy and the Internalisation of Business: Recent Approaches', *Managerial and Decision Economics*, 8, 31–40.

Young S., J. Hamill, C. Wheeler and J.R. Davies (1989) *International Market Entry and Development: Strategies and Management* (Hemel Hempstead: Harvester Wheatsheaf).

Young, S. and N. Hood (1976) 'Perspectives on the European Marketing Strategy of US Multinationals', *European Journal of Marketing*, 10, 240–56.

Zucker, L. (1977) 'The Role of Institutionalisation in Cultural Persistence', *American Sociological Review*, 42(5), 726–43.

Index

acquisitions and mergers, within EU 91–111
Aerospatiale/Alenia/de Havilland case 99, 106–7
affiliates, foreign 7, 37, 217
Africa
  lack of FDI in 12
  South Africa 219
Agarwal, S. 155, 164
Aharoni, Y. 87
Alcatel/AEG/Kabel case 97–8, 99
Alcatel/Telettra case 99
alliances, international corporate 8–9, 66–8
Andersen, O. 193
Anderson, E. 156
anti-dumping measures 8, 26
ASEAN (Association of South-East Asian Nations) 33–4, 36
Asia
  Apec 38, 41n39
  ASEAN 33–4, 36
  effect of NAFTA on 33
  FDI in Asia Pacific region 10–12
  IPOs in 217–18
  outward FDI from 38
  see also China; Hong Kong; Japan; Japanese firms; Macao; Taiwan; Taiwanese firms; Thailand
Asia Pacific Economic Co-operation (Apec) 38, 41n39
Association of South-East Asian Nations (ASEAN) 33–4, 36
Atlas Copco 200
ATR/de Havilland case 106–7, 111
AT&T/NCR case 106
Australia 153
automobile industry 200
Awadzi, W.K. 175
Aydin, N. 151n5

Balasubramanyam, V.N. 39
Belgium 97, 214
Bernard, K.N. 208, 210, 216
Bilkey, Warren 193
Britain *see* UK; UK firms
BSN, French food manufacturer 103–6
Buckley, P.J. 172, 197, 200, 202, 204
Bundeskartellamt, Germany 98
business format franchising 136
business networks 6, 80–2, 86–7
Burton, F.N. 151n9

Canada
  de Havilland case 106–7
  FDI in 10
  and NAFTA 31–2, 44, 47, 66, 68
  trade with China 153
  UK firms operating in 58–60, 63–6
Canadian firms operating in EU 47–58, 60–3
cartels 93–4
Casson, M.C. 155, 172
Caterpillar 214
Cavusgil, S.T. 193, 198
Cecchini Report 91, 100
CEN (European Committee on Standardisation) 47
CENELEC (Committee for Electrotechnical Standardisation) 47
chemical industry 200
Child, J. 197
China, People's Republic of
  EU firms in 159–61, 168
  foreign joint ventures in 174–91
  growing FDI in 166, 167, 168
  as manufacturing base 165–6
  'open door' policy 153, 166, 171
  overseas Chinese investing in 171, 176–7, 178–91 *passim*
  production and transaction costs in 154–5
Churchill, G.A. 159, 160, 161
Clark, T.A.R. 200
cognitive categorisation 117–18
common market, definition of 20
communications industries 9, 27, 47–56, 66–8
Companhia Vale du Rio Doce, Brazil 213
Continental Can 95
corporate culture 113–14, 124–5, 128

cost motives 154–5
  transaction costs 173
Council for Mutual Economic Assistance 40n16
counterfeiting 4
countertrade 9–10
country risk, perceptions of 155, 162, 164
Cross, A.R. 151n9
cross-border acquisitions *see* under European Union
cross-border franchising *see* franchising, international
cultural differences
  between markets 60–2, 69, 147
  and choice of foreign market entry strategy 113–15, 156, 162, 164
customers, of service firms 88
customs unions 20, 26
Cyert, R.M. 72
Czinkota, M.R. 193

Daniels, J.D. 154
Davidson, W.H. 155, 164
Delta Airlines/PanAm case 106
developing countries 32–5, 39
  see also less developed countries
Digital/Kienzle case 106
Digital/Philips case 106
distribution channels, service sector 81–2
Drager/IBM/HMP case 106
Du Pont/ICI case 99
Dunning, J.H. 72, 78, 130, 156, 158
Dutch firms *see* Netherlands

East Asian countries 33, 38
Eastern European countries 168, 169
eclectic paradigm model 72, 78–9
Edvardsson, B. 75, 84
Edvinson, L. 84
electronics industry 200
entrepreneur, theory of 114–15, 120–1, 125–6
entry-mode choice, factors affecting 153–69
establishment chain 73, 77–80
EU *see* European Union
European Commission
  investigation of mergers 95–7, 100–7
  limitations of 101
  powers 91, 93–5, 97
European Economic Area (EEA) 30, 31, 36–7, 38, 207
European firms
  in China 153–69, 176–91 *passim*
  international procurement by 217, 221–4
European Free Trade Area (EFTA) 29, 30–1
European Union (EU) (formerly European Community (EC); European Economic Community (EEC))
  acquisitions and mergers 91–111
  competition policy 93–5, 110–11
  creation of Single European Market (SEM) 8, 29–30
  cultural diversity within 60–2, 69
  deregulation of service industries 38
  development and expansion of 28–30, 38
  effects of competition within 61–2
  FDI in 35–6, 56
  non-tariff barriers 29
  outward FDI in China 153–69
  promotion of technological development 47, 67
  public procurement within 56
  trade creation 37
  see also European Commission; European firms; Single European Market
Exor, France 105
exporting 6–7, 194

Facit 200
Felstead, A. 151n3
financial services sector 57–8, 59–60, 61, 64
Finnish firms 194
firm size, effect on foreign market entry 156–7, 165, 167
food and drink industry 59, 61, 103–6, 200
Ford Motor Company 214
foreign direct investment (FDI)
  in China 153, 171, 173
  eclectic paradigm model 72
  effects of technological development on 67–8
  establishment chain 73, 77–8
  franchising as form of 142, 150

global sourcing through 218
global trends 34–6
intra-industry 8
motivations for 21–3
in NAFTA 68–9
political instability and 155
preferred to licensing 4
and regional trading blocs 10–12, 24–5, 57
Uppsala model 72–3, 194–5, 205
foreign market entry 135, 153–69, 196, 198
foreign market experience 156, 165, 167–8, 194, 195, 201, 205–6
foreign market servicing
between mode shifts 197–9
mixed marketing approaches 203–4, 205
no single route 197, 205
retrenchment 199, 204–5
within mode shifts 197, 199–200
France 148
firms in 97, 99, 103–6, 111
franchising, international
agency issues 145–6
definition 136
degree of equity investment 140–2
distinguished from licensing 135, 137–8, 142–3
as foreign market entry mode 135
organisational forms 138–42
transaction costs 146–9
free trade areas 20, 26

Gatignon, H. 156
GATT (General Agreement on Tariffs and Trade)
abuses of 8
basic principles 26
effect on world trade 4–5
failures leading to trading blocs 36–7
Geneva Round (1947) 26, 28–9
Kennedy Round (1964–67) 26, 29, 40n12
Tokyo Round (1973–79) 26, 29, 40n12
Uruguay Round (1986–93) 26–8 (*see also* Uruguay Round)
George, K. 91
Germany, firms in 97, 99
Giunipero, L. 209, 217
global markets, demands of 43
see also liberalisation of world trade
government policy, effects on FDI of 21
Greenaway, D. 39
Guisinger, S. 239
Gummesson, E. 75

Hackett, D.W. 151n5
Hedlund, G. 194
Herzberg, F. 123
Hickman, J. 209
Hickman, S.C. 209
Hoffman, R.C. 151n5
Holton, R. 181
Hong Kong 153, 154, 171
Hymer, S. 6

IKEA 85
import tariffs 7
importing strategy 217
intellectual property rights 4, 27, 39, 136, 166
international franchising *see* franchising, international
international licensing *see* licensing, international
International Organisation Observatory (IOO) 200
international sourcing 207–25
internationalisation
definition 3
changing environment 4
stages of 73–4, 193
see also foreign market servicing; Uppsala Internationalisation Model
intra-firm trade 7
Italy, firms in 97, 99

Jacquemin, A.P. 91
Japan
FDI in 10–12, 35
influence of national culture 130
outward FDI from 38–9 (*see also under* Japanese firms)
service multinationals in 74
trade with China 153
Japanese firms
approach to international sourcing 217, 218, 221–4
FDI in China 153, 171, 176–91 *passim*

Japanese firms *cont.*
  FDI in EU 36
  saw Single European Market as threat 44
Jenny, F. 106
Johanson, J. 3, 87, 155, 193, 195
joint ventures, international 93–4, 108, 139, 141, 150
  benefits and disadvantages 172–3
  in China 162–8, 172, 189–91
  disadvantages of 173
  duration of 190–1
  in EU 96, 108, 154–9
  location strategy 190
  motivations for establishing 177–80
  partner selection 180–2
  performance 173–4, 187–9
  size of investment and percentage foreign equity 176
  in sourcing 218
  share of control 182–7

Kacker, M. 151n5
Kagono, T. 130
Kawasak 213
Kindleberger, C.P. 6
Kirkpatrick, C. 33
Kitching, J. 100
Knickerbocker, F.T. 6
Kverneland, A. 194

Larimo, J. 194
Latin America, trading blocs in 32–3
Lawrence, P.R. 197
less developed countries (LDCs) 4, 7–10
Li, J. 74
liberalisation of world trade
  effects on FDI 24–6, 35–6
  effects on internationalisation strategy 5, 7, 9
  effects on sourcing 207
  under GATT 26–8
licensing, international
  compared with franchising 135, 137–8, 142–3
  factors affecting EU firms' choice 154–9, 162–8
  motivations for 202
Likert, R. 123
Lo, W-C. T. 154
Lorsch, J.W. 197
Lowendahl, B. 82

Luostarinen, R. 194

Maastricht Treaty 30
Macao 171
McFetridge, D.G. 155, 164
McGregor, D. 123
Mallory, G.R. 200
Mannesmann/Hoesch case 98, 99
manufacturing industries 200
March, J.G. 72
market servicing *see* foreign market servicing
marketing mix, standardisation of 164–5, 167
markets, need for knowledge about 8, 195
master international franchisors 140, 150
mechanical engineering industry 200
mergers and acquisitions, within EU 91–111
Meyer, J. 128
Mexico 10, 32
Milner, C. 29
Mirus, R. 156
Monczka, R.M. 209, 217
Monopolies and Mergers Commission (UK) 98
Moscovici, S. 119
MSA (UK firm) 219
multinational firms 7, 208–9

NAFTA *see* North American Free Trade Agreement
national culture 129–30
Nestlé/Perrier case 99, 103–6, 111
Netherlands, firms in 97, 99
networks, business 6, 80–2, 86–7
non-tariff barriers 8–9, 26, 29–30, 40n12
Normann, R. 85
North America 10, 74
North American Free Trade Agreement (NAFTA) 31–2
  established in response to SEM 36–7, 44
  expansion of 38
  failure to deregulate market 64
  legislative differences within 60
  international trade and 4, 33
  need for competition policy 59, 66, 68
  US dominant within 63–4

Norton, S.W. 151n5
Nunnally, J. 161
NV Koninklijke/VRG case 99
Nystrom, H. 84

Office of Fair Trading (UK) 98
offshore production 7
OLI-framework 78–9
Oman, C. 137
organisational culture 116–17, 124–31
Overbury, C. 97, 98
overseas Chinese 171, 176–7, 178–91 *passim*

Parker, A. 172
Pass, C.L. 197, 200
patent controls 58–9, 158
Pearce, R.D. 130
Perkins, J.S. 142
Perrier/Nestlé case 103–6
pharmaceutical industry 58–9, 66–8, 200
Philip Morris case 94
political and economic factors affecting foreign market entry 156, 162, 164
Porter, M.E. 85
Preble, J.F. 151n5
Prescott, K. 197, 200, 202
procurement, international *see* sourcing, international
product life cycles 5
production costs 154–5
protectionism 5, 8–9
psychic distance of foreign markets 155–6
public procurement access 56–7, 60–1
Pugh, D.S. 206n2
purchasing, international *see* sourcing, international

Qua, C.F. 217

Rajagopal, Shan 208, 210, 216
Ramaswami, S.N. 155, 164
Ramirez, R. 85
regional integration
  and FDI 10–12, 20–6
  historical development 19, 28–34, 36–7
  impact on member and non-member countries 46–7
  promotes external protectionism 47–58
  and reorganisation of production and distribution 62, 67
Reid, S. 193
Renault/Volvo case 102
retrenchment of foreign operations 199
Robock, S. 155
Root, F.R. 137, 194
Rowan, B. 128
Rugman, A.M. 216
Russia, trade with China 153

Sandvik 200
Schein, E. 114, 122–4
second generation franchising 136
Securitas 84
service industries
  brought under GATT 5, 27
  business networks in 80–2
  deregulation of 38, 43
  differences from manufacturing 74–7, 194
  foreign market servicing strategies 77–80, 82–3, 86–8
  increasing investment in 23, 35, 71, 74
  value-sharing with customers 85–6, 88
Sharma, D. 87
Sicind/CEAC case 99
Siemens/Nixdorf case 106
Siemens/Philips case 98, 99
Singapore 153, 200, 217
Single European Market (SEM)
  creation of 8, 30, 36
  effect on mergers 100–1, 110–11
  effect on other regional trading groups 31, 33
  and FDI in EU 35–6
  movement of capital and trade in services 36–7
  perceived as protectionist threat 43–4, 58, 68
sourcing, international 207–25
South Africa 219
South Korea 153
Spain 97
Steetley/Tarmac case 98
Sticht, J.P. 87
strategic alliances 8–9, 66–8

subsidiary international franchising 139, 141, 150
Swann, D. 91
Sweden 84, 130
Swedish firms 99, 193–4, 200
Switzerland, firms in 99

Taiwan 153
Taiwanese firms 153, 217
technology
 developments in 47, 69
 joint ventures involving 157
Teece, D.J. 158
telecommunications industry 9, 27
Terpstra 216
Tesar, G. 193
Tetra Pak/Alfa Laval case 99
Thailand 217
Thomassen Drijver 95
Thompson, R.S. 151n4
Thian, T.C. 217
trade creation and diversion 20–1
trademarks 136
trade-related investment measures (TRIMS) 27–8, 39
trading blocs,
 definitions 20
 development of 19, 28–34
 effects on FDI 10–12
 increased competitive pressures within 157, 164, 166–7
 see also regional integration
transaction complexity 157, 164, 166–7
transaction costs 154–5, 173
transaction uncertainty 153, 163
transportation equipment industries 27, 66–8
Treaty of Rome 91
Turnbull, P.W. 194

UK (United Kingdom) 60, 97, 130
UK firms
 international sourcing strategies 220–4
 operating in Canada 68–9
 operating in USA 58
Uppsala Internationalisation Model
 definition of FDI 202
 effects of market knowledge 155
 limitations of 193–6, 200, 201, 203
 predicts sequential development 195, 205
Uruguay Round of GATT (1986–93) 26–8, 207
 effect on regional integration 33, 37
 inclusion of service industries 4–5, 38
 intellectual property rights covered 4, 39
US firms
 choice of foreign market entry mode 155, 164
 in EU 34, 99
 investing in China 158
 international sourcing of 217, 221–4
USA (United States of America)
 alliances in 65
 cultural influences 130
 disclosure legislation in 148
 FDI in 10, 58
 import tariffs 7
 and NAFTA 31–2, 65–6
 and SEM 44
 trade and investment in China 153, 166, 171
 see also US firms

Vahlne, J-E. 3, 155, 193, 195
value–added tariffs 7
Van Miert, K. 111
Varta/Bosch case 98, 102
Volvo 200

Welch, L.S. 151n5
Western Europe 10, 74
 see also European Union
Wiedersheim-Paul, F. 193
Williamson, J. 29
Williamson, O.E. 146, 158
WM-Data 84–5
Woodward, J. 197
World Trade Organisation (WTO) 4, 27, 38
 see also GATT
Wright, M. 151n4